The
American Common School

AN HISTORIC CONCEPTION

BY

LAWRENCE A. CREMIN, Ph.D.

BUREAU OF PUBLICATIONS
TEACHERS COLLEGE · COLUMBIA UNIVERSITY
NEW YORK · 1951

To
T. B. C. and A. T. C.

FOREWORD

The American Common School is a brilliant study into the origins
of some of our educational conceptions and institutions. It deals
with the most creative period in the history of American education
and with the most basic unit of our educational system—the common school. The general field of inquiry embraced by the study
is of course not new. Many scholars have directed their energies
and talents to the study of the age which witnessed the establishment of the broad outlines of our democratic system of public
schools. Yet Dr. Cremin has added something new and vital to our
understanding of American education in general and of the common school in particular.

First of all, he has related more clearly and fully than any of his
predecessors, the origin of the common school to the play of social
forces and ideas agitating the young republic. With due regard for
balance and proportion he has brought into the record the conflicting interests of political and economic groups, the egalitarianism
of the frontier and the rural neighborhood, the dynamism of the
town and the beginnings of industrialism, the divisive influence of
cultural and religious diversity, the integrating power of a growing nationalism, and the insistent demands of democratic conceptions and institutions. Dr. Cremin has also given due attention
to that "spirit of reform" which, according to Professor A. M.
Schlesinger, has characterized the American temper from early
colonial times and which showed extraordinary vigor during the
second quarter of the nineteenth century.

Secondly, Dr. Cremin has demonstrated through abundant documentation that the "founding fathers" of the common school understood the relation between education and political systems.
They rejected the idea that education is an autonomous process
conducted according to its own laws, welcomed by free societies
and feared by despotisms. They accepted as axiomatic the view

that there is an appropriate form of education for every society, that the educational practices developed in the monarchical states beyond the Atlantic were unsuited and even dangerous to republican America, and that the American people should develop a very special kind of school appropriate to their free institutions and democratic ideas. This profound insight into the nature of education was often lost or obscured in later generations. Today, as we marshal our resources to halt the worldwide thrust of totalitarian aggression, it is peculiarly imperative that we recover, enrich, and apply with power and vision this insight of the generation that launched the common school.

Thirdly, Dr. Cremin has laid bare the original meaning of the designation *the common school*. The central idea here is distinctly a product of American genius. It is the idea that this school is common, not because it is intended for the common people, the masses, as distinguished from the classes, like its counterpart in Europe, but rather because it is intended for all the people, regardless of social, class, religious, national, or racial condition. Here undoubtedly is a cardinal feature of any school that professes loyalty to the democratic ideal. And here too is an idea that is being threatened today by the current effort on the part of sectarian groups to obtain public funds for the support of private schools.

The American Common School is obviously more than a fine historical study. It is also a study that throws light on a number of the most fundamental problems confronting American education in these critical times. I trust that it will be widely read and pondered.

GEORGE S. COUNTS

PREFACE

THE American public school is today the center of a storm of controversy. Perceiving with ever greater clarity the power of education, Americans have begun increasingly to examine this institution, the assumptions under which it arose, and the principles according to which it now functions. Witnessing with apprehension the vast educative systems of the dictatorships, they have manifested a growing interest in their schools as instruments of democracy in a world of potential authoritarianism. Perhaps the most conclusive evidence of such interest is the spirited, often heated, and sometimes embittered discussion of educational questions in the press, in Congressional debates, and in Supreme Court decisions. As in every such instance of singular import, profound disagreements have emerged; for within the broader limits of democracy, different men and different groups envision different ends for the individual and society.

Inevitably, in seeking to establish their respective points of view with the public, such conflicting interests will turn to the past for support. They will assert with resolve and vigor that this or that position is the authentic American tradition, evolved by former generations as the course truly compatible with democracy and republican institutions. Though much of such argument will be specious, a goodly proportion will most certainly represent the sincere efforts of citizens to arrive at tenable and intelligent decisions. The understanding of its cultural heritage will not only save a society from the pitfalls of its ancestors; it will also enable it to profit from their wisdom. Such insight provides the vital foundation of intelligent social action.

The history of the public—or common—school reveals that although some of its roots stem from the early colonial settlements, its conceptual, legal, and practical beginnings emerged during the

first half-century of national life. It seems fitting that this should
be so; for these decades also saw the beginnings of many other elements which have since stood at the heart of the American tradition. Universal manhood suffrage, the separation of church and
state, and the organization of labor are but a few of the patterns
which, along with the common school, developed during this
period.

Thus it seems logical that any attempt to examine the basic
principles and assumptions of the American public school would
turn back to these years in an effort to understand its beginnings.
What were the social and intellectual factors which stimulated its
growth? Who were the men and groups who conceived it and
attempted to establish it in practice? What distinctive tasks did
they assign to this school? How successful were they in their
efforts? What was the nature of the schools which emerged? These
are some of the questions which occur to one seeking to compre-
hend the heritage of American public education. It is in the hope
of providing suitable answers that the study at hand has been conceived and pursued.

Few authors can hope adequately to acknowledge the extent of
their intellectual and personal indebtedness to teachers, fellow
scholars, and friends. In the case of the present volume, the following expressions of sincere appreciation must suffice: to Profes-
sors John L. Childs, R. Freeman Butts, Edward H. Reisner, and
Ryland W. Crary, all of Teachers College, Columbia University,
for generous and helpful counsel and continuing interest throughout the progress of the study; to Professor Henry Steele Commager
of Columbia University, for valuable criticism of the final draft;
to Miss Martha L. Counts, for her untiring efforts in checking the
documentation; to Mrs. Alma Fogarty, Miss Priscilla S. Aiken, and
Miss Elizabeth V. Rowland, for typing the manuscript; to the staff
of the Teachers College Library, for considerable aid and advice
in the search for sources; and to the staffs of the Columbia University Libraries, The New York Public Library, the New York Historical Society Library, the Massachusetts Historical Society Library, and the Library of Congress, for similar services. Finally, I
wish to express my very great debt of gratitude to the sponsor of
this study, Professor George S. Counts. In addition to giving freely

of his guidance, encouragement, criticism, and friendship, he has inspired a priceless devotion to the ideals and canons of historical scholarship.

What strengths this study possesses can be traced in large measure to these friends. Responsibility for its shortcomings most assuredly rests with the author.

LAWRENCE A. CREMIN

New York, 1949

CONTENTS

The
American Common School

And hence it is, that the establishment of a republican government without well-appointed and efficient means for the universal education of the people, is the most rash and fool-hardy experiment ever tried by man.

—HORACE MANN

PART 1

THE CULTURAL ROOTS OF
THE COMMON SCHOOL

THE American common school emerged as a response to the conditions of American life. Its development during the Middle Period [for purposes of this study, 1815–1850] may be closely related to four basic social and intellectual trends in the early life of the Republic: (1) the democratizing of politics; (2) the growth of the struggle to maintain social equality; (3) the change in the conception of man and society; and (4) the rise of nationalism. Essentially, the common school represented one means by which citizens of that era sought consciously to meet certain of the problems implicit in these broad cultural changes. In view of their importance, then, it seems necessary briefly to describe these trends as a framework within which to examine the educational developments of the period. Only against such a background can the latter be viewed with insight and perspective.

1. THE DEMOCRATIZING OF AMERICAN POLITICS

"All communities," said Alexander Hamilton in 1787, "divide themselves into the few and the many. The first are the rich and well born, the other the mass of the people. . . . The people are turbulent and changing; they seldom judge or determine right. Give, therefore, to the first class a distinct, permanent share in the government. They will check the unsteadiness of the second; and as they cannot receive any advantage by a change, they therefore will maintain good government." [1] Hamilton was stating the traditional English principle of politics which had dominated the colonial scene for nearly two hundred years. At the close of the Revolution, it was everywhere evident in practice. Five states maintained real estate qualifications for voting,[2] while five others maintained them with alternatives (i.e., other property or payment of taxes).[3] The remaining three demanded either ownership of a given amount of personal property or payment of public taxes.[4] It has been estimated that even when Washington took office a decade later, only one free male in seven was eligible to vote in the nation as a whole.[5]

When Hamilton died in 1804, however, he had lived to see the unmistakable beginnings of the twilight of his philosophy. Fed by the vigorous surge of democracy from the frontier areas, the growing demands for more liberal suffrage enactments were heard throughout the nation. Vermont and Kentucky came into the Union in 1791 and 1792 respectively with neither property nor taxpaying qualifications. By 1821 Connecticut, Delaware, Massachusetts, and New York had liberalized their suffrage provisions regarding property, while Georgia, New Hampshire, and South Carolina had removed such requirements completely. The newer western states enjoyed a unique experience; for in keeping with the vigorous equality of the frontier, there was little if any question concerning the exclusion of certain classes or groups from the franchise. Ohio, Louisiana, and Mississippi came in with only tax-

---

[1] Alexander Hamilton, quoted in Jonathan Elliot, ed., *The Debates in the Several State Conventions, on the Adoption of the Federal Constitution, as Recommended by the General Convention at Philadelphia, in 1787* (J. B. Lippincott Company, Philadelphia, 1888), Vol. 1, pp. 421–22.

[2] Virginia required ownership of a given number of acres of real estate; North Carolina required ownership of fifty acres of land to vote for state senators, but only the payment of public taxes to vote for members of the lower house; New Hampshire, Rhode Island, and New York required ownership of real estate of definite value.

[3] Delaware, Connecticut, and Massachusetts provided the alternative of other property; South Carolina provided payment of taxes as an alternative; and Maryland simply designated ownership of a given sum of money as an alternative.

[4] New Jersey and Georgia required property of given value; Pennsylvania required prior payment of public taxes.

[5] David Saville Muzzey, *The United States of America* (Ginn and Co., Boston, 1933), Vol. 1, p. 348.

paying qualifications;[6] and after 1817 every state which joined did ✓ so with provision for universal manhood suffrage. By 1840 Rhode Island remained the only state where the colonial policy of exclusion prevailed unmodified.

This tremendous extension of the franchise, coupled with the growing interest in politics of the people in general, led to a vast increase in the number of active voters during the 1820's. The movement had gained such force by 1830 that practically every election campaign thereafter was directed principally toward the great mass of the people whose rule Hamilton had so greatly feared.[7]

Paralleling this movement toward extension of the franchise were a series of moves tending to democratize the actual business of politics and government. In keeping with their faith in the ability of the few to govern best, the framers of the Constitution vested the election of the President and Vice-President in a small body of electors to be selected at the discretion of the various state legislatures. As the Beards have stated it, they "hoped to introduce a quiet, dignified procedure about as decorous as the selection of a college rector by a board of clerical trustees." [8] The legislatures, again in keeping with the theory of the few governing the many, reserved these powers for themselves. Such provisions, reinforced by the practice of sending unresolved elections to the Senate (a body also chosen by the legislatures) and only in the last resort to the House of Representatives, were regarded by the founding fathers as one of the many checks on a possible "tyranny of the majority." Indeed, even such a liberal as Alexis de Tocqueville called the process "a happy expedient" whereby "the respect due to the popular voice is combined . . . with those precautions which the interests of the country demand." [9] Gradually, however, the people of each state sought to wrest this power, too, from the

---

[6] An interesting exception is Tennessee, which, although its neighbor Kentucky was able to come into the Union with universal manhood suffrage, fell to the conservative forces and entered with a freehold property requirement not removed until 1834.

[7] See Jacob H. Freid, "The Log Cabin Symbol in American Presidential Politics" (Unpublished Ph.D. Thesis, Columbia University, 1948).

[8] Charles A. Beard and Mary R. Beard, *The Rise of American Civilization* (Macmillan, New York, 1946), Vol. I, p. 545.

[9] Alexis de Tocqueville, *Democracy in America* (Phillips Bradley, ed.; Alfred A. Knopf, New York, 1946), Vol. I, p. 134.

few; and popular choice of presidential electors spread until by 1832 there was only one state, South Carolina, in which the legislature continued to designate them.

The democratizing forces also made headway within the structures of the political parties themselves. Hitherto, the choice of candidates for the highest offices had been made by the members of Congress and the state legislatures assembled in party caucuses. Now, these duties began to fall to popular conventions displaying a more adequate representation of the rank-and-file elements of the parties. Spurred by influences from the frontier states and from the working people in the towns, a new attitude began to develop concerning the nature of requisites for public office. The common people, having gained control of elective offices, could not very well conceive of these offices as filled only by representatives of a benevolent aristocracy. More and more the notion of eligibility for public office regardless of social or economic position began to govern the selection of candidates.

The result of these three major changes—the extension of the franchise, the rise of popular interest in the functions of government, and the conception of universal eligibility for public office—was a vital new political role for the common man. To the great body of the people, these broad changes meant that at last they were to exercise the power which they considered their "natural and inalienable right." To the more conservative upper classes, the moves represented the culmination of the trend toward complete "tyranny of the majority." Many were pessimistic as to the chances for national survival, fearing that the long-dreaded rule of the masses had finally come. "The country," wrote John Randolph of Roanoke, "is ruined past redemption: it is ruined in the spirit and character of the people." [10] Yet, in spite of efforts to avert the change, political power rapidly slipped from the hands of the seaboard freeholders, planters, merchants, and factory owners into the hands of the western farmers and the working people of the growing cities. The latter swiftly used it to win the bloodless "revolution of 1828" by electing their beloved Andrew Jackson to the Presidency.

[10] Randolph to J. Brockenbrough, Jan. 12, 1829, in Hugh A. Garland, *The Life of John Randolph of Roanoke* (D. Appleton, New York, 1850), Vol. 2, p. 317.

2. THE STRUGGLE TO PRESERVE SOCIAL EQUALITY

Although certain segments of colonial society had favored the development of an aristocracy similar to the great landed nobilities of the Old World, the actual chances of such a pattern taking root were weak. Drawing on the lower and middle classes of Europe for its population, the New World offered to every man willing to work the opportunity to carve out a life of plenty. The history of the colonies records a gradual modification of the laws of inheritance and entail to the point where there was little chance of a landed aristocracy perpetuating itself. The economic and political conditions which prevailed led Tocqueville to remark in 1835: "Men are there seen on a greater equality in point of fortune and intellect . . . more equal in their strength, than in any other country of the world, or in any age of which history has preserved the remembrance." [11]

Although there were classes in America, by the 1830's the gulf between them had become slight. Francis Grund, a German visitor, observed that the "laboring classes in America are really less removed from the wealthy merchants and professional men than they are in any part of Europe; and the term 'mob,' with which the lower classes in England are honored, does not apply to any portion of the American community." [12] Most arguments concerning the relative position of the rich and the poor, he continued, "are more founded on theories and analogies, than on actual observation of the different classes of society in the United States. There is no distinct line of demarcation between the rich and the poor, as in Europe; the deserters from both ranks, but especially from the latter, being more numerous than those who remain; and the number of new comers putting computation altogether out of the question." [13] Within such a context of vertical social movement, it is not difficult to see how class lines would fail to harden.

What aristocracy there was in America—those men who had

---

[11] Alexis de Tocqueville, *op. cit.*, Vol. I, p. 53. The journals of a number of European visitors to America seem to afford particularly rich illustrative material for this section because of the perspective with which they viewed the American social scene.

[12] Francis Grund, *The Americans, in Their Moral, Social, and Political Relations* (Marsh, Capen & Lyon, Boston, 1837), p. 38.   [13] *Ibid.*, p. 238.

begun to amass the great trading fortunes or land holdings—
was careful to remain ever close to the great body of the people.
Tocqueville noted that there was no class in America in which "the
taste for intellectual pleasures is transmitted with hereditary fortune and leisure and by which the labors of intellect are held in
honor." [14] He observed an actual mistrust of the indolent wealthy
by the common people.[15] The more opulent citizens took "great
care not to stand aloof from the people. . . ." [16] What distinguished them more than any other factor from members of contemporary European aristocracies was their insistence that every
member engage in some kind of productive labor. "I have sometimes met in America," Tocqueville continued, "with young men
of wealth, personally disinclined to all laborious exertion, but who
had been compelled to embrace a profession. Their disposition
and their fortune allowed them to remain without employment;
public opinion forbade it, too imperiously to be disobeyed." [17] Sir
Charles Lyell, on disembarking in New England, observed ". . . we
seemed to have been in a country where all, whether rich or poor,
were laboring from morning till night, without ever indulging in a
holiday." [18] Even in the realm of dress, class distinctions became
less and less obvious. By 1830 gentlemen of the well-to-do classes
no longer wore knee breeches and shirts of lace. Although there
were still differentiating signs, such as frills and coats, there was a
growing tendency toward uniformity in dress.[19]

Both Grund and Tocqueville observed the lack of contempt for
the more humble occupations. Nor was the idea of working for
economic remuneration looked down upon as it was among the
European aristocracy. "In the United States," remarked Tocqueville, "professions are more or less laborious, more or less profitable; but they are never either high or low: every honest calling is
honorable." [20] With the upper classes linked firmly to the mass,
the myth of high social status being within the personal reach of
everyone was widely held. "No Americans," he continued, "are

[14] Alexis de Tocqueville, *op. cit.*, Vol. I, p. 52.
[15] *Ibid.*, Vol. I, p. 278.   [16] *Ibid.*, Vol II, p. 104.   [17] *Ibid.*, Vol. II, p. 237.
[18] Charles Lyell, *A Second Visit to the United States of North America* (Harper &
Brothers, New York, 1849), Vol. II, p. 91.
[19] Carl Russell Fish, *The Rise of the Common Man* (Macmillan, New York, 1927),
p. 8.
[20] Alexis de Tocqueville, *op. cit.*, Vol. II, p. 153.

devoid of a yearning desire to rise . . . All are constantly seeking to acquire property, power, and reputation. . . ." [21]

In keeping with these standards, the humbler classes of society bore a pride which fascinated visitors from Europe. "The spirit of the institutions of the States," wrote the Frenchman, Marryat, "is so opposed to servitude, that it is chiefly from the emigrants that the Americans obtain their supply of domestics." [22] Grund pointed to the continual appearance of complaints in the diaries of European aristocrats visiting America regarding the inefficiency of servants; [23] while Sir Charles Lyell advised Europeans contemplating the journey to America to leave their domestics at home, lest they become infected with the above-mentioned spirit, and ruined in terms of further usefulness. [24] In general, the lot of the people was a good one and a secure one. The spirit of optimism and of progress was everywhere to be seen; and if it had been a prime purpose of this generation to weaken the potential aristocracy which existed in its youth, it had succeeded to a large degree.

Hard on the heels of this victory of the common man, however, the rumblings of the new industrialism presaged changes in the near Utopia. Factories were springing up over the countryside, and around them, bustling towns and cities. Trading centers thrived as the steamboat, the railroad, and the telegraph revolutionized commerce and communication. Everywhere, the beginnings of the great movement from farm to city were in evidence. Those who perceived these changes—those who foresaw the social inequalities they portended—took two approaches. One group sought to stem the tide, their futile efforts resembling a crumbling dike in the face of a gigantic torrent. The other sought to impress upon those in greatest danger of losing their new-found democracy the consequences which industrialism bore for them. The former were the dying remnants of the agrarian Republicans; the latter were the leaders of the eastern "labor movement." When they joined forces, they became the backbone of the new Jacksonian movement and its political instrument, the Democratic Party.

The Jeffersonian Republicans saw the only hope for the preser-

[21] *Ibid.*, Vol. II, p. 243.

[22] Frederick Marryat, *A Diary in America* (Longman, Orme, Brown, Green and Longmans, London, 1839), Vol. 1, Pt. II, p. 144.

[23] Francis Grund, *op. cit.*, p. 236.   [24] Charles Lyell, *op. cit.*, Vol. II, p. 167.

vation of democracy based on a nation of agrarian freeholders—a hardy, independent stock close to the soil, proud and independent. Indeed, it was such a group of freeholders which Thomas Jefferson called the "chosen people of God." [25] On the other hand, they feared the emergence of a new class of laborers whose freedom was linked to the wage system. "The mobs of great cities," Jefferson held, "add just so much to the support of pure government, as sores do to the strength of the human body." [26] They saw political democracy resting only on the strong economic base of a well-distributed agricultural economy. Their warnings were published and circulated widely during the first decades of the nineteenth century. John Taylor, sage of Virginia, saw in the growing system of finance and industrialism a threat which could lay waste the natural economic order and establish, through the legalized plunder of private property, a new aristocracy of "paper and patronage." [27] His warnings, however, and similar ones from such men as John Randolph of Virginia and Nathaniel Macon of North Carolina, went relatively unheeded.

The "mobs of the cities" which Jefferson despised were growing, for the new industrial machine demanded human labor in ever increasing amounts. They were the beginnings of a great army that was to form the working class of the United States. It must be borne in mind, however, that the pre-Civil War American worker in no way resembled his later counterpart. Steeped in a heritage of social equality, he was both psychologically and functionally still a petty-bourgeois producer. As a matter of fact, one fails to note any genuine feeling of class consciousness among American laborers until well into the 1850's.

Yet, even in light of this fact, by 1830 there were unmistakable changes in the economic and social life of workingmen. In the cities, the subsistence farm was a thing of the past, and whole families, including the male breadwinner, were dependent on the wage system. Although the great majority still belonged to the class of independent artisans, there was a growing number fully tied to a productive system in which they owned little. The latter typified

[25] Thomas Jefferson, "Notes on the State of Virginia," in *The Writings of Thomas Jefferson* (Paul Leicester Ford, ed.), Vol. III, p. 268.   [26] *Ibid.*, Vol. III, p. 269.
[27] John Taylor, *An Inquiry into the Principles and Policy of the Government of the United States* (Fredericksburg, 1814).

what the former feared most—the loss of economic independence. It was principally in connection with the growth of these urban groups that the workingmen's organizations experienced their rise to prominence during the 1820's and 30's.

The banding together of workingmen for their mutual interest had precedents in America during the last years of the eighteenth century—in the organization of the Federal Society of Journeymen Cordwainers in Philadelphia in 1794. Collective action by such groups had its beginning when this society conducted its first strike in 1799 to resist wage cuts by the masters. During the next decades, even though the courts declared strikes conspiratorial actions in restraint of trade, such associations multiplied and flourished—experiencing ups and downs with the variations of the economic situation. By the time of Jackson's election, artisans in every craft had organized in the larger towns; and by 1836 there were fifty-three unions reported in Philadelphia, fifty-two in New York, twenty-three in Baltimore, and sixteen in Boston. It seemed inevitable, especially during a period of political unrest, that these workingmen's organizations would develop political arms; and accordingly, workingmen's parties sprang up in Philadelphia in 1828, in New York in 1829, and throughout New England during the early 1830's.

It was principally through the intellectuals, writers and reformers associated with or in sympathy with the labor movement, that the great wealth of "labor literature" emerged. This literature, at heart a literature of social protest, was a potent influence in determining the problems with which the common man concerned himself. It provided one philosophical base for the great controversies over the National Bank, education, land policy, the tariff, and the monetary system.

According to these intellectuals, the struggles were between the great body of the people—workers, small producers, and small farmers—on the one hand, and the small minority comprising capitalist and financier, on the other. Whereas the former were "woefully unorganized," the latter had extended its "well-ordered tentacles" over the state, the financial system, the press, and education. "The rich perceive, acknowledge, and act upon a common interest, and why not the poor?" asked William Leggett, fiery radical editor of *The Evening Post* (New York).[28] "The few have always . . . seen the necessity of the closest union among themselves in order to maintain their ascendency, while the many have not only been ignorant of this fact, but have always regarded the few as their benefactors, protectors, and friends," inveighed Frederick Robinson before the Trades' Union of Boston in an Independence Day Oration in 1834.[29] As it had been the purpose of the previous generation to put an end to the growing landed aristocracy of the Colonial Period, so it became the driving purpose of these leaders to break these privileges of the new aristocracy.

They saw in the financial systems of an expanding merchant and industrial capitalism ogres which would destroy the broad base of social democracy in America. "Thus far . . . we perceive our constitution of *equal rights* to be the merest untenanted skeleton of liberty that the imagination of man can conceive; which, by its *operation,* creates aristocracy, privileges, extortion, monopoly, and overgrown fortunes, and which, by its *letter,* declares that equality of rights shall be guaranteed to all and the pursuit of happiness to be a common boon secured to industry by the equity of her principles and the simplicity of her laws," wrote Stephen Simpson, early leader of the Philadelphia Working Men's Party.[30] "Property is no longer secure, and life in jeopardy . . . ," cried Leggett; "The scrip nobility of this Republic have adopted towards the free people of this Republic the same language which the Feudal Barons and the despot who contested with them the power of oppressing the people, used towards their serfs and villains, as they were opprobiously [*sic*] called." [31]

How were the small planters, farmers, mechanics, and laborers, whom Jackson called "the bone and sinew of the country," [32] to meet the problem? The intellectuals provided two responses: (1) the organization and unifying of their own forces and (2) the de-

---

[28] William Leggett, *The Evening Post* (New York), Nov. 4, 1834, p. 2, col. 3.

[29] Frederick Robinson, "An Oration Delivered before the Trades' Union of Boston and Vicinity," July 4, 1834, quoted in Joseph Blau, ed., *Social Theories of Jacksonian Democracy* (Hafner, New York, 1947), p. 321.

[30] Stephen Simpson, "The Working Man's Manual: A New Theory of Political Economy, on the Principle of Production the Source of Wealth," quoted in Joseph Blau, ed., *op. cit.,* pp. 141–42.   [31] William Leggett, *op. cit.,* p. 2, col. 3.

[32] *Gen. Jackson's Farewell Address to the People of the United States, together with His Proclamation to South Carolina* (Harrisburg, 1850), p. 11.

centralization of the power elements in society—the state, the banking system, etc.[33]

As for hindrances to the organization of workers, the restraint of the courts has been mentioned above. There was also probably much in the tradition of individualism, economically and politically, which further restrained such movement. The "laborite" intellectuals waged a constant war against these restraints. Thus Leggett wrote:

> But let us ask what and where is the danger of a combination of the labouring classes, in vindication of their political principles, or in defence of their menaced rights? Have they not the right to act in concert, when their opponents act in concert? Nay, is it not their bounden duty to combine against the only enemy they have to fear as yet in this free country, monopoly and a great paper system that grinds them to the dust? Truly this is strange republican doctrine, and this is a strange Republican Country, where men cannot unite in one common effort, in one common cause, without rousing the cry of danger to the rights of person and property. Is not this a Government of the People, founded on the rights of the People, and instituted for the express object of guarding them against the encroachments and usurpations of power? And if they are not permitted the possession of common interest; the exercise of a common feeling; if they cannot combine to resist by constitutional means, these encroachments; to what purpose were they declared free to exercise the right of suffrage in the choice of rulers, and the making of laws? [34]

According to these intellectuals, the only way for workingmen to fight the power of the "well-organized" upper middle classes was to organize, and to make their organized strength felt at the polls. Through their newly-won franchise, "the people" would eventually triumph over this new "aristocracy." "Teach the lawgivers a salutary lesson at the polls . . . ," preached Theophilus Fisk, "vote for no man who is not pledged to maintain your cause at all risks and at every hazard. If you are united, your strength is well nigh omnipotent." [35]

If this "labor literature" was not entirely accepted by the working groups, it did sensitize them to some of the sweeping changes

---

[33] This latter plan seems the logical reconstruction of the earlier efforts at political and economic decentralization advanced by the Jeffersonian Republicans.

[34] William Leggett, *op. cit.*, p. 2, col. 4.

[35] Theophilus Fisk, "Capital Against Labor," in *The Evening Post* (New York), Aug. 6, 1835, p. 2, col. 2.

which were taking place. Though the spirit of equality described by the foreign travelers still pervaded the scene, the insecurity of long hours, low pay, and sporadic employment was already in evidence in the mill towns and cities. Slums and poor working conditions were beginning to appear; and the huge immigrations of the 1840's rapidly accelerated their development. The writings of such men as Robert Owen carried reports of the dreadful conditions which industrialism had wrought among the English artisans,[36] while pamphlets like Mathew Carey's *Appeal to the Wealthy of the Land* [37] revealed similarly distressing conditions in America. All these things were viewed with increasing alarm by the lower middle classes; and though industrialism had not yet destroyed their economic independence, they became both frightened of its desolation elsewhere and determined to counter its unfavorable effects at home.

3. Changes in the Conception of Man and Society

Two intellectual trends, perhaps more than any other, reflect the broad changes in the conception of man and society which occurred during the early years of the Republic: one, the liberalizing of Christianity; the other, the growth of dynamic democracy. Together, they provided the spiritual force behind the tremendous wave of reform movements which swept the nation between 1820 and 1850.

It will be recalled that the Puritan fathers, following Calvin's dictum that "civil government is designed, as long as we live in this world, to cherish and support the external worship of God . . ." [38] had provided for the strictest ecclesiastical regulation of their community. The established church, enjoying legal support and preference, stood as the ultimate repository of political as well as reli-

[36] According to Joseph Dorfman (*The Economic Mind in American Civilization*), the ideas of the European socialists, though they were reinterpreted in terms of the American scene, provided a source of inspiration for much of the "laborite" literature.

[37] Mathew Carey, *Appeal to the Wealthy of the Land, Ladies as Well as Gentlemen, on the Character, Conduct, Situation, and Prospects of Those Whose Sole Dependence for Subsistence Is on the Labour of Their Hands* (Second Edition, Philadelphia, 1833).

[38] John Calvin, "Institutes of the Christian Religion," quoted in Columbia University, *Introduction to Contemporary Civilization in the West; A Source Book* (Columbia University Press, New York, 1946), Vol. 1, p. 514.

gious authority. The suffrage was restricted to its members, tithes were levied for the support of its clergy, and dissent from its peculiar doctrines was vigorously suppressed. While all of the colonial governments were by no means of a similar theocratic character, some such cooperation between the civil authority and a given established church usually characterized the early years of most of them.

Two factors during the eighteenth century provided the philosophical springboards for the struggle against the colonial establishments: the Great Awakening and the influences of eighteenth century Rationalism in the new world.[39] The former, embodying the spirit of a more personal, evangelical religion, saw the birth of the Separatist movements in the various states. Fed by an ever increasing membership, the more "popular" denominations, such as the Baptists and the Methodists, formed a powerful opposition to the entrenched forces of the established orders. Eighteenth century Rationalism, on the other hand, embodied the scientific reason of the Positivists and the humanism of the French Enlightenment. It sought to challenge the ascendancy of the established orders through the theory of natural rights. Indeed, these currents reached their culmination when such a document as the Virginia Declaration of Rights proclaimed in 1776:

That Religion, or the duty we owe to our CREATOR, and the manner of discharging it can be directed only by reason and conviction, not by force or violence, and therefore all men are equally entitled to the free exercise of religion, according to the dictates of conscience; and that it is the mutual duty of all to practise christian forbearance love and charity toward each other.[40]

Yet, at the beginning of the Revolution, there were established churches in nine of the thirteen colonies. New Hampshire, Connecticut, and Massachusetts had established the Congregationalist, while in New York and the majority of the southern states,[41] it was the Episcopalian that held sway.

The Revolutionary War strengthened the forces making inroads

[39] Evarts Green, *Religion and the State* (New York University Press, New York, 1941), p. 65.
[40] Gaillard Hunt, ed., *The Writings of James Madison* (G. P. Putnam's Sons, New York, 1900–10), Vol. I, p. 40.
[41] Virginia, Maryland, North Carolina, South Carolina, and Georgia.

into these church-state unions.[42] It not only provided a need for the support of the dissenting sects; it also sharply accentuated the inconsistencies of an established clergy with a natural rights philosophy.[43] Although pressures were brought to bear with increasing force, the tithes for the support of official religion did not immediately disappear. By the time of the Constitutional Convention in 1789, and the debates over the Bill of Rights in the Congress of 1791, nine of the original thirteen states had effected disestablishment.[44] At this stage of the movement, the First Amendment to the Federal Constitution was framed, both reflecting on a national scale the growing sentiment favoring separation, and serving to reinforce further the forces aiming at disestablishment. Though the struggles were long and bitter, separation was finally secured in Maryland in 1810, in Connecticut in 1818, and in Massachusetts in 1833. For all practical purposes, this latter date marked the final achievement of disestablishment on the American scene.[45]

If the Americans of this period saw fit to disestablish their religion, however, it was not for any lack of interest. ". . . there is no country in the world," remarked Tocqueville, "where the Christian religion retains a greater influence over the souls of men than in America. . . ." [46] Sunday Laws were still observed to differing extents; and foreign travelers, with the exception of the British, were constantly impressed by the character of Sunday observance. Church attendance remained the fashion; and on the frontier it was limited only for lack of available facilities. Although religious tithes had been discontinued, religion was, on a basis purely volun-

[42] J. Franklin Jameson, *The American Revolution Considered as a Social Movement* (Princeton University Press, Princeton, 1940), p. 85.

[43] Evarts Green, *op. cit.*, p. 76.

[44] Delaware, Georgia, New Jersey, New York, North Carolina, South Carolina, Pennsylvania, Rhode Island, and Virginia. For an excellent report of the dynamics of the achievement of separation, see R. Freeman Butts, *The American Tradition in Religion and Education* (Beacon Press, Boston, 1950).

[45] New Hampshire provided that "no portion of any one particular religious sect or denomination, shall ever be compelled to pay towards the support of the teacher or teachers of another persuasion, sect or denomination," but "continued to authorize towns to provide funds for the support of public protestant teachers of piety, religion, and morality." See Francis Newton Thorpe, *The Federal and State Constitutions, Colonial Charters, and Other Organic Laws of the States, Territories, and Colonies Now or Heretofore Forming the United States of America* (Government Printing Office, Washington, 1909), Vol. IV, pp. 2454 and 2493.

[46] Alexis de Tocqueville, *op. cit.*, Vol. I, p. 303.

tary, better supported than ever before.[47] Ministers held a favored place in public life; and the moral base known as "Christian Principles" was widely accepted in the area of values.

Within the area of content, this same period also witnessed extensive changes among the theological systems themselves. The movement amounted essentially to a destruction of the authoritarian predestination of Calvinism in favor of a more individual and personalized form of religious experience. Conducting a searching examination of the Calvinist theology in terms of the new liberal thought, Unitarianism provided what Parrington has called a bridge between colonial times and the world of the Middle Period.[48] Incorporating a profound respect for the dignity of the human individual, Unitarianism moved from an angry autocratic God to a warm, loving, embracing God, from a world of Elect and Damned to a world where each could achieve his own individual salvation. In its appeal to "known reason in every step of its progress," it was for many the true "democracy of religion." [49] Related to the spirit of Unitarianism, and yet in many ways antithetical to it, was the spirit of Protestant evangelicism growing out of the Great Awakening. Emphasizing the highly personal, vividly emotional appeal of individual conversion, this form of religious experience rapidly took root in rural and frontier areas where life so often meant hardship, boredom, loneliness, and fear.

Closely paralleling this religious movement away from the authoritarian predestination of Calvinism was the rise of an American philosophy of democracy. The protection of the oceans, the distance from powerful neighbors, the huge tracts of fertile land—all had contributed from the beginning to a sense of physical security not to be found in Europe. The vigorous equality of an independent yeomanry, kept always alive by the frontier, had pervaded American society from its earliest years. Now, the influx of ideas from the European Enlightenment richly fertilized the roots of democratic thought.

That trend of thought which perhaps more than any other ex-

---

[47] Carl Russell Fish, *op. cit.*, pp. 179–80.
[48] Vernon Louis Parrington, *Main Currents in American Thought* (Harcourt, Brace & Co., New York, 1930), Vol. 2, p. 341.
[49] See, for instance, Thomas Hamilton, *Men and Manners in America* (W. Blackwood, Edinburgh, 1833), Vol. 1, pp. 167–68.

pressed the prevailing optimism of the American scene was the humanitarian doctrine of progress—of the infinite perfectibility of mankind. Insisting that through the rational treatment of the problems besetting him, man could aspire to ever higher levels of happiness, it vigorously asserted the dawn of a new era. Differences between men were minimized; the accent was thrown on the dignity of man and mankind. In the new science and reason of the Enlightenment, optimistic philosophers saw the tools for the fulfillment of these aspirations. Man's perfectibility is indefinite, they urged; it has no other limit than the duration of the globe upon which nature has placed him.[50] This was the faith of dynamic democracy.

Out of this faith emerged a new conception of the common man. Nowhere was it better indicated than in the growing respectability of *democracy* in the eyes of the people and their leaders. For the Jeffersonian Republicans, the freehold farmer and the independent artisan had been the only firm foundation of a free society. Yet they still conceived of government as the job of the enlightened upper class representatives who would inevitably be chosen by such an electorate. It remained for the liberal forces of the Jacksonian movement to transform this classical Jeffersonian republicanism into a working conception of democracy.

Fed by the ideas and ideals of the West, it became the common man—"the planter, the farmer, the mechanic and the laborer . . . the bone and sinew of the country" [51]—who stood as the symbol of the American people. Gradually, the literature of the "laborites" and of the Democratic Party began to speak of *the people* in romantic tones suggesting the ideal society. "The exact measure of the progress of civilization," wrote the Democrat, George Bancroft, "is the degree in which the intelligence of the common mind has prevailed over wealth and brute force; in other words, the measure of the progress of civilization is the progress of the people." [52] His contemporary, Ralph Waldo Emerson, similarly declared: "Ours

[50] Condorcet, *Esquisse d'un Tableau Historique des Progrès de l'Esprit Humain* (Librarie de la Bibliothèque Nationale, Paris, 1886), p. 19.

[51] *General Jackson's Farewell Address to the People of the United States, Together with His Proclamation to South Carolina*, p. 11.

[52] George Bancroft, "The Office of the People in Art, Government, and Religion," *Literary and Historical Miscellanies* (Harper & Brothers, New York, 1855), p. 427.

is the country of poor men. Here is practical democracy; here is the human race poured out over the continent to do itself justice; all mankind in its shirt-sleeves; not grimacing like poor, rich men in cities, pretending to be rich, but unmistakably taking off its coat to hard work. . . ." [53] By the age of Jackson, it was a foregone conclusion that the common man was to rule American society. It remained only for history to bear out the fears of conservatives or fulfill the fond hopes of liberals.

It was essentially a synthesis of the two intellectual currents described above—of liberalized Christianity and dynamic democracy—which gave birth to the wave of reform movements that swept the nation in the 1840's and 50's. While the older theological systems had insisted that life in this world was simply a preparation for life in the next, humanitarian optimism now saw man fulfilling his destiny in the here and now. Predestination gave way to unbounded possibilities for individual and social progress. Thus, the way was opened for needed social reforms to be accomplished in the lifetime of a generation.

Taking up the new ideas concerning the worth of the common man, the dignity of the human personality, and the possibility of infinite progress, eager reformers organized for the struggle to alleviate social evil. Recruits flocked to their standards, for it was an age when practically anyone with a new idea could gain a following. Universal peace, prison conditions, the militia system, capital punishment, temperance, imprisonment for debt, care of the insane, women's rights, education, working conditions and slavery—all provided areas for their zealous efforts. The struggles these groups experienced were often long, bitter, and fruitless. Inevitably, the movement bred a lunatic fringe which brought down criticism on genuine and spurious alike. But their victories were apparent in the wealth of pioneering social legislation they secured. Though they had failed in their Utopian attempt to achieve the perfect society, they had opened America's eyes to certain conditions clearly incompatible with her professed ideals of democracy, and stimulated her first imperfect steps in the direction of their amelioration.

[53] Ralph Waldo Emerson, "The Fortune of the Republic," *Miscellanies*, Vol. 11 of *Emerson's Complete Works* (Houghton Mifflin and Co., Boston, 1893), p. 408.

4. THE RISE OF NATIONALISM

The ratification of the Constitution and the election of the first administration in 1789 marked the birth of the United States as a sovereign and independent nation. Born of a federation of thirteen formerly independent states, however, young America was wracked by internal dissension and conflicting allegiances. Actually, it was a matter of decades before the new nation could boast a faithful and devoted citizenry of its own. Yet, the development of this new nationalism constituted one of the most powerful forces on the American scene during the Middle Period.

Economically, the growth of nationalism was closely allied with the interests of the growing class of merchant and industrial capitalists. Concerned over the ever increasing productivity of the more advanced British capitalism, American capitalists saw in a plan of economic independence the means of furthering their own interests and at the same time minimizing the effects of European competition. Thus, the forces of nationalism were firmly tied to such proposals as Henry Clay's American Plan and the protective tariff.[54]

The political implications of these proposals were powerfully in favor of a stronger central government. Although both the Jeffersonian and Jacksonian conceptions of government centered in weak powers on the national level, it was evident that if the commercial interests were going to expand, such items as currency regulation, waterway development, harbor improvement, and tariff protection were of dire necessity. Inasmuch as the Constitution had reserved these to the federal government, it was apparent that only through a strong and active national authority could they be secured. Politically, then, it seems likely that the forces favoring economic nationalism were a potent factor in effecting the coalescing of the formerly loosely bound states into a single, stable, integrated unit.

Ideologically, the concept of this new nationalism was rooted deeply in the democratic faith of the *mission of America*. Bound up with the currents of the Doctrine of Progress and of Protestant

---

[54] The former would vastly improve the transportation facilities of the West, linking it with Eastern manufactures. The latter would keep the infant industries of the East on their feet until they could more easily endure a free competition with foreign products.

Christianity, this faith revolved around the American's notion that it was his divinely inspired duty not only to carry out his democratic principles at home, but also to carry them to peoples all over the world. "He has been educated," observed Marryat, "to despise all other countries, and to look upon his own as the first in the world; he has been taught that all other nations are slaves to despots, and that the American citizen only is free, and this is never contradicted." [55] It was to these other nations that the nineteenth century American was to carry the torch of liberty, the bright fire of democracy, and the saving grace of Christianity.

One of the first evidences of the new nationalism was the appearance of a profound interest in the nation's past. During the two decades from 1830 to 1850, at least thirty-five historical societies were organized and began the momentous task of gathering together the documents and other historical materials which were to become the symbols of the great past.[56] The necessity for a new history of the United States, written from a patriotic point of view, was fulfilled by George Bancroft in his first comprehensive history of the American people,[57] while numerous lesser works appeared on the scene for school and popular consumption.[58] And if reverence for the past developed as an integral aspect of the new American patriotism, it was matched equally by a reverence for the future. ". . . the Americans," observed Grund, *"love* their country, not, indeed, *as it is,* but *as it will be.* . . . They live in the future, and *make* their country as they go on." [59] Society was looking forward; progress was inevitable. If the American past was unique and to be revered, the fulfillment of its future was the aspiration of all mankind. Thus, continued Grund: "An American considers the history of his country as the beginning of a new era; and cares, therefore, less for the past, than he does for the present and the future." [60] The young society looked optimistically forward to the fulfillment of its manifest destiny.

[55] Frederick Marryat, *op. cit.,* Vol. II, Pt. 2, p. 82.
[56] Merle Curti, *The Growth of American Thought* (Harper & Brothers, New York, 1943), p. 410.
[57] George Bancroft, *History of the United States from the Discovery of the American Continent* (D. Appleton and Co., 1892–95).
[58] See *American Annals of Education,* Vol. II, p. 378.
[59] Francis Grund, *op. cit.,* p. 151.   [60] *Ibid.,* p. 135.

A loyalty value always remains a nebulous, abstract thing unless it can be attached to a concrete symbol—a symbol which becomes the sentimental rallying point for all the emotions and attitudes connected with the loyalty value itself. The development of such symbols during these first decades of the nineteenth century served further to crystallize the common attachments which American society was building. The flag, the hero symbol, the patriotic song, the cartoon representation, the festive celebration—all served to translate loyalty, as it developed on a local level, into a sentiment of nationality. Thus, beginning with the Bunker Hill Monument near Boston, a series of monuments commemorating the great battles, heroes, and events of the Revolutionary War was begun.[61] By the end of the period, the myth and symbol of Washington had taken its place as the ideal of democratic man and hero, and the process had also begun with some of the lesser figures of the Colonial Period. They were to be, as Ralph Gabriel has pointed out, the newly canonized saints of the young national faith.[62] The flag, changing numerous times during the early years of national life, became among the most concrete of these rallying points, while such graphic symbols as "Brother Jonathan" and "Uncle Sam" appeared widely in popular songs, sketches, and cartoons. The Fourth of July, in its opportunities for patriotic declamation and celebration, lent itself neatly to the cultivation and expression of nationalist sentiment. There seems little doubt that these more popular symbols of the new spirit helped tremendously to engender patriotic sentiments in the great body of the people.

Another important relationship centered in the close support which Christianity tendered to American nationalism. Revolving around the dual conception of "a higher moral law" and "the American mission," many saw the role of the patriot as the role of the good Christian carrying his Christianity to the world. An article in the *Southern Literary Messenger*, entitled "Christianity and Patriotism," [63] is illustrative of many dealing with this theme. Christianity, in furnishing "the best culture to the human mind"

[61] George Edward Ellis, *History of the Battle of Bunker's (Breed's) Hill, on June 17, 1775 from Authentic Sources in Print and Manuscript* (Lockwood, Brooks, and Company, Boston, 1875).   [62] Ralph Gabriel, *op. cit.*, p. 93.
[63] "Christianity and Patriotism," in *Southern Literary Messenger*, Vol. VIII (1842), No. 9, pp. 600–06, signed "Elm."

(because of its capacity to direct the mind to the noblest ends and aspirations), provides the "safest preservative to social institutions." It requires and creates a healthy body of literature, it stimulates everywhere wholesome laws, and it protects with divine sanction the inalienable rights of man. Therefore, Christianity furnishes the best "guarantee to national perpetuity"; for in providing national states with the capacity to raise the level of the masses and to inspire individuals to the highest ideals, it provides the stuff of leadership and the foundation of justice. Essentially, the argument ran that Christianity alone could maintain liberty, that the maintenance of liberty was the basis of the national welfare, and thus, that Christianity supported the national welfare.[64]

It must be borne in mind that for many the relationship went two ways, and that if given churches had been disestablished, this fact was far removed from the general moral duty of the government to further the principles of Christianity. Thus, for instance, Justice Joseph Story noted that "it is impossible for those who believe in the truth of Christianity, as a divine revelation, to doubt that it is the especial duty of government to foster and encourage it among all the citizens and subjects. This is a point wholly distinct from that of the right of private judgment in matters of religion, and of the freedom of public worship according to the dictates of one's conscience." [65] The Protestantism of the Americans was just one more of those unique factors in their national heritage which they could identify with patriotism. In view of this, the Bible rapidly became identified as a patriotic symbol of the first order;[66] and through it, the missionary zeal of Christianity easily lent part of its emotional force to the furtherance of the new patriotic sentiments.

When this growing nationalism encountered the new waves of immigration from Northern Europe, it yielded a phenomenon alien to the American scene: nativism. Until the 1830's, America had beckoned to the weak and downtrodden of the world, welcoming all who would come, to the vast expanse of her bosom. On

[64] See also Alexis de Tocqueville, *op. cit.*, Vol. I, p. 306.

[65] Joseph Story, *Commentaries on the Constitution of the United States* (Little, Brown & Co., Boston, 1858), Vol. 2, p. 661.

[66] See, for example, Alfred B. Ely, *American Liberty, Its Sources—Its Dangers, and the Means of Its Preservation* (New York, 1850).

his individual ability to carve a life for himself and his family rested society's evaluation of the immigrant; on successfully coping with this task, he was duly qualified to participate in the affairs of the community. "The American commonwealth," noted Grund, "consists of a community of reason and good sense; its empire, therefore, is the largest, and its basis the most unalterable on which the prosperity of a people was ever established. . . . Whoever thinks as they do, is, morally speaking, a citizen of their community; and whoever entertains opinions in opposition to their established theory of government, must be considered a natural enemy to their country." [67]

But the new nationalism began drastically to alter this picture; and for the first time in earnest, the potential loyalty of the immigrant was called into question. Much of this hostility can probably be understood in such economic terms as labor's resentment of the immigrant's willingness to accept an inferior standard of living. Further understanding must also be sought on the intellectual level—in the feeling that the newcomers, stemming as they did from monarchical traditions, could not possibly participate in a republican community. "The foreigner, who attempts to drive the chariot of American freedom," inveighed a speaker before the Order of United Americans, "is but another Phaeton rashly and fatally seeking to guide the fiery coursers of the Sun; and that, which in its proper course, would give light, and heat, and happiness to man, will, once astray, not only spread terror and dismay abroad, but bring swift destruction upon the ignorant adventurer who sought to control an unknown power." [68] Doubtless many holding such sympathies earnestly feared the inundation of the young republic by a flow of immigration far in excess of the number it could healthfully absorb.[69] Others probably welcomed the opportunity to extend their own deeply felt bigotry.

The apex of all this mounting resentment toward foreigners, perhaps, was evidenced in the ever sharper hostility toward the

---

[67] Francis Grund, *op. cit.*, pp. 148–49.   [68] Alfred B. Ely, *op. cit.*, p. 27.

[69] See, for instance, Samuel F. B. Morse, *Imminent Dangers to the Free Institutions of the United States Through Foreign Immigration, and The Present State of the Naturalization Laws* (New York, 1835). In this, as in much of such literature, it is difficult to ascertain how much of this genuine concern is present, and how much is simply an expression of prejudice.

Catholic. As regards numbers, the Catholics in 1830 constituted but a small minority of the population; and it was not until the successive Irish potato famines of the 1840's that huge waves of immigrants swelled their numbers. Apparently, though, in light of the traditional Protestant suspicion of Catholicism, they were the logical scapegoats of nativism. Viewing with concern the hierarchical organization of the Catholic clergy—with its spiritual roots in Europe—and noting the failure of Catholic congregations in the several cities to gain control of their church property, the Protestant American turned increasing resentment toward this "undemocratic ecclesiastical organization." Even in the face of substantial opposition holding that the United States was the haven of *all* the world's oppressed, the nativist movement rapidly gained force. Terrorism against Catholic churches, convents, and individuals appeared in many places. Secret societies, such as the Sons of the Sires, the Supreme Order of the Star-Spangled Banner, and the Order of United Americans were organized and took on the work of defamation.

The waves of Irish and German Catholics who entered the United States during the 1840's only served to aggravate the situation. Although they were first welcomed as an unskilled labor force they soon began to settle down and take industrial jobs— driving out American labor with its higher standard of living. Tending to settle in groups, distinguished by their religious tenets, and scorned for their unified efforts in local politics, they stimulated the further development of nativism. ". . . the question of Popery and Protestantism, or Absolutism and Republicanism, which in these two opposite categories are convertible terms," wrote Samuel F. B. Morse, "is fast becoming and will shortly be the *great absorbing question,* not only of this country but of the whole civilized world." [70] "The Irish element," wrote Charles Dickens on his visit to the United States, "is acquiring such enormous influence in New York City, that when I think of it, and see the large Roman Catholic cathedral rising there, it seems unfair to stigmatise as 'American' other monstrous things that one also

[70] Morse to R. S. Willington, Esq., May 20, 1835, in Edward Lind Morse, ed., *Samuel F. B. Morse, His Letters and Journals* (Houghton Mifflin, Boston, 1914), Vol. 2, p. 36.

sees." [71] The nativist movement finally culminated in the formation of a Native American Party in the 1850's—a party which essentially amalgamated all of the forces of the nativist movement.[72] It was a short-lived effort, however, in the face of the approaching turmoil. Sectional conflicts were gaining ascendancy; and by 1861 the political influence of the nativists had declined to the point of relative insignificance.

If the nativist movement represented a kind of fanatical fringe of nationalism, its vehemence characterized one essence of this new force which had emerged. Shaping the course of national expansion in the role of Manifest Destiny, it seemed powerful enough by 1846 to be in large measure responsible for the initiation and successful prosecution of the Mexican War. It was no longer the harmless bravado of the young child, but had become the raucous bullying of the adolescent. In developing, however, it had provided a unifying element in an age of increasing sectionalism. It was a force which had knitted elements of the most heterogeneous sort—of diverse population stocks and conflicting regional and ideological affiliations—into a mesh of common loyalty and belief that was the new American nationality.

5. Footnote on the South

Conditions below the Mason-Dixon line during the early nineteenth century indicate a profound cleavage between the South, as a region, and the rest of the nation. By the latter half of the Middle Period, this uniqueness had developed to the point where a sense of regional pride, of a peculiar past, present, and future, and of a physical and spiritual unity, was rapidly pervading the southern way of life.[73] Therefore, although each of the principal trends which have been discussed eventually emerged in the South (at varying intervals with different degrees of vigor), the contradictory elements in its culture were powerful enough to warrant brief discussion at this point.

[71] John Forster, *The Life of Charles Dickens* (Lippincott, Philadelphia, 1872–74), Vol. III, p. 413.

[72] It was an oath-bound secret fraternity with an elaborate ritual. A candidate had to be descended from two generations of Protestant-American ancestors to qualify for admission.

[73] Merle Curti, *The Growth of American Thought*, pp. 427–28; 451–53.

Perhaps the principal point of difference between the South and the other regions lay in its economic system. The plantation[74] represented not only a geographical unit for agricultural production, but, in a fashion, a whole way of life. Constituted as the basic economic institution for the production of cotton and tobacco it set the whole tempo of southern life.[75] Around this miniature society revolved the political, social, religious, and intellectual life of the region. Furthermore, in its role as the dominant economic pattern, it was also instrumental in determining the social pattern and the inevitable range of class relationships.

Developing largely around the conception of the English gentleman which they borrowed from Europe,[76] the large landholders viewed society in terms of what Parrington has so aptly called "the dream of a Greek democracy." It was to be a humane and cultivated society, "set free from the narrow exactions of economics to engage in the higher work of civilization." [77] The conception easily rationalized a pyramidal type of class structure, with the small, select body of gentlemen landholders at the top and the great mass of the slaves at the broad base. In between was an almost caste-like array of classes based largely on the extent and kind of agricultural holdings.

Just below the large planters on the social scale were the smaller planters—those who did not possess as many slaves or as much land as the aristocracy. Working the smaller farms of the back country, these became the first to experience the economic squeeze of the plantation system in the rising cost of slaves and the decreased productivity of the land. Next in line were the independent yeomen farmers who, although they could not afford the luxury of

[74] The movement toward the unification of the small farms of the Colonial Period into the large plantations was a phenomenon of the eighteenth and early nineteenth centuries. By the latter period, though, they had emerged as the vast estates which set the tone of Southern life.

[75] For an excellent description of life on these plantations, see Philip Vickers Fithian, *Journals and Letters, 1767–74* (John Rogers Williams, ed.; Princeton Historical Society, Princeton, 1900); Ulrich Bonnell Phillips, *Life and Labor in the Old South* (Little, Brown, and Co., Boston, 1930); and John R. Commons *et al., Documentary History of American Industrial Society* (The Arthur H. Clark Co., Cleveland, 1910), Vol. 1–2.

[76] Louis Booker Wright, *The First Gentlemen of Virginia; Intellectual Qualities of the Early Colonial Ruling Class* (The Huntington Library, San Marino, 1940).

[77] Vernon Louis Parrington, *op. cit.,* Vol. 2, p. 99.

slaves, still held their land as a freehold. Had they tilled their land in the West, or in New England, they would have been among the prouder members of society. Within the social structure of the South, they were ever aware of the vast social distance between their own status and that of the plantation aristocracy. At the bottom of white society were the poor whites, the class who tilled the marginal and submarginal lands of the sand stretches or hills. Probably a principal difference between their lot and the lot of the Negro was color—a difference which they sought to preserve at all possible costs.

It is interesting to note the lack of any vigorous commercial class in this pyramidal scheme. In general, the tendency was for each planter to deal directly with the English and Dutch traders and shippers. The decentralized economy of largely independent plantation communities was not at all conducive to the development of mercantile towns. By 1860 there were only six southern communities with populations in excess of 20,000—Charleston, Richmond, Mobile, Memphis, Savannah, and New Orleans.[78] These towns were inhabited principally by the type of independent artisan characteristic of earlier European society. Bankers, lawyers, doctors, and other professional men were not found in large numbers; for these men usually pursued their professions only in addition to their duties as lords of their own plantations. If there was no ample evidence of an expanding merchant capitalism, there was considerably less illustrating any impact of industrialism. Manufactures like clothing, implements, etc., were largely produced on the plantations proper, or by the artisans of the towns. What other materials were needed were almost always supplied directly from outside sources.

Basically, then, this culture reflected as strong a pattern of landed aristocracy as existed anywhere in North America. Nurtured by the ideals of the British gentry, undisturbed by the commercial and industrial expansion of a growing middle class, it bred a society which became largely static, ideologically and intellectually. The preservation of southern "Greek democracy" rested on fundamental class solidity. "I am an aristocrat," cried John Ran-

---

[78] Eighth Census of the United States, Mortality and Vital Statistics of the United States (Washington, 1866), p. xviii.

dolph; "I love liberty, I hate equality." [79] The change from the older concept of republicanism into the newer concept of democracy was skillfully avoided. The humanitarian influences which had dominated the Virginia scene during the days of Jefferson and Madison were now retreating in the face of a vigorous desire to perpetuate the economics of the plantation system by every possible means. The effects of diminishing returns, high slave prices, and exhausted lands, increasingly apparent during the 1840's, only strengthened the determination to preserve the status quo. The capitalistic ways of northern industry were repudiated as utterly plebeian; the strengthening of the national government to aid this capitalism, as authoritarian. The southern response was centered in reaction, in a return to decentralized agrarian ways—to local economics and politics.

In the face of such political and economic realities, the forces of dynamic democracy made little headway. With no industrial enterprise developing, there was little of the labor unrest of the North. Receiving fewer and fewer of the new immigrants, the South experienced little of the influence of European socialism. What new ideas did manage to find their way into its thinking were quickly stamped out. The society as a whole was little receptive to change; it bred few leaders to carry the torch of reform. If there had been some hope for a gravitation toward more liberal ends in the Jeffersonian democracy of the early South, it was crushed in the militant political and economic regionalism of John C. Calhoun. Whereas the former philosophy had looked to the early natural extinction of the slave system, slave trading was now more profitable than ever. The spirited equality of Jefferson's freehold farmer had changed into the caste-like, benevolent oligarchy of a plantation aristocracy. The new system denied democracy in favor of a monarchical kind of republicanism, and it challenged the ways and power of the vigorous, youthful middle class. It retreated into its reactionary agrarianism until the jolt of the Civil War brought to a head the impending disaster of economic collapse, and left only ruin on which to build a new society.

[79] William Cabell Bruce, *John Randolph of Roanoke, 1773–1833* (G. P. Putnam's Sons, New York, 1922), Vol. II, p. 203.

PART 2

THE COMMON SCHOOL AS
AN EDUCATIONAL IDEAL

O NE of the principal attributes of every culture, or way of life, lies in the close relationships which its various components bear to one another. As such, any new element or change introduced into a culture will inevitably set off a chain of responses in other aspects of that culture, until the parts again achieve a new equilibrium. In this way, cultures are constantly undergoing reconstruction. They continually seek readjustment, never quite achieving it because of the rapidity of change and innovation.[1]

Education is just one among the countless activities comprising a society's way of life. As such, it cannot help but be materially affected by major changes in other realms of the culture. The preceding section undertook to describe briefly four principal developments during the early years of the American nation: (1) the democratizing of politics; (2) the growth of the struggle for social equality; (3) the change in the conception of man and society; and (4) the rise of nationalism. It was inevitable that these developments would exercise a profound influence on American education. Actually, they gave rise to certain demands which eventually determined the character of the common school. It

---

[1] See Ralph Linton, ed., *The Science of Man in the World Crisis* (Columbia University Press, New York, 1945), pp. 78–106, 206–10. See also the article on "Culture" by Malinowski in the *Encyclopaedia of the Social Sciences,* for an extended discussion of the culture construct as well as its specifically organic aspects.

is to these demands, then, that we must next turn in our effort to understand the state educational systems which eventually emerged.

1. THE DEMANDS OF REPUBLICAN GOVERNMENT

The first, and perhaps the most widespread, demand on education grew out of the new pattern of republicanism. It was increasingly argued that if there was to be universal exercise of the rights of suffrage and citizenship, all of society would have to be educated to this task. Although the liberal intellectual envisioned such education as a means of equipping the citizenry to make intelligent political choices, his conservative counterpart saw it largely as a propaganda agency to save society from the "tyranny of democratic anarchy." [2] In education, the latter saw the only way of counteracting the incipient radicalism of the newly enfranchised lower classes.[3] The end result of both, however, emerged as a vigorous demand for the universal education of the people—a demand conceived by its proponents to be at the very heart of republican society and government.

The argument itself was certainly not novel, having appeared prominently in the thinking of the founding fathers. Washington had counseled in his "Farewell Address": "Promote then as an object of primary importance, Institutions for the general diffusion of knowledge. In proportion as the structure of a government gives force to public opinion, it is essential that public opinion should be enlightened." [4] Similarly, Jefferson had reflected almost a half century of effort on behalf of universal education when he wrote in 1816: "If a nation expects to be ignorant and free, in a state of civilization, it expects what never was and never will be." [5]

[2] For an excellent intensive analysis of these differing qualities and bases of demands for universal education, see Sidney Jackson, *America's Struggle for Free Schools* (American Council on Public Affairs, Washington, 1941).

[3] Charles White, "On the Literary Responsibility of Teachers," in *The Lectures Delivered Before the American Institute of Instruction, at Lowell, (Mass.) August, 1838; Including the Journal of Proceedings, and a List of the Officers* (William D. Ticknor, Boston, 1839), p. 20.

[4] *The Writings of George Washington from the Original Manuscript Sources* (John C. Fitzpatrick, ed.; Government Printing Office, Washington, 1940), Vol. 35, p. 230.

[5] Thomas Jefferson to Colonel Charles Yancey, Jan. 6, 1816; in *The Writings of Thomas Jefferson* (Paul Leicester Ford, ed.; G. P. Putnam's Sons, New York, 1899), Vol. X, p. 4.

James Madison, too, had asserted in 1822: "A popular Government, without popular information, or the means of acquiring it, is but a Prologue to a Farce or a Tragedy; or, perhaps both. Knowledge will forever govern ignorance: And a people who mean to be their own Governors, must arm themselves with the power which knowledge gives." [6]

The theme was treated more frequently than ever during the Jacksonian period, appearing on the heels of universal manhood suffrage. It was nowhere more convincingly presented than by Charles Stewart Daveis, a young New England lawyer, in an address at Portland, Maine, on May 19, 1825.[7] Daveis exhibited no less than a passionate faith in the capabilities of the people to govern themselves.

Experience has certainly shown no sufficient reason to question the general aptitude of the People for self-government. When we observe the capacity discovered by the members of society in all their concerns, sagacity entering into all subjects, extending to all relations, and equal to all occasions, carried also into duties of administering its authority; and when we observe them indiscriminately executing or aiding in all its departments, civil and judicial, as jurors, magistrates, legislators, governors, acting as trustees of all the interests of the community for the benefit of the public and as guardians of all those rights for which law was designed as security, taken continually from all classes and returning to the general mass by the perpetual elective process, can we any longer doubt the efficacy of this great principle which is thus receiving constant refreshment and vigor from its original fountains? [8]

Daveis saw the power of the people basically as a moral one; thus it was "of the utmost consequence that its intellectual principle should be well informed." On this point, he made interesting reference to Machiavelli's *The Prince*. The safety of the state, he inferred from Machiavelli, depends principally on the educa-

---

[6] Madison to W. T. Barry, Aug. 4, 1822, in *The Writings of James Madison* (Gaillard Hunt, ed.; G. P. Putnam's Sons, New York, 1910), Vol. IX, p. 103. The theme was also central in the thinking of many intellectuals of the later eighteenth century who drew heavily on the thought of the French Enlightenment. See Allen Oscar Hansen, *Liberalism and American Education in the Eighteenth Century* (Macmillan, New York, 1926).

[7] Charles Stewart Daveis, "An Address Delivered on the Commemoration at Fryeburg, May 19, 1825," quoted in Joseph L. Blau, ed., *Social Theories of Jacksonian Democracy*, pp. 38–53.   [8] *Ibid.*, p. 45.

tion of the sovereign. As the power of the sovereign becomes greater, so in proportion does the necessity of his being well informed. The implications for democracy were crucial:

With a view to improve the principles of self-government in a state of society that subjects everything to its sense, in a country where the whole sovereignty is lodged in the people and all authority is exercised upon the strictest responsibility to the end of its universal welfare, *the education of the whole becomes the first interest of all.* The diffusion of knowledge becomes, therefore, the distribution of power. Where authority is appropriated for other purposes than the general good under any partial organization, a part is studiously educated for the government of the rest, who are deliberately left in ignorance to support the fundamental principles of the government. The proper system of republican education should *combine* the regular course of useful elementary instruction with that species of education which naturally "results from the political order of society." In this manner the moral education of *the prince,* if I may use the expression, becomes of the first importance, and it is a happy circumstance that there is always a generation of young and fair minds springing up among the people, free from any false impressions, in proper season to assume the real reins of power and exemplify the true principles and influence of education.[9]

In closing his argument, Daveis carefully pointed out that such an education as the republican system demands cannot be influenced by narrow or insidious purposes. "It pleads the cause of no party, it advocates no profession, is propitious to no predominance." It should call only on the highest of aims and emotions, for: "With its success is identified almost every rational hope of the future welfare of our race, extending to the suppression of the most fruitful causes of vice and misery, and embracing the widest spread of peace and happiness beneath the cope of heaven." [10]

The convincing nature of the argument was clearly evidenced by its increasing appearance in the utterances of public figures. Prominent among these were the governors of many of the northeastern, middle-eastern, and midwestern states.[11] Illustrative of their approach are the remarks of Governor Edward Everett of Massachusetts before an educational convention in the autumn of

[9] *Ibid.,* p. 46.
[10] *Ibid.,* p. 47.
[11] See, for instance, the *American Annals of Education,* Vol. I (1831), p. 125.

1838.[12] Concerning the duty of a popular government with regard to the elective franchise, the governor stated:

I do not mean, that it is necessary that every citizen should receive an education, which would enable him to argue all these questions at length, in a deliberative or popular assembly. But while it is his right, and his duty, to give effect to his judgment at the polls, and while the constitution necessarily gives as much weight to the vote of the uninformed and ignorant as to that of the well-instructed and intelligent citizen, it is plain, that the avenues to information should be as wide and numerous as possible; and that the utmost practicable extension should be given to a system of education, which will confer on every citizen the capacity of deriving knowledge, with readiness and accuracy, from books and documents.[13]

Not only did the governor see an educational responsibility in connection with suffrage rights, but also in relation to the other functions of citizenship. Concerning the constitutional guarantees of the right to keep and bear arms, he asserted:

It will not then be a matter of indifference, whether the honor and peace of the community are committed to an ignorant and benighted multitude, like those which swell the ranks of the mercenary standing armies of Europe, or to an educated and intelligent population, whose powers of reflection have been strengthened by exercise, and who are able to discriminate between constitutional liberty and arbitrary power, on the one hand, and anarchy on the other.[14]

Next he saw fit to mention the administration of justice through trial by jury. "But I may appeal," he said, "to every professional character and magistrate in this convention, that, in an important case, if he were to be called on to select a jury on which he could place full reliance, he would select men of good common sense, who had received a good common education." [15] Finally, he brought up the all-important question of the capability of the common people to fill high positions of public trust, particularly those offices which allowed the individual wide latitude in the definition and administration of power.

There are three courses, between which we must choose. We must have officers unqualified for their duties;—or we must educate a privi-

[12] Edward Everett, "Remarks at the Taunton Common School Convention," in *The Common School Journal*, Vol. I (1839), pp. 220–21.
[13] *Ibid.*   [14] *Ibid.*, p. 221.   [15] *Ibid.*

leged class to monopolize the honors and emoluments of place;—or we must establish such a system of general education, as will furnish a supply of well-informed, intelligent, and respectable citizens, in every part of the country, and in every walk of life, capable of discharging the trusts which the people may devolve upon them. . . . It is superfluous to say, which of the three courses is most congenial with the spirit of republicanism.[16]

Thus, in the dual responsibility of leading his government and participating in its decisions, the average citizen could not be allowed to contribute in ignorance. The necessity of universal education for citizenship appeared as a primary demand of the new political patterns of republicanism.

2. The Demands of Republican Equality

A second crucial demand on education came from the increasingly vocal labor groups in the larger cities. Fearful of the political and social consequences of the new industry and commerce, and mindful of the gaps between principle and reality in the democratic ethic of the nation, they waged a vigorous campaign for "equality of citizenship." The newly enfranchised workingmen saw in the equal education of all children the only means by which the sense of community among the American people might be perpetuated, and rigid class stratification avoided. This view was expressed in all its optimistic vigor by Robert Dale Owen, early leader of the labor movement:

I believe in a National System of Equal, Republican, Protective, Practical Education, the sole regenerator of a profligate age, and the only redeemer of our suffering country from the equal curses of chilling poverty and corrupting riches, of gnawing want and destroying debauchery, of blind ignorance and of unprincipled intrigue.[17]

Revealing as it did the contemporary faith that a given reform could rectify a multitude of social evils, the cry of "Free, Equal, and Republican" education became both a focus and a rallying point of early labor agitation. One after another, the various workingmen's associations and political parties went on record vigorously urging such a system on their respective state legislatures. Their pressures rose to the extent where some historians have held

[16] *Ibid.*   [17] *Free Enquirer,* Vol. 2, No. 2, Nov. 7, 1829, p. 14.

them to be the deciding factor in the institution of the American free school systems.[18]

In general, two distinct patterns may be delineated in the approach of this early agitation. One represented the efforts of workingmen, through their associations and parties, to secure the improvement and extension of existing public facilities. The other represented the efforts of intellectuals in the movement to develop a drastically new system which they saw befitting an age of industrialism. In view of the importance with which labor looked on educational reform during this period, it is not surprising that the conflicting claims of these courses of action became so highly controversial that in New York, for example, they actually destroyed the very unity of the movement itself.

I

Illustrative of the first approach is the report of a joint committee of Philadelphia workingmen appointed in September, 1829 "to ascertain the state of public instruction in Pennsylvania." [19] The report was unanimously adopted at a meeting of the "friends of general and equal education" at the beginning of February, 1830.[20]

The committee's examination revealed that except in Philadelphia, Lancaster, and Pittsburgh, Pennsylvania was practically destitute of the means of education. The report declared the provisions of the Law of 1809 (appropriating public funds for the education of indigent children in convenient private schools) "incomplete and frequently inoperative" because of embezzlement of funds and irresponsibility among the private institutions involved.[21] As for the schools in the three leading cities, it saw their most prominent feature as pauperism:] insert

They are confined exclusively to the children of *the poor*, while there are, perhaps, thousands of children whose parents are unable to afford

---

[18] See Herbert Harris, *American Labor* (Yale University Press, New Haven, 1939), p. 19, and Philip R. V. Curoe, *Educational Attitudes and Policies of Organized Labor in the United States* (Teachers College, Columbia University, New York, 1926). It is interesting to note that this concern in education on the part of labor showed that much of the force of the early labor movement was directed primarily against social and political inequalities rather than economic inequalities. *History of Labour in the United States* (Macmillan, New York, 1918–24), Vol. 1, p. 223.

[19] *The Working Man's Advocate* (New York), Vol. I, No. 19, March 6, 1830, p. 1.
[20] *Ibid.*   [21] *Ibid.*

for them, a good private education, yet whose standing, professions or connexions in society effectually exclude them from taking the benefit of a *poor law*. There are great numbers, even of the poorest parents, who hold a dependence on the public bounty to be incompatible with the rights and liberties of an American citizen, and whose deep and cherished consciousness of *independence* determines them rather to starve the intellect of their offspring, than submit to become the objects of public charity.[22]

The committee also accused these schools of teaching a curriculum which "extends, in no case, further than a tolerable proficiency in reading, writing, and arithmetic, and sometimes to a slight acquaintance with geography," [23] and deplored the fact that no provision had been made for the large number of children under five years of age. It was frequently necessary, they observed, for poor families to deny school-aged children an education in order that they might care for younger brothers and sisters while both parents worked away from home.

The remedies, as proposed in the report, centered in destroying the "monopoly of talent" held by the higher classes—a monopoly constituting the "original element of *despotism*"—and making education universally available as the "common property of all classes." The essence of its analysis is summed up in the following paragraphs:

It appears, therefore, to the committees that there can be no real liberty without a wide diffusion of real intelligence; that the members of a republic, should all be alike instructed in the nature and character of their equal rights and duties, as human beings, and as citizens; and that education, instead of being limited as in our public poor schools, to a simple acquaintance with words and cyphers, should tend, as far as possible, to the production of a just disposition, virtuous habits, and a rational self governing character.

When the committees contemplate their own condition, and that of the great mass of their fellow laborers; when they look around on the glaring inequality of society, they are constrained to believe, that until the means of equal instruction shall be equa [sic], secured to all, liberty is but an unmeaning word, and equality an empty shadow, whose substance to be realized must first be planted by an equal education and proper training in the minds, in the habits, in the manners, and in the feelings of the community.[24]

[22] *Ibid.*   [23] *Ibid.*   [24] *Ibid.*

Specifically, the committee's proposals involved *first,* the extension of public education to all districts of the state; *second,* the placing of the management of such public facilities "under the control and suffrage of the people"; *third,* the extension of educational privileges not as an act of charity to the poor but as the equal right of all classes supported, therefore, at the expense of all; and *fourth,* the establishment of infant schools for younger children. The report pointedly left "the door open to every possible improvement which human benevolence and ingenuity may be able to introduce." [25] It is interesting to note also that the committee wisely despaired of the chances for so great a change "being accomplished suddenly throughout the state." "No new system of education," they held, "could probably be devised with consequences so manifestly beneficial, as to awaken at once in the public mind, a general conviction and concurrence in the necessity of its universal adoption." [26]

One further aspect of this document is worthy of note—the section dealing with the manual labor schools established by Fellenberg at Hofwyl, Switzerland. After discussing the advantages of teaching children agriculture, gardening, and the mechanical arts, the committee described the organization of Hofwyl as "an independent, selfgoverning community, regulated by a constitution and bylaws formed by the pupils themselves." Such a plan, the report maintained, awakened in the youth "an interest in the public welfare, and a zeal for the public good, which might in vain be sought in older but not wiser communities." [27] Furthermore, in the demands of such a system on the students' time and attention, the committee saw "the only rational hope of ultimately averting, the ruin which is threatened" by the extensive vice of intemperance among the youth of the state.

The report closed by acknowledging that the committee was fully aware of certain influences vehemently opposed to their recommendations. In fact, they expected their proposals to meet with "more than an ordinary share of opposition."

It is to be expected that political demagogueism, professional monopoly, and monied influence, will conspire as hitherto (with several exceptions more or less numerous) they ever have conspired against every

[25] *Ibid.*   [26] *Ibid.*   [27] *Ibid.,* p. 2.

thing that has promised to be an equal benefit to the whole population.[28]

However, they were convinced that the newly awakened interest of the public, the press, the governor, and the legislature was more than powerful enough to resist these reactionary efforts. Positive legislation, they optimistically prophesied, awaited only a decision concerning the fundamental principles and policy to be pursued. Two proposed bills were appended to the report.[29] One called for the establishment of a system of common schools "in which some principle should be adopted, calculated to obviate the defects that have been alluded to, and by which the children of all who desire it, may be enabled to procure, at their own expense, a liberal and scientific education." [30] The other called for the establishment of high schools or model schools based on "a union of agricultural and mechanical with literary and scientific instruction." [31] Also included was a document suggesting that the necessary funds to support these proposals be raised through a tax on "Dealers in Ardent Spirits." [32] After the report had been considered and unanimously adopted, a "committee of correspondence" was appointed to cooperate with all persons interested in the cause of education, and a memorial was addressed to the legislature requesting passage of the appended bills.[33]

II

The disclosures and proposals of the Philadelphia report were instrumental in raising to a heightened pitch the discussion concerning educational reform. Certainly its ideas were given wide attention in the labor publications of Philadelphia and New York throughout the winter and spring of 1830.[34] There seems little doubt that they were among the principal factors responsible for the subsequent publication of Robert Dale Owen's six essays on "Public Education" in April of 1830.[35]

Owen, the son of the English socialist Robert Owen, had long been active in American labor and reform movements. Gradually,

[28] *Ibid.*   [29] *Ibid.*, pp. 1, 3.   [30] *Ibid.*, p. 2.   [31] *Ibid.*

[32] *History of Labour in the United States,* Vol. 1, p. 226.

[33] *Ibid.*, Vol. 1, pp. 226–27.   [34] *Ibid.*, Vol. 1, p. 227.

[35] Richard W. Leopold, *Robert Dale Owen, A Biography* (Harvard University Press, Cambridge, 1940), pp. 92–93.

since the failure of his communal experiment at New Harmony, he had become more and more convinced that reform of the educational system was the only solid foundation on which a more extensive reform program could rest. In the New York labor movement, with its workingmen's party, he saw the opportunity to put his ideas into effect.

Insisting that the new party would do well to concentrate on a few basic reforms rather than a widespread, inarticulate program, Owen urged that a system of republican education be placed at the head of its platform.[36] In December of 1829, the party appointed a subcommittee to study the situation and draw up a suitable plan for the platform. But early in 1830, when the Philadelphia report was published, the New York committee had yet taken no action. In April, prompted both by the findings in Pennsylvania and by the inaction in New York, Owen published his essays.

Asserting that "No system of education which embraces any thing less than the whole people, deserves the name of republican; and no other system will reform a nation," [37] Owen proposed a system that would be *"open and equal to all."* Funds would be provided from two sources: first, by "a tax . . . for each child throughout the state from the age of two or three, to the age of twelve or fourteen; and this to be levied without distinction; whether the parents chose to send their children to the State Schools or not," [38] and second, if the first was insufficient, by an appropriation from the state treasury, supplemented, when necessary, by a direct income tax. "To make a mere matter of dollars and cents of it," asked Owen, *"is not the tax of ignorance a much heavier tax than any tax for education?"* [39]

The quality of the education provided was to be the best that the nation, in its wisdom, was able to provide. Its academic scope would include—in addition to the standard reading, writing, and common arithmetic—history, modern languages, chemistry, drawing, and music. "If it be," said Owen, "only as scientific, as wise, and as judicious, as modern experience can make it, it will regenerate America in one generation. It will make but one class out of

---

[36] See R. D. Owen to Mrs. Robert Owen, Jan 4, 1830, quoted in Richard W. Leopold, *op. cit.,* p. 92.

[37] *The Working Man's Advocate,* Vol. I, No. 25, April 17, 1830, p. 4.

[38] *Ibid.*   [39] *Ibid.*

the many that now envy and despise each other; it will make American citizens what they once declared themselves, *free and equal.*" [40]

It was in his practical proposals that Owen actually made the greatest departure from the American scholastic tradition. For he held that in the system of day schools then in operation there were factors which served only to negate the ideals which a free school should be seeking.

If state schools are to be, as now in New England, common day schools only, we do not perceive how either of these requisitions are to be fulfilled. In republican schools, there must be no temptation to the growth of aristocratical prejudices. The pupils must learn to consider themselves as fellow citizens, as equals. Respect ought to be paid, and will always be paid, to virtue and to talent; but it ought not to be paid to riches, or withheld from poverty. Yet, if the children from these state schools are to go every evening, the one to his wealthy parent's soft carpetted drawing room, and the other to its poor father's or widowed mother's comfortless cabin, will they return the next day as friends and equals? He knows little of human nature who thinks they will.[41]

He cited further evidence to support his point. Differences in quality of clothing, for instance, invoked envy on one side and disdain on the other—feelings which Owen thought unvirtuous and improper in young republicans. Moreover, what of the hours which the poorer children spent after school, on the city streets "learning rudeness, impertinent manners, vulgar language, and vicious habits?" [42] Further, what of the laborer who, even though the school facilities were free, could not afford the luxury of feeding and clothing a nonproductive member of his family? Would not his children be effectively denied an education? It was only in a public school which engaged the full time of the young of all classes that Owen saw the neutralizing of these inconsistencies with republican theory.

We conceive, then, that state schools, to be republican, efficient, and acceptable to all, must receive the children, not for six hours a day, but altogether; must feed them, clothe them, lodge them; must direct not their studies only, but their occupations and amusements; must care for them until their education is completed, and then only abandon them to the world, as useful, intelligent, virtuous citizens.[43]

[40] *Ibid.*   [41] *Ibid.*, Vol. I, No. 26, April 24, 1830, p. 4.   [42] *Ibid.*   [43] *Ibid.*

As regards the curriculum, Owen also incorporated in his proposals mention of the Hofwyl system which had been cited so extensively in the Philadelphia report. In the introduction of vocational training and the mechanical arts into his curriculum, he saw the destruction of one more element of class distinction. Citing the many areas in which the democratic thought of America had made progress, Owen argued:

We have yet to learn, that the world can go on without two classes, one to ride and the other to be ridden; one to roll in the luxuries of life, and the other to struggle with its hardships. We have yet to learn how to amalgamate these classes; to make of men, not fractions of human beings, sometimes mere producing machines, sometimes mere consuming drones, but integral republicans, at once the creators and the employers of riches, at once masters and servants, governors and governed.

How can this most desirable and most republican amalgamation take place? By uniting theory to practice, which have been too long kept separate. By combining mechanical and agricultural with literary and scientific instruction. By making every scholar a workman, and every workman a scholar. By associating cultivation and utility, the productive arts and the abstract sciences.[44]

Thus, if all children were taught some useful trade or occupation in addition to the basic practices of agriculture, everyone would be able to support himself by the labor of his own hands. This, according to Owen, in no way implied that all men would have to work as craftsmen or husbandmen—merely, that in the event of necessity, all men should have the necessary skills and capabilities. Furthermore, the labor of the pupils could go to the partial support of the schools themselves, thus lightening the burden on the taxpayers. And finally, when all children had participated in manual labor during their youth, the pride of the workingman and small farmer would forever be secure against any disdain on the part of an intellectual leisure class.[45]

Owen thus saw fit to take the proposals of the Philadelphia report for boarding schools on the secondary level, and extend them to the whole public school system. Only in this way could the public schools become "not schools of charity, but the schools of the nation; to the support of which all contribute; and instead of being almost a disgrace, it would become an honor to have been

[44] *Ibid.*   [45] *Ibid.*

educated there." [46] In his concluding essay, he summed up his proposals as follows:

The system of Public Education, then, which we consider capable, and only capable, of regenerating this nation, and of establishing practical virtue and republican equality among us, is one which provides for all children at all times; receiving them at the earliest age their parents chose to entrust them to the national care, feeding, clothing, and educating them, until the age of majority.

We propose that all the children so adopted should receive the same food; should be dressed in the same simple clothing; should experience the same kind treatment; should be taught (until their professional education commences) the same branches; in a word, that nothing savoring of inequality, nothing reminding them of the pride of riches or the contempt of poverty, should be suffered to enter these republican safeguards of a young nation of equals. We propose that the destitute widow's child or the orphan boy should share the public care equally with the heir to a princely estate; so that all may become, not in word but in deed and in feeling, free and equal.[47]

In spite of the radical position which was their essence, the essays met with a surprising degree of support. They were copied into sixteen newspapers in their entirety, and were approved by many others.[48] Some of the rural newspapers are even reported to have given them "kindly notice." [49] Unfortunately, though, because of a political rift which had been developing in the New York Workingmen's Party since the latter part of 1829, the "state guardianship plan," as Owen's scheme was called, became the center of a storm of controversy which split the ranks of the party asunder and made concerted action on its behalf relatively impossible.

With all the discussion the plan received, it yet seems evident that the majority of the workingmen were not in favor of the kind of changes it proposed.[50] Opposition came on several counts, the essence of which is perhaps best expounded by Harris:

The average workingman, with that *arriviste* attitude which, from the beginning, seems to have been imbibed with the American air, wanted for his offspring the fashionable "classicist" education with all its rotund Latin tags, the same kind of education, indeed, that the rich

[46] *Ibid.,* Vol. I, No. 27, May 1, 1830, p. 1.
[47] *Ibid.,* Vol. I, No. 26, April 24, 1830, p. 4.
[48] Richard W. Leopold, *op. cit.,* p. 93.   [49] *Ibid.,* p. 94.
[50] Herbert Harris, *op. cit.,* pp. 26–27, and *History of Labour in the United States,* Vol. 1, p. 252.

and well born were getting in their academies and colleges; an outlook which was but another facet of labor's economic views. . . .

In short, labor as a whole didn't want anything basically new or different; it wanted to share more fully in the advantages of existing commercial and industrial arrangements. It wanted for itself what the "haves" possessed. It wanted its children to rise in the world. It wanted them to be farmers with a great deal of land; or even better, perhaps, it wanted them to be merchants, shipowners, lawyers, doctors, politicians, contractors, bankers, manufacturers, to wear high starched stocks, the period's equivalent of the white collar.[51]

Faithful to a powerful family tradition in America, the workingmen could not approve a system which would separate children from their parents during their most formative years. They further feared the possible effects of relieving young married couples of the responsibility of supporting their children. This latter argument carried such weight that Owen saw the plausibility of charging parents a small annual sum for the upkeep of their children in the state schools.

When these considerations were coupled with a vigorous political rivalry in the leadership of the party, a rivalry in which Owen headed one of the competing factions, it is not difficult to see where a rift was inevitable. The actual crisis was precipitated when the General Executive Committee rejected a minority report of its subcommittee on education—one incorporating in essence the proposals of Owen—in favor of a majority report which held generally that

While they [the committee] are unchangeably in favor of granting to all men the free enjoyment of their own private opinions on all subjects of this nature, they are solemnly resolved, never to support any attempt to palm upon any man, or set of men, the peculiar doctrines of infidelity, agrarianism, or sectarian principles.[52]

The issues raised by the report roused a storm of controversy which literally wrecked the party. The legitimacy of the executive committee's action in accepting the report of the subcommittee was challenged by the Owen faction; and as the struggle carried through the next few months, there were actually two executive

[51] Herbert Harris, *op. cit.*, pp. 26–27.
[52] "Report of the Majority of the Sub-Committee on Education to the General Executive Committee," in *The Working Man's Advocate*, Vol. I, No. 31, May 29, 1830, p. 2, and *Documentary History of Industrial Society*, Vol. 5, p. 176.

committees in operation. Dissension reached the point where each faction nominated a different candidate in a special election during July of 1830. As the split became wider, the chances for reconciliation narrowed. The fundamental differences between the two camps, sharpened by personal animosities among their respective leaders, stood as an unsurmountable barrier to unity. In a very short time, the workingman's organization no longer presented a political threat of any significant force to the established parties of the city.[53]

Although the party had not succeeded as a political force, its intellectual influence cannot be discounted. Owen, whose chief contribution to the early movement centered in his state guardianship plan, never actually hoped for any result other than the awakening of public figures to educational inadequacies.[54] In general, his hopes enjoyed a reasonable fulfillment in the 1830's. Primarily, the workingmen now looked upon public education as a movement definitely bound up with their interests. They saw in a system of "equal and republican" education the means for preserving what social equality they possessed and winning whatever extensions of it they sought. And even if the actual provisions of the Owen plan for state guardianship had been turned down by the party itself, its principles had left their indelible impression. In reaffirming the principles of tax support, of equal education for the whole citizenry, and of vocational as well as academic education, the plan had sensitized a significant body of people to the educational demands of a republican social system. Doubtless, reports asserting the same or similar principles but implemented in a way more in keeping with the American tradition were instrumental in bringing about necessary legislation in many states. For example, it is probable that the Philadelphia report of 1829 had a considerable influence in preparing the way for the progressive legislation of the middle 'thirties.

Thus, principally through its literature, yet also, in places, through direct political agitation, the labor movement asserted its

[53] Richard W. Leopold, *op. cit.*, p. 99.
[54] *Ibid.* The continuity of Owen's thought, however, is evidence in his adherence to the "state guardianship" plan in his educational writings of the 1840's. See R. D. Owen and Frances Wright, *Tracts on Republican Government and National Education* (J. Watson, London, 1847).

demands on the educational system of the United States. Curoe has most adequately summed up its effect in his *Educational Attitudes and Policies of Organized Labor in the United States:*

What the political workingmen's parties and the trades' unions really did for the development of American education was *first*, to educate their own membership to the value of education, thus counteracting the inertia or cupidity of laboring parents and changing apathy towards education into active interest; *second*, to contribute with other organizations towards stirring up an interest in educational reform among the more complacent members of legislatures and of the general public; and *third*, to "sell" the idea that a voting citizen cannot discharge his obligations without a modicum of education nor without some leisure for self-improvement.[55]

In the efforts of labor, then, to secure for themselves an education equal to the best which could be procured lay a second fundamental demand on the school—that it play a critical role in the maintenance and perpetuation of the social equality and the equality of opportunity upon which American republicanism was founded.

3. THE DEMANDS OF AMERICAN NATIONALITY

A third fundamental demand on education grew out of the newly emergent American nationality; and, as with the latter, it was sharply accentuated by the steadily increasing immigrations of the 1830's and 40's. Tending as they did to live in homogeneous communities apart from the rest of the population, the immigrants contributed to a rising illiteracy rate. Their gregariousness, when combined with their poor economic status, made it practically impossible for them to allow their children any schooling. The adults, nurtured in a foreign culture, tended to follow the older patterns with but a few adjustments to the new way of life.

With the rise of nationalism among the American people, leaders began to fear the presence of a large body of persons whose patterns of thought and living were incompatible with the American way of life. They felt that such persons could well become a debilitating influence on the virility of the republic. Gradually they began to call for some means of educating them in the basic concepts and practices of democracy, in order that they might be

---

[55] Philip R. V. Curoe, *op. cit.*, p. 33.

more readily integrated into the community. In the proposals which came forth the school figured prominently as an Americanizing institution.

An interesting formulation of a liberal position on this question is evidenced in an address by Benjamin Labaree, President of Middlebury College, Vermont, before the American Institute of Instruction in 1849.[56] In his remarks, Labaree sought to define a twofold role for the schoolmaster in assimilating the newcomers into the American community. Its first aspect involved his task as an agent in changing the newcomers' habits of thought and modes of action. Labaree argued as follows concerning this function:

The multitude of emigrants from the old world, interfused among our population, is rapidly changing the identity of American character. These strangers come among us, ignorant of our institutions, and unacquainted with the modes of thought and habits of life peculiar to a free people. Accustomed to be restrained by the strong arm of power, and to look upon themselves as belonging to an inferior class of the human race, they suddenly emerge from the darkness of oppression into the light and liberty of freemen. The transition is instantaneous, and admits of no preparation for the new life. Will not this sudden change in their political relations produce a corresponding change in their views respecting personal rights and duties? Would it be strange if in such circumstances, many should mistake lawless freedom from restraint, for true and rational liberty? Shall these adopted citizens become a part of the body politic, and firm supporters of liberal institutions, or will they prove to our republic what the Goths and Huns were to the Roman Empire? The answer to this question depends in a great degree upon the wisdom and fidelity of our teachers and associated influences.[57]

Thus, Labaree saw as a principal task of the school the inculcation of those values vital to adequate participation in the American community. The schoolmaster must act the part of a master-builder, "and by degrees mould these unprepared and uncongenial elements into the form and character which the peculiar nature of the edifice demands, and in due time the youth especially

[56] Benjamin Labaree, "The Education Demanded by the Peculiar Character of Our Civil Institutions," in *The Lectures Delivered Before the American Institute of Instruction, at Montpelier, Vt., August, 1849; Including the Journal of Proceedings and a List of the Officers* (Ticknor, Reed, & Fields, Boston, 1850), pp. 27–58.
[57] *Ibid.*, p. 34.

may become intelligent, enterprising and liberal-minded supporters of free institutions." [58]

The second aspect of the schoolmaster's task seems particularly
interesting in view of the fact that the nativist movement was
reaching its climax during these years. In addition to the job of
inculcating American traditions into the newly arrived, Labaree
saw the schoolmaster also preparing the native population "for
the suitable reception and treatment of these strangers. . . ." [59]
The instructor must teach the native population "to lay aside
prejudices and animosities, to meet the newcomers in the spirit
of kindness and benevolence, and to enlist their sympathies and
good-will on the side of liberty, humanity and truth." [60] Thus,
Labaree was seeking the aid of the school in preserving American
traditions both in the immigrants and in the native population
itself. He saw both aspects as equally important for the maintenance of the American way of life.

If our country is to remain, as it has been, the asylum of the oppressed,
and the home of the free, a wise and liberal policy must be pursued
towards foreigners; resolute and persevering exertions must be made
to engraft them upon the republican stock, and to qualify them for the
duties of free and enlightened citizens.[61]

Very much as Protestant Christianity was related to nationalism
as a conservative and morally guiding influence, so was it related
to the prevailing conception of how to Americanize immigrants.
If the political and civil restraints of law were to be relaxed in the
American community, the power of religion would prevent people
from conceiving and committing "what is rash or unjust." And in
this way, the training involved in Americanization—in *engrafting,*
as Labaree stated it, immigrants upon the republican stock—involved teaching them not only the techniques of republicanism,
but also the moral and spiritual creed which regulated it and provided its foundation.

Under the guise of this conception, many of the more conservative nativists saw fit to urge the actual "Christianizing" of
the immigrants; and in the case of the large groups of Catholic
newcomers, there is little doubt that this implied Protestant Christianizing. "It is admitted on all hands," cried George Cheever in

[58] *Ibid.,* pp. 34–35.   [59] *Ibid.,* p. 35.   [60] *Ibid.*   [61] *Ibid.*

1854, "that we are in great danger from the dark and stolid infidelity and vicious radicalism of a large portion of the foreign immigrating population." [62] The one way he saw of rectifying the potential danger centered in the public schools.

What, then, can be done to ward off this danger, and how can we reach the evil at its roots, applying a wise and conservative radicalism to defeat the working of that malignant, social, anti-Christian poison? How can the children of such a population be reached, except in our free public schools? If the Bible be read in them, its daily lessons cannot but be attended by the Divine blessing, and in many instances may beget such a reverence for the Word of God, and instil such a knowledge of its teachings, that the infidelity of their home education shall be effectually counteracted.[63]

The temper of this passage, and the whole presentation of Cheever, differs markedly in its nativist antagonism from the more liberal and tolerant position of Labaree. Yet, as has been noted in other instances, if the liberal and conservative positions differed in content, they nevertheless converged in a recognition of the necessity for a school that could embrace all newcomers—acting to assimilate them into the American republican community. The school was to be the means not only of teaching the young from foreign lands the elements of the republican political system, but also of bringing these children of diverse religious faiths into contact with Protestant Christianity. These several elements, pressing together in the direction of an extended, more embracing educational system, constituted a third basic factor lending its weight to the demand for a new kind of education.

4. The Demand for a Functional School

What, then, was the total effect of these forces upon the character of educational institutions? What new qualities in the American schools would they require in adjustment to the new cultural developments? Any synthesis seems to revolve largely around a demand for a new, functional, and positive conception of the school's role in society.

In recognizing the demands of a republican system on its all-

[62] George B. Cheever, *Right of the Bible in Our Public Schools* (New York, 1854), p. 112.
[63] *Ibid.*, pp. 112–13.

important electorate, certain groups demanded that the school provide universal preparation for the exercise of citizenship. They acknowledged, then, that the school had to do something which could no longer be haphazardly left to the family, the church, or even simple participation in the life of the community. The school was now entrusted with a responsibility on which depended the perpetuation and progress of the society.

Similarly, demands from the growing laboring classes cast another functional role for the school. It now took on the role of a democratizing institution—an agency for preventing that rigid class stratification which these groups saw inherent in the new industrial system. While some saw the fulfillment of this role merely in the provision for universal education, others carried it further. Feeling that it was only out of an experience common to all groups that intergroup hostilities might be rendered ineffectual and class lines kept fluid, they urged the establishment of institutions cutting across traditional family, class, and religious lines. Essentially, they maintained, valid republican education could be carried on only within the social context of a miniature of the broader community. Such experience would tend to neutralize the undemocratic qualities inherent in the life of the wider society —thereby serving constantly to bolster equality of citizenship.

In the demands for the school as an Americanizing institution, an agency for integrating newly arrived immigrants into the American community, lay a third positive role for the school. For in this area, leaders saw the school actually changing the habits of thought and action of people—molding them in such a way that they could adequately participate in the unique way of life required by republican society. The school, then, had not only to accomplish for newcomers all that it did for the native young (as implied above), but also to combat vigorously the undemocratic patterns which it encountered in the acculturation process. Admittedly, the newcomer could no longer integrate through mere social intercourse with American society. His tendency to live among his own fellows, when coupled with the increasing complexity of American social and political institutions, made the task almost insurmountable. Only through a vigorous, positive effort, utilizing a special institution such as the school, could American society hope to make the newcomer an effective participant in the democratic community.

Thus, the effects of these new pressures on the American school all converge at one significant point: namely, the demand for an education which would exercise a positive and necessary influence on the life of *every* member of American society—uniquely providing each with those basic skills, techniques, attitudes, and loyalties necessary for a proper exercise of the prerogatives of republican citizenship.

5. The Reform Group Conceives an Ideal School

The men who, perhaps more than any other, unified, integrated, and attempted to realize in practice the proposals of these diverse social groups were the educational reformers. They might best be described as the men who saw in education the means of elevating the whole condition of society and thereby bringing about human progress. Although in some aspects they might be regarded simply as personalities who mediated the educational demands of other groups, one must remember that the movement of reform was itself an important cultural development of the period. Thus, in its own right, this group stood as a social force exerting its demands on education.

The figures who led the movement played an auspicious role in the educational activity of the period. In New England, James G. Carter and Horace Mann in Massachusetts and Henry Barnard in Connecticut stand out as the giants of the educational scene. In the South, such men as Calvin Wiley of North Carolina and Charles Fenton Mercer of Virginia are distinguished for their efforts; while the West boasted a host of figures—Caleb Mills in Indiana, Calvin Stowe, Samuel Lewis, and Samuel Galloway in Ohio, Ninian Edwards in Illinois, John D. Pierce and Isaac Crary in Michigan, Robert Breckinridge in Kentucky, and John Swett in California. These men, in combination with friendly public figures in every state, were the leaders who pointed the way for public education. Generally, they employed three means of enunciating and pressing their demands.

First, the reformers worked through groups and organizations. Tocqueville had remarked about the general tendency of Americans who "have taken up an opinion or a feeling which they wish to promote in the world" to look for mutual assistance.[64] And this was as true of the educational movement as of any. Among the better known of these groups was the American Lyceum, organized by Josiah Holbrook in 1826. Its purposes included not only the improvement of its members in useful knowledge, but also the advancement of popular education (1) by introducing uniformity and improvements in common schools, and (2) by becoming auxiliary to boards of education.[65] In 1827 a branch of the Pennsylvania Society for the Promotion of Public Economy became the Pennsylvania Society for the Promotion of Public Schools. Its object was:

. . . the promotion of education throughout the State of Pennsylvania, by encouraging the establishment of Public Schools . . . ; for the attainment of the end, the Society shall open and maintain a correspondence with such zealous, intelligent and patriotic citizens, as may be induced to cooperate with it, and shall from time to time communicate to the public, through the medium of pamphlets and newspapers, such information as it may deem expedient, and adopt such other measures as may appear to be best calculated to accomplish the object of its creation.[66]

In the West, in 1829, a similar organization was launched in the Western Academic Institute and Board of Education, established in Cincinnati by Albert Pickett in cooperation with Samuel Lewis, Lyman Beecher, Calvin Stowe, and others. Reorganized in 1832 as the Western Literary Institute and College of Professional Teachers, the organization carried out a broad program of agitation through lectures, lobbying, meetings, memorials, publications, and the like. And finally, there was the American Institute of Instruction, established in New England in 1830 for similar purposes. These organizations were only the principal ones. There were hundreds of lesser associations of teachers, reformers, and educational enthusiasts. They held countless conventions in the several states, and generally carried on at a local level the work of the larger bodies.

[64] Alexis de Tocqueville, op. cit., Vol. II, p. 109.

[65] American Journal of Education, Vol. III (1828), pp. 753–58. See also Cecil Branner Hayes, The American Lyceum; Its History and Contribution to Education, U. S. Office of Education Bulletin No. 12, 1932.

[66] The Register of Pennsylvania, Vol. I (1828), p. 300.

Second, the reformers, singly and through their organizations, worked through the press. About twenty educational journals were instituted by the year 1840, though few survived more than several issues. The principal periodicals which enjoyed a more extended life were the *American Journal of Education* (1826–31; William Russell, ed.) and its successor, the *American Annals of Education* (1831–39; W. C. Woodbridge, ed.); the *Common School Assistant* (1836–40; J. Orville Taylor, ed.); the *Connecticut Common School Journal* (1838–42; Henry Barnard, ed.); and the *Common School Journal* (1839–52; Horace Mann, ed.). These journals published materials concerning every aspect of public education, and vigorously campaigned for educational improvements of every kind. In addition to the regular periodical literature, there were thousands of reports, lectures, pamphlets, brochures, memorials, and petitions. In all, they provided an extensive body of literature reflecting the views of the educational reform movement.

A third, and perhaps the most important, means by which the reformers exerted their influence was through actual positions in the state governments or school systems. In this way they were able to serve a double purpose of helping to crystallize public opinion to the point of action, and then shaping the course of that action by administering it. Thus, Horace Mann as secretary of the Massachusetts Board of Education, Henry Barnard as chairman of a similar board in Connecticut, Calvin Wiley as state superintendent in North Carolina, Caleb Mills as state superintendent in Indiana, and Samuel Lewis as state superintendent in Ohio—all were influential in their capacity as early molders of educational policy and practice.

The ideas of these men and the groups with whom they worked represent the forging of an educational conception compatible with the political, social, and economic institutions of a republican society. In formulating this conception, it was inevitable that they would not only draw on certain historical and contemporary traditions, but also evolve innovations for which there was little in the way of precedent. Working as they were, out of different backgrounds, in different places, and under different conditions, it was also inevitable that disagreements and inconsistencies would arise. It seems possible, however, on perusing the literature of this group

—their speeches, their books, their memorials, and their resolutions—to extract certain basic premises and patterns which seemed fundamental to their efforts. It was these patterns which constituted the fundamental elements of the novel and unique function they envisioned for American education. In their synthesis rested the ideal of the American common school.

I

At the base of the conception, and perhaps the most important element involved in it, was the idea that the means of education must be made available to all members of the community. This evolved as the result of two separate commitments. First, it was the responsibility of the republican community, in the preservation and furtherance of its own ends, to provide for the education of its constituents. "Believing," stated the *Common School Assistant,* "that the mind of every citizen of every republic is the common property of society, and constitutes the basis of its strength and happiness, it is considered the peculiar duty of a free government, like ours, to encourage and extend the improvement and cultivation of the intellectual energies of the *whole*." [67] Second, it was the responsibility of the republican community to fulfill the natural right of individuals to an education, a right which accrued through the existence of "a great, immutable principle of natural law, or natural ethics,—a principle antecedent to all human institutions and incapable of being abrogated by any ordinances of man,—a principle of divine origin, clearly legible in the ways of Providence as those ways are manifested in the order of nature and in the history of the race." [68] In satisfying the responsibilities of this dual commitment, it was incumbent upon the community to provide educational facilities for *all* of its members.

It was apparent, though, that if such facilities were to be truly "available," two conditions would have to be fulfilled. First, they would have to be free; for it was evident that even the slightest cost for education automatically excluded large segments of the

[67] Quoted from the preamble of one of the School Laws of Illinois. *Common School Assistant,* Vol. 1 (1836), p. 87.

[68] *Tenth Annual Report of the Board of Education, Together with the Tenth Annual Report of the Secretary of the Board* (Dutton and Wentworth, Boston, 1847), p. 112.

population. Each parent, then, must be made to feel "that a free education is as secure a part of the birth-right of his offspring, as Heaven's bounties of light and air," [69] or the goal of universal education would be destroyed. "Unless the Common Schools," remarked Samuel Lewis, "can be made to educate the whole people, the poor as well as the rich, they are not worthy [sic] the support of the patriot or the philanthropist." [70] And as James G. Carter so aptly phrased this premise:

And just in proportion as you lose sight of, or abandon the true principle of the free schools; you lose sight of, and abandon all the moral, political, and religious blessings which result from them. You check the diffusion of knowledge through all classes of people. You stop the circulation through the extremities of the body politic of the very life-blood, which must nourish and sustain them. You may preserve and amuse yourselves with the name of free institutions, and of a republican government, but you will not be blessed with the reality. You may incorporate in your constitution, if you like, the articles, "that all men are born free and equal," and "that all are eligible to the highest offices;" but this is not freedom, while ninety-nine hundredths of the community have not the means of fitting themselves or their children, for discharging the duties of those high offices. As well might you tie the legs, and pinion the arms of a man, and tell him he has as fair a chance to win the race, as one who is free and trained to the course.[71]

Only as education was made available without cost could the wide diffusion of knowledge required by a republican community be adequately realized. The theories of popular government were mere vocalizing—ideals never to be realized—if the great mass of the people who could not afford to obtain it through private means were entirely deprived of it.

A second condition of true "availability" was that such schools as furnished this free education would have to be of high quality —equivalent to any institution which could be established through private means. If the "birthright" of the American citizen was tainted through poor quality with the stigma of a "pauper's educa-

[69] Ibid., p. 233.
[70] William G. W. Lewis, Biography of Samuel Lewis (Cincinnati, 1857), p. 245.
[71] James G. Carter, Essays upon Popular Education, Containing a Particular Examination of the Schools of Massachusetts, and an Outline of an Institution for the Education of Teachers (Bowles & Dearborn, Boston, 1826), p. 21. See also Remarks upon Mr. Carter's Outline of an Institution for the Education of Teachers (Bowles & Dearborn, Boston, 1827), pp. 7–8.

tion," it too would be scorned by the proud and independent citizens of a republic—as repugnant to every ideal enunciated in republican theory.[72] Thus, in New Jersey, Bishop George W. Doane, chairman of a committee appointed by an educational convention to draft an address to the legislature, formulated a stirring statement of the incompatibility of the pauper school with the universal exercise of citizenship:

We utterly repudiate as unworthy, not of freemen only, but of men, the narrow notion that there is to be an education for the poor, as such. Has God provided for the poor a coarser earth, a thinner air, a paler sky? Does not the glorious sun pour down his golden flood as cheerily upon the poor man's hovel as upon the rich man's palace? Have not the cotter's children as keen a sense of all the freshness, verdure, fragrance, melody, and beauty of luxuriant nature as the pale sons of kings? Or is it on the mind that God has stamped the imprint of a baser birth so that the poor man's child knows with an inborn certainty that his lot is to crawl, not climb? It is not so. God has not done it. Man can not do it. Mind is immortal. Mind is imperial. It bears no mark of high or low, of rich or poor. It heeds no bound of time or place, of rank or circumstance. It asks but freedom. It requires but light. It is heaven-born, and it aspires to heaven. Weakness does not enfeeble it. Poverty can not repress it. Difficulties do but stimulate its vigor. And the poor tallow chandler's son that sits up all the night to read the book which an apprentice lends him lest the master's eye should miss it in the morning, shall stand and treat with kings, shall add new provinces to the domain of science, shall bind the lightning with a hempen cord and bring it harmless from the skies. *The Common School is common, not as inferior, not as the school for poor men's children, but as the light and air are common. It ought to be the best school because it is the first school; and in all good works the beginning is one half.*[73]

It is apparent that Bishop Doane's statement well expressed the views of the reform group; for within a short time after its publication it was reprinted in part in the *Connecticut Common School Journal,*[74] in *The Common School Journal* [75] of Massachusetts, and

[72] "Memorial of the Education Convention, Assembled at Clarksburg, Harrison County, Virginia, September 8th and 9th, 1841," in *Journal of the House of Delegates,* 1841–42, Doc. No. 7, p. 28.

[73] *American Journal of Education,* Vol. XV (1865), pp. 8–9. (Italics mine.) See also *American Annals of Education,* Vol. I (1831), p. 361, for a similar conception in Pennsylvania.

[74] *The Connecticut Common School Journal,* Vol. II (1839–40), p. 152.

[75] *The Common School Journal,* Vol. I (1839), pp. 381–82.

in the *Common School Advocate*[76] of Cincinnati, Ohio. Evidently, many seemed aware of the fact that the pauper school, as in Europe, could educate only toward a class-stratified society. They were equally aware of the fact that common schools, as they viewed them, were incompatible with such a society. Thus, at an educational convention in Clarksburg, Virginia, Alexander Campbell made the following comments concerning the aims of the people of Virginia's western sections:

> But it is obvious to all that we want common schools for the common wants; and the question is, how shall we get them. We do not want poor schools for poor scholars, or gratuitous instruction for paupers; but we want schools for all at the expense of all. . . .
> Our brethren of the east have difficulties, that lie not in our way. They have two sorts of population of great political disparity. We are not so unfortunate. That misfortune tends to aristocracy. Now common schools and aristocracy are not quite so homogeneous. A patrician will not have a plebeian system of education. It would undignify his son to learn out of the same grammar, under the same teacher, and in the same schoolroom with the son of a plebeian.[77]

Thus, availability of educational facilities to the whole population involved making such facilities free and of high quality. Only in this way could it be conclusively established that the means of education were really open to every member of society. The common school had to be common to all citizens before it could fulfill its function in the American republic.

II

Every school system, consciously or otherwise, educates toward some future social structure. In terms of this, a school system which is common by availability might, according to the extent of its usage, maintain any number of relationships with the structure of the larger society in which it functions. The role of such a system certainly varies according to whether it lies dormant through lack of employment, whether it is used only by certain segments of society, or whether it is used by the whole of society. In the first role, such a system, though available, maintains a rather neutral

[76] *Common School Advocate* (Cincinnati), Vol. 2 (1838), No. 20.
[77] Address of Alexander Campbell before the Clarksburg Educational Convention, Sept. 8, 1841, quoted in *Journal of the House of Delegates of Virginia*, 1841–42, Doc. No. 7, p. 39.

position; in the latter two, it affects positively, in a given direction, the institutions about it. It becomes, then, a matter of importance to examine further the conceptual ideal of the reformers in order to gain clarity on this crucial aspect of the question.

Analysis reveals that this group was certainly sensitive to the importance of these relationships between the school and social structure; and in terms of their commitment to the republican form of society, a positive role for the school emerged. This centered in a conception of the common school as a leveling institution —one which would, during early childhood, remove the barriers which inevitably arose from different standards of living among different socio-economic groups. Only a common school which was attended by the whole community contained the seeds of a fully republican society. Only in a school where children of all classes, faiths, temperaments, etc., mingled freely together could the odious distinctions of a rigidly hierarchical society be neutralized. Thus the reformers sought to effect a conception of education which would embrace the young of the whole community in one great democratic effort.

Among the first to enunciate this conception of common education was a Virginian Federalist named Charles Fenton Mercer. The occasion was a meeting of the American Whig and Cliosophic Societies at Princeton, New Jersey on September 26, 1826.[78] In his address, Mercer analyzed the political and economic foundations of American society, pointed out the necessity for the wide diffusion of popular knowledge,[79] and then cited the dangers associated with wide differences in economic status.[80] As he saw the acceleration of these differences inherent in the vigorous commercial activity of the period, he looked to other institutions to neutralize them, settling upon the school as the primary means for accomplishing his end. Some excerpts from his speech indicate the progress of his argument:

If it be one of the most salutary effects of popular instruction, to diminish the evils arising to social order from too great a disparity of wealth, it should be so dispensed as to place the commonwealth with regard to all her children, in the relation of a common mother.

[78] Charles Fenton Mercer, *A Discourse on Popular Education* (Princeton, Sept. 26, 1826).
[79] *Ibid.*, pp. 16–18.   [80] *Ibid.*, p. 21.

A discrimination, therefore, in the same schools, between the children of different parents, which is calculated to implant in very early life, the feelings of humiliation and dependence in one class of society, and of superiority and pride in another, should be avoided as alike incompatible with the future harmony and happiness of both. And it is no more an answer to this objection, that time and necessity gradually overcome, among the poor, the natural indisposition to send their children to schools so organized, than that the same lenient effect of familiar habit, reconciles man to every other species of degradation, as it but too often does to guilt itself and all its consequences. It is one of the most beneficent effects of that education, which aims at the equal improvement of the understanding and the heart, to elevate the sentiments and character of every citizen of the commonwealth; and no distinction among its pupils should be retained in its first lessons, inconsistent with this benevolent and useful end.[81]

Intellectual and moral worth constitute in America our only nobility; and this high distinction is placed by the laws, and should be brought in fact, within the reach of every citizen.

Where distinct ranks exist in society, it may be plausibly objected to the intellectual improvement of the lower classes of the community, that it will invert the public sentiment, or impose on the privileged orders the necessity of proportional exertion to protect themselves from the scorn of their inferiors. But the equality on which our institutions are founded, cannot be too intimately interwoven in the habits of thinking among our youth; and it is obvious that it would be greatly promoted by their continuance together, for the longest possible period, in the same schools of juvenile instruction; to sit upon the same forms; engage in the same competitions; partake of the same recreations and amusements, and pursue the same studies, in connexion with each other; under the same discipline, and in obedience to the same authority.[82]

Mercer saw in this kind of equalizing or leveling education a means of perpetuating the American democratic structure by preventing differences in economic status from undermining it.[83]

This positive, leveling role of the common school permeated the thinking of the reform forces throughout the next two decades. "In these schools," said Gardner Perry in one of the early lectures before the American Institute of Instruction, "are children of different ages, education, temperament, inclinations, and pursuits. A wide field of human character is spread out before each, a little

[81] *Ibid.*, p. 58.   [82] *Ibid.*, p. 76.
[83] The close resemblance between these proposals and those of Owen and Wright is evident here.

world, from which they are to gather a knowledge of men, and upon which they can exercise their own skill and power to influence and control." [84] Four years later, before this same body, Theodore Edson noted that in such schools the child mingles with the good and bad alike—as he will have to do in the world—and learns to distinguish between them.[85] The Reverend Caleb Stetson of Medford argued before the Middlesex County Association for the Improvement of Common Schools:

/I want to see the children of the rich and the poor sit down side by side on equal terms, as members of one family—a great brotherhood—deeming no one distinguished above the rest but the best scholar and the best boy—giving free and natural play to their affections, at a time of life when lasting friendships are often formed, and worldliness and pride, and envy have not yet alienated heart from heart. . . . The different classes of the community will love and honor each other, when they come to remember these intimate associations of their childhood and the great lesson they taught—namely, that true dignity and worth depend not upon the outward but upon the inward man.[86]

And Samuel Lewis, after noting the role of the common school in forming "one people" out of a population representing so many different castes, states, nations, languages, and prejudices,[87] made the following proposal:

Take fifty lads in a neighborhood, including rich and poor—send them in childhood to the same school—let them join in the same sports, read and spell in the same classes, until their different circumstances fix their business for life: some go to the field, some to the mechanic's shop, some to merchandize: one becomes eminent at the bar, another in the pulpit: some become wealthy; the majority live on with a mere competency—a few are reduced to beggary! But let the most eloquent orator, that ever mounted a western stump, attempt to prejudice the minds of one part against the other—and so far from succeeding, the

[84] Gardner B. Perry, "On Primary Education," in *The Introductory Discourse and the Lectures Delivered Before the American Institute of Instruction, in Boston, 1833. Including a List of Officers and Members*, p. 110.

[85] Theodore Edson, "On the Comparative Merits of Private and Public Schools," in *The Introductory Discourse, and the Lectures Delivered Before the American Institute of Instruction, at Worcester (Mass.), August, 1837. Including the Journal of Proceedings, and a List of the Officers*, pp. 102–04.

[86] *The Common School Journal*, Vol. I (1839), p. 60.

[87] Samuel Lewis, "Remarks on Common Schools," in Calvin Stowe, *The Prussian System of Public Instruction* (Truman and Smith, Cincinnati, 1836), Appendix, pp. 95–96.

poorest of the whole would consider himself insulted, and from his own knowledge stand up in defence of his more fortunate schoolmate.[88]

Periodicals, both educational and literary, sounded the same theme. "We say then, again, let the common school," wrote Orville Taylor in the *Common School Assistant*, *"be made fit to educate all, and let all send to it.* This alone will secure an education for every one, and this is republican. More than all," he continued, *"this is duty."* [89] Taylor then argued:

. . . the spirit of common schools—schools where the rich and the poor meet together on equal terms, where high and low are taught in the same house, the same class, and out of the same book, and by the same teacher—is a republican spirit. And this is a republican education.[90]

Speaking on the subject in *The New England Magazine* in 1832, another writer remarked:

There the rich and the poor should meet together; there their children should join—the rich man's son to learn that it is by a rough contest with the rougher members of society, that he is to work his way through life; and the poor man's son to catch some of the embellishments of higher stations and more polished minds. It is this mixture of character that improves our minds, and forms the harmony of this sometimes jarring world.[91]

Nor was this conception confined to the northern states. In the report of a convention committee in Virginia in 1841, for instance, it was recommended that "public schools should be *free* to all the white youth within the districts of a proper age to go to school. This provision will be important to the success of the *whole system.* Unless the schools be free to *all* they cannot succeed. It will destroy the success of the whole system to allow any distinction between the rich and the poor." [92] Thus, this leveling role of the common school was advanced at many points and through many media by the reformers. It seems valid to infer that it constituted a basic element in their thinking about the new education.

---

[88] *Ibid.,* p. 97.   [89] *Common School Assistant,* Vol. II (1837), p. 1.
[90] *Ibid.,* Vol. II (1837), p. 41.
[91] *The New England Magazine,* Vol. 3 (1832), p. 200. See *Southern Literary Messenger,* Vol. 4 (1838), p. 224, for this conception in the South.
[92] "Memorial of the Education Convention, Assembled at Clarksburg, Harrison County, Virginia, September 8th and 9th, 1841," in *Journal of the House of Delegates of Virginia,* 1841–42, Doc. No. 7, p. 28.

An argument intimately bound up with this positive conception of the common school as a leveling institution was one which saw private schools as competing factors detracting from the efficiency of the former. It was an argument which was central in the thinking of James G. Carter during the early years of the educational revival,[93] and one which appeared almost universally in the writings of reformers during the next two decades. In virtually every case, several detracting influences are cited: *First,* and perhaps most important, was the fact that the private schools tended to destroy the ability of the common school to function as a leveling institution. As Orville Taylor stated it:

The child of a rich parent is sent to a private school—a school, the child is told, that is better than the common school. The daily talk before the little one is, "I would not have my child associate with the children in the common school for any consideration."—Thus the first lesson given, is one of pride and selfishness. The child is taught from infancy, in a private school, to look upon certain classes as inferior, and born to fewer privileges. This is not republican. This is not allowing all, as far as possible, a fair start in the world.[94]

As more and more of the children who could afford it withdrew from the common school, it was increasingly less probable that the interplay among children of all stations in life could operate. *Second,* the money that went into the maintenance of private schools, if applied to the public school fund, could increase the quality of the common schools to a point far beyond the capacity of the public or private schools operating separately. Thus, another writer in *The Common School Journal* urged:

The resources of the State . . . which are now applied to school education are crippled by division. Let that part, which the wealthier classes now choose to expend for private tuition, be added to that which must be expended for Common Schools, and we shall have a system of instruction, thorough, ample and various enough to meet the wants of all classes of the community. And I have no doubt that the rich would find it greatly for their advantage to have their children educated along with the rest, instead of supporting one class of schools for themselves and another to satisfy the demands of the law.[95]

[93] James G. Carter, *Essays upon Popular Education* . . .
[94] *Common School Assistant,* Vol. II (1837), p. 41.
[95] *The Common School Journal,* Vol. I (1839), p. 59.

Third, in proportion as certain groups in the community withdrew their children from the common schools, to that extent would they be less interested in the cause of the common schools. Speaking of this phenomenon in Massachusetts, Horace Mann stated that such schools tend

to withdraw, also, the guardian care and watchfulness of some of the most intelligent men in the district . . . and . . . as in most country districts, there were no surplus intelligence and public spirit that could be spared from the cause of public education, the transfer of the sympathies and interest of a considerable number of the most intelligent citizens left the Common School to languish, or, what is infinitely worse, to acquire, through neglect, a pernicious efficiency in the formation of bad habits and character.[96]

It is clear that to a certain extent the ideal of a common school receiving *all* classes and groups in the community in the role of "common mother" was incompatible with the existence of private schools. And although the reformers maintained that they could not possibly deny the rights of private schools without doing violence to the legal and moral principles of an individualist-capitalist economy,[97] the incompatibility of the two commitments was evident. The resolution, perhaps, rested in the argument that if the common schools were good enough, there would be no reason for people to send their children to private ones. That this resolution was possible in reality is illustrated, for instance, in Boston during the late 1840's, when Charles Lyell remarked:

The high schools of Boston, supported by the state, are now so well managed, that some of my friends, who would grudge no expense to engage for their sons the best instructors, send their boys to them as superior to any of the private establishments supported by the rich at great cost.[98]

Thus, although nothing could be done to restrain the operation of private institutions while remaining loyal to the commitment of private enterprise, the mores of competition dictated that if the

[96] *Ibid.,* Vol. III (1841), p. 285. See also *The Connecticut Common School Journal,* Vol. I (1838–39), p. 11, and *Common School Assistant,* Vol. II (1837), p. 61.

[97] *Eleventh Annual Report of the Board of Education, Together with the Eleventh Annual Report of the Secretary of the Board* (Dutton and Wentworth, Boston, 1848), p. 124.

[98] Charles Lyell, *A Second Visit to the United States of North America* (Harper & Brothers, New York, 1849), Vol. I, p. 151.

common school was made good enough, few would forsake it for private institutions.

The availability of the common school, then, was far from a neutral conception in the ideal of the reformers. It was a most positive one. It was a conception which held that the common school, through the experience of common participation, could teach equality and fraternity better than any other institution. It was a role which held that there was "no limit to the modes and forms by which, in the process of such an education, the noble and generous principles of pure patriotism may be illustrated and enforced, and all narrow and sectional prejudices checked and controlled, if not rooted out." [99] It was a conception which placed upon the school a positive responsibility of neutralizing the antirepublican tendencies of economic individualism—one which looked to the reaffirmation and perpetuation of a democratic social structure. It is only when the ideal of an "available" common school is viewed in the light of this conception that its full import as a positive commitment is adequately realized.

III

Given the concept of a school which would reach the whole community—a school which would finally be capable of extending its influence to all the children of the commonwealth, what would be the content of its offering? What would be its influence on the young? In terms of the educational philosophy which dominated the early nineteenth century, any approach to this question must be discussed in terms of subjects.[100] When the educators of this period wanted the school to deal with this area or that, it was always regarded as a matter of the teacher *teaching* a given body of material to the student, and the student *learning* this material. Although there was much discussion about the cultivation of certain desirable attitudes, the means of cultivation always involved a certain body of content, the mastery of which would give rise to the desired values in the student. Thus, although the literature

[99] F. A. Packard, *Thoughts on the Condition and Prospects of Popular Education in the United States* (No place, no date), p. 28.

[100] Though the newer educational theories from Europe were beginning to appear on the scene, they had not permeated educational thinking to any great extent by this time.

of the period attempts to deal rather explicitly with the curriculum of the common school, it does so largely in terms of a subject-centered approach. In light of this, it is possible to delineate certain tasks which the friends of education sought to delegate to the school—tasks which a republican school would have to undertake if the perpetuation of a republican society was to be guaranteed.

"It is the object of education," noted a speaker before the American Institute of Instruction,

to prepare men for their duties. To attain this object, a course of study is prescribed, to impart to the young a knowledge of those duties, and to develope and strengthen the mind for the proper discharge of them. The neglect of instruction in any one class of general duties, important to the general good, is obviously a defect in education. . . . The common weal is the end, of which education, as promoted by State patronage, is the means.[101]

Generally, the task of the common school was to teach the "common branches" of education,[102] those studies which "embrace what is necessary to qualify men for the discharge of the ordinary duties of life."[103] The common schools were to occupy themselves with the "rudiments of education,"[104] since the instruction they furnished would provide "the great mass of the community with all the education they are to receive, except so much as they obtain afterwards by their own unaided efforts."[105] Thus, it became incumbent upon the reformers to formulate the curricular elements which were vitally necessary to all members of the community, to choose that minimum without which life in society could not effectively function. As they considered the problem, their thinking tended to center in three general areas: (1) education for ordinary everyday living, (2) education for moral adequacy, and (3) education for the intelligent and responsible exercise of citizenship.

[101] Edward A. Lawrence, "On the Elementary Principles of Constitutional Law, as a Branch of Education in Common Schools," in *The Lectures Delivered Before the American Institute of Instruction, at Boston, August, 1841; Including the Journal of Proceedings, and a List of the Officers,* p. 179. See also *Tenth Annual Report of the Board of Education . . . ,* p. 112.

[102] Clement Durgin, "On Natural History as a Branch of Common Education," in *Introductory Discourse and Lectures Delivered Before the American Institute of Instruction,* (n.p., n.d.), p. 209.

[103] *Common School Assistant,* Vol. II (1837), p. 47.

[104] "Education of the People," in *Massachusetts Quarterly Review,* Vol. 1 (1847–48), p. 208.   [105] *American Annals of Education,* Vol. I (1831), p. 155.

Although there was disagreement on exactly what education was necessary for ordinary living, the conclusions of these men usually revolved around the common branches—the tools of reading, writing, spelling, arithmetic, and then perhaps some geography, history, and grammar.[106] There was a great deal of discussion on how to render these most useful to young citizens-to-be. Thus, a pamphlet in Pennsylvania, pointing to the shortcomings of contemporary "documents of various municipal offices, such as the receipts, orders, reports, accounts, records, etc. of commissioners, guardians, administrators, arbitrators, and magistrates," concluded: "Surely we are within bounds when we say that to write a common business letter, promissory note, receipt, bill, or account, legibly and in proper form, is the least that should be required of our common schools in this department." [107] Similarly, regarding arithmetic, this same writer pleaded for instruction which "shall qualify the pupil for the ordinary business of a farmer, or mechanic." [108] The values of communication accruing through an adequate knowledge of reading and writing were stressed. The purpose of the common school was to train, not scholars, statesmen, and philosophers, but "practical business men, or intelligent, independent citizens." [109]

Hard on the heels of these demands for a more practical and functional offering in the common branches were demands for wide expansion of the curriculum. Exponents of the inclusion of natural history,[110] natural science,[111] government,[112] physical train-

---

[106] Daniel Kimball, "On the Duties of Female Teachers of Common Schools," in *The Lectures Delivered Before the American Institute of Instruction, in Boston, August, 1836. Including the Journal of Proceedings, and a List of the Officers*, pp. 108–09.

[107] F. A. Packard, *op. cit.,* p. 8.   [108] *Ibid.*

[109] Robert Rantoul, Jr., "Introductory Discourse," in *The Introductory Discourse, and the Lectures Delivered Before the American Institute of Instruction, at Springfield (Mass.), August 1839. Including the Journal of Proceedings, and a List of the Officers,* p. 21.

[110] A. A. Gould, "On the Introduction of Natural History as a Study to Common Schools," in *The Introductory Discourse and the Lectures Delivered Before the American Institute of Instruction, in Boston, August, 1834. Including the Journal of Proceedings, and a List of the Officers.*

[111] A. Gray, "On the Importance of the Natural Sciences in Our System of Popular Education," in *The Lectures Delivered Before the American Institute of Instruction, at Boston, August, 1841.*

[112] Joseph Story, "On the Science of Government as a Branch of Popular Education," in *The Introductory Discourse and the Lectures Delivered Before the American Institute of Instruction, in Boston, August, 1834.*

ing,[113] constitutional law,[114] and a host of other areas vigorously pronounced their subjects of crucial importance to the adequate education of a free people. Others saw the need, both from practical considerations and from the necessity of removing the tendency to regard manual labor with "disgust and scorn," [115] for the introduction of manual training along with intellectual training.[116] Only by these means could a happy balance between the two be reached, and a truly practical education be offered to the young. Thus, sporadically, recommendations appeared advising the inclusion of agriculture and the mechanical arts in the common school curriculum. In 1831 the *American Annals of Education* cited a speech by Governor Enos Thompson Throop of New York publicly recommending that some attention be given to agriculture and the industries in common schools. "I feel confident," he stated, "that under proper regulations, a vast amount of knowledge in arts and sciences, connected with agriculture and handicraft, which are simple in their principles, and easily comprehended, might be taught to children during those years which are usually spent at common schools." [117] Similarly, William A. Alcott, in a prize essay published by the American Institute of Instruction a year later, stated that he could not "help anticipating a period when every common school will have the means of attending to agricultural and mechanical pursuits more or less every day, and be furnished with all the necessary *implements,* made of a proper size for the smaller, as well as the larger pupils." [118] Still others saw the need for inculcating an appreciation of the more aesthetic areas, and

[113] *Sixth Annual Report of the Board of Education, Together with the Sixth Annual Report of the Secretary of the Board* (Dutton and Wentworth, Boston, 1843), pp. 56–83. See also Henry Barnard, First Annual Report, in *The Connecticut Common School Journal*, Vol. I (1838–39), p. 169.

[114] Edward A. Lawrence, *op. cit.*

[115] Charles Fenton Mercer, *Discourse on Popular Education*, p. 31.

[116] Beriah Green, "On Uniting a System of Education, Manual with Mental Labor," in *The Introductory Discourse and the Lectures Delivered Before the American Institute of Instruction, in Boston, August, 1834* . . .

[117] *American Annals of Education*, Vol. I (1831), p. 125.

[118] William A. Alcott, "On the Construction of School-Houses," in *Introductory Discourse and Lectures Delivered Before the American Institute of Instruction, 1831.* See speech of Mr. A. Kinmont in 1835 before the Western Literary Institute and College of Professional Teachers, quoted in *Transactions of the Fifth Annal Meeting of the Western Literary Institute,* p. 109, for a view of an educational leader opposing the movement to introduce vocational training into the common school.

consequently recommended the inclusion of music[119] and drawing[120] as aspects of the common branches. Finally, there were the hundreds of treatises on improved means and methods for teaching these diverse subject areas with maximum efficiency.[121]

The enthusiasm over the introduction of these new areas into the school curriculum met with a reaction on the part of the more conservative. Some took refuge in the contention that if the original common branches, providing the basic tools of reading, writing, and arithmetic, were thoroughly mastered, the other subjects would not be difficult to attain.[122] Others threw up their hands in disgust, and perhaps agreed with the writer who exclaimed:

> The *passion* for improving the common schools has become a complete madness, and if it should grow upon us a few years longer, as it has for a few years past, every county in the state will need an insane hospital, and every district school-house will become a receptacle for the furiously, if not the incurably, mad attempts that have been made, . . . to introduce text books of Anatomy, Botany, Geology, Chemistry, and other sciences into the public schools. A knowledge of all these sciences is desirable; but the common school is not the place where that knowledge is to be acquired.[123]

Thus, there was general agreement that the common schools should teach the common branches or rudiments of knowledge, and that this should include at least the tools—reading, spelling, writing, and arithmetic—plus certain other necessary subjects. The implications intrinsic in this contention were that the common school was to be the first stage of training—that stage necessary to all members of the community—from which those who desired could go on to other pursuits, whether in the academic or in the non-academic world.

IV

If education was to put into the hands of the citizenry the knowledge that was power, it was inevitable that the ethical use of this newly found power would become a prime concern of those who

---

[119] *The Common School Journal,* Vol. IV (1842), pp. 257–60.

[120] *The Common School Journal,* Vol. IV (1842), p. 209.

[121] See, for instance, J. Orville Taylor, *The District School; or, National Education* (Carey, Lea, and Blanchard, Philadelphia, 1835), Chap. XI–XXIII.

[122] *The Common School Journal,* Vol. XII (1850), p. 13.

[123] *Ibid.,* Vol. XII (1850), p. 147.

sought to bestow it. ". . . intellectual education alone," inveighed one E. W. Robinson before the American Institute of Instruction, *"will not lead men in the way of virtue.* The best mental endowments, the highest cultivation, and the most polished manners have been often connected with loose morals, a bad temper, and dissipated habits." [124] Indeed, the fear engendered in people of the powers of knowledge unrestrained by moral virtue was one factor in the anti-intellectualism of areas like the West. Speaking of the campaign problems of a well-schooled candidate for the Indiana legislature in 1828, Baynard Rush Hall noted that his ability would easily have prejudiced his cause "had any doubt existed as to his moral integrity; for, a bad man out there was very properly dreaded in proportion to his cleverness, and therefore, power to harm. Indeed, we always preferred an ignorant bad man to a talented one; and hence attempts were usually made to ruin the moral character of a smart candidate." [125] Thus, if any conception was to involve granting to the entire population the power accruing from knowledge, it would immediately have to provide the moral and ethical restraints to guarantee that this power would be turned to the good only.

It was almost inevitable, in view of the religious and ethical traditions of the period, that the reformers would turn to Christianity for this moral guidance. But in turning to this body of doctrine, they were immediately confronted with a problem which threatened their ideal of a community school available to all. In the nineteenth century, the moral good was so intimately bound up with religious faith that the two were practically inseparable in the minds of the people. Thus, morality would have to be inculcated through a religious faith. But how could this be done in view of the multiplicity of churches, each holding its own doctrinal interpretation of the Christian tradition? The teaching of any given religious faith in the schools would be tantamount to proselytism and the eventual exclusion, by reason of conscience, of members

[124] E. W. Robinson, "Moral Culture Essential to Intellectual Education," in *The Lectures Delivered Before the American Institute of Instruction, at Boston, August, 1841 . . .* , p. 122. See also Henry Barnard, First Annual Report, in *The Connecticut Common School Journal*, Vol. I (1838–39), p. 169.

[125] Baynard Rush Hall, *The New Purchase or, Seven and a Half Years in the Far West* (James Albert Woodburn, ed.; Princeton University Press, Princeton, 1916), p. 176.

of other faiths. Mann pointed this out emphatically in his Twelfth Annual Report:

. . . if a man is taxed to support a school, where religious doctrines are inculcated which he believes to be false, and which he believes that God condemns; then he is excluded from the school by the Divine law, at the same time that he is compelled to support it by the human law. . . . The principle involved in such a course is pregnant with all tyrannical consequences. It is broad enough to sustain any claim of ecclesiastical domination, ever made in the darkest ages of the world.[126]

This, then, was the problem which faced the reformers as they turned to the Christian ethic for the moral foundation of common education.

Its seeming insurmountability, however, found resolution in a position which attempted to preserve two crucial values: (1) a morally founded curriculum in the common school, and (2) the rights of individual conscience:

The diversity of religious doctrines, prevalent in our community, would render it difficult to inculcate any religious truths, . . . were it not for two reasons: *first,* that the points on which different portions of a Christian community differ among themselves are far less numerous than those on which they agree; and, *secondly,* were it not also true, that a belief in those points in which they all agree, constitutes the best possible preparation for each to proceed in adding those distinctive particulars, deemed necessary to a complete and perfect faith.[127]

The solution, then, rested in culling from the various creeds the common elements on which all agreed, and teaching these as the moral foundation of common education, "leaving to the family, the pulpit, and the Sabbath School, that more full doctrinal instruction which parents may desire." [128]

[126] *Twelfth Annual Report of the Board of Education, Together with the Twelfth Annual Report of the Secretary of the Board* (Dutton and Wentworth, Boston, 1849), p. 118.

[127] *The Common School Journal,* Vol. I (1839), p. 14.

[128] Report of a Committee of the Convention of Delegates from the several associations of Orthodox Congregational Churches in Massachusetts at Roxbury, June 26, 1849, on the "Connection Between Common School Education and Religion," in *The Common School Journal,* Vol. XI (1849), p. 212. See also Annual Report of Superintendent Dix, New York, 1839, in S. S. Randall, *Common School System of the State of New York* (New York, 1871), pp. 43–44; speech of Reverend Alexander Campbell before the Clarksburg Educational Convention in Virginia, 1841, in *Journal of the House of Delegates of Virginia,* 1841–42, Doc. No. 7, pp. 36–37; and the *Common School Advocate* (Jacksonville, Ill.), Vol. 1 (1837), p. 35.

Two means presented themselves as far as the actual teaching of these common elements of Christianity were concerned. One involved the use of certain ethical concepts basic to Christian morality in contexts other than religious ones. Thus Mann quoted in 1843 from the report of the Michigan superintendent of schools:

. . . in excluding sectarianism from all schools supported by the public purse, the cardinal virtues must not be banished. Without virtue, no system of instruction can perfect its work. If the teacher is fit to be placed over a school, he will, by precept and his own exemplary conduct, teach all that the most rigid morality can ask. More than this, would be trenching on forbidden ground; less, would be conclusive evidence of unfitness for his place. Let justice, for instance, be taught on every occasion that presents itself in the school. Make the child understand that stealing, false dealing, lying, fraud, oppression, bribery, and all other forms of injustice, are wrong, and, if indulged in, surely productive of unhappiness. Let him talk against avarice, and, while recommending the pursuits of industry and honest gain, keep constantly in mind the maxim that "the love of money is the root of all evil." Let him condemn slander, hypocrisy in social and religious intercourse, anger, blasphemy, evil communications, and other pernicious practices; and, by conversation interwoven with instruction, depict their consequences. Let him inculcate brotherly love, duties to parents and society, and the peace-giving pleasures of benevolence, kindness, amiable manners and forgiveness of injuries. Let him talk about temperance, and the terrible evils of intemperance. A teacher, who feels right on these subjects, and whose daily example is made to prove it, will make himself familiar with such maxims as these,—"Do as you would be done by,"—"Abhor evil and cling to that which is good,"—"Evil communications corrupt good manners,"—"Honor thy father and mother,"—"Love your enemies,"—"Forgive injuries,"—and a multitude of similar maxims that can be gleaned from the Scriptures and other good writings. Above all, let distinct ideas of the greatness and all-pervading goodness of God be given, and but little of moral instruction will be left untaught.[129]

In this use of the great moral truths of the Christian tradition rested the possibility of presenting a moral foundation which was related in no way to the peculiar dogma or doctrine of any given sect. While it was far from an irreligious or nonreligious morality, it did move far along in the direction of establishing a nondenominational ethic.

[129] *The Common School Journal*, Vol. V (1843), pp. 120–21.

The other means of providing a moral base for the teaching of the common school was the introduction of the Bible, without comments, as a part of the school exercises.[130] "That our Public Schools are not theological seminaries," wrote Horace Mann in his Twelfth Annual Report, "is admitted. . . . But our system earnestly inculcates all Christian morals; it founds its morals on the basis of religion; it welcomes the religion of the Bible; and, in receiving the Bible, it allows it to do what it is allowed to do in no other system,—*to speak for itself.*" [131] The rationale behind the introduction of Bible reading lay in the contention that the Bible was given by God, while sectarianism was made by man; and thus only in the Bible itself did one find the true moral principles which must be subsumed by all sectarian philosophies.[132] In turning to the Bible, the overwhelming predominance of Protestantism on the American scene led rather naturally to the adoption of the Protestant-Christian version. In a culture of such homogeneity, it was difficult to question the contention that "a Christian teacher with the New Testament in his hand need not be a sectarian teacher." [133]

Thus, in an attempt to secure a moral base for the common school curriculum, the educational reformers turned to the common elements of Protestant Christianity. This moral foundation, which entered the schools in the reading of the Bible without comments and the teaching in a nonreligious context of basic Christian ethical values, represented an important response to the dual commitment of a community school teaching moral values. It asserted for the first time that moral education could be given outside the context of the sectarian religious beliefs of a given denominational faith.

V

"It may be an easy thing to make a Republic," stated Horace Mann in his Twelfth Annual Report; "but it is a very laborious

---

[130] See Reverend George B. Cheever, *Right of the Bible in Our Public Schools,* for the arguments advanced in this report.

[131] *Twelfth Annual Report of the Board of Education* . . . , pp. 116–17.

[132] Quoted from *Journal of Commerce* in *The Common School Journal,* Vol. X (1848), p. 30. See also F. A. Packard, *Thoughts on the Condition and Prospects of Popular Education in the United States,* pp. 26–27.

[133] *Common School Advocate,* Vol. 1 (1837), p. 35.

thing to make Republicans." [134] If the common school was to be an instrument embracing the whole population, a third phase of its universal influence would have to be the preparation of the citizenry for the exercise of its political responsibilities. This influence, as the reform group envisioned it, centered in two closely interrelated areas: (1) the perpetuation of the values and institutions which constituted the basis of republican society and government, and (2) the training required to make sound decisions within the framework of these institutions. [135]

The role of the common school in perpetuating the values of republicanism is subsumed in practically every argument advanced in favor of universal education. "To the citizens of the United States," wrote one educator in 1838, "is committed the solemn charge of perpetuating that liberty, and of maintaining those institutions, civil, social, literary, and religious, which it cost our fathers so much blood and treasure to establish. . . . To maintain our free institutions, then, and to transmit them unimpaired to posterity, is no light trust, to be committed to rash hands and rasher heads." [136] The answer lay in the school's carefully inculcating in the young the values implicit in republicanism as a form of government and as a way of life. [137] "However elevated the moral character of a constituency may be," noted Horace Mann; "however well informed in matters of general science or history, yet they must, if citizens of a Republic, understand something of the true nature and functions of the government under which they live. That any one who is to participate in the government of a country, when he becomes a man, should receive no instruction respecting the nature and functions of the government he is afterwards to administer, is a political solecism." [138]

Implicit in the necessity of teaching "an understanding of the nature and functions" of republican government was the same problem that existed on the religious scene; namely, how could these basic principles be taught without encountering the ferocity

[134] *Twelfth Annual Report of the Board of Education* . . . , p. 78.
[135] E. C. Wines, *Hints on a System of Popular Education* (Philadelphia, 1838), pp. 90–92. [136] *Ibid.*, pp. 89–90.
[137] See, for instance, Horace Mann's proposed lesson on republicanism in *The Common School Journal*, Vol. I (1839), pp. 31–32.
[138] *Twelfth Annual Report of the Board of Education* . . . , p. 84.

of party strife? [139] "It is obvious," observed Mann, ". . . that if the tempest of political strife were to be let loose upon our Common Schools, they would be overwhelmed with sudden ruin. Let it be once understood, that the schoolroom is a legitimate theatre for party politics, and with what violence will hostile partisans struggle to gain possession of the stage, and to play their parts upon it!" [140] Once again, however, the problem did not present an irresolvable dilemma; for in a similar culling of principles common to all political camps stood the resolution of this pressing difficulty. "Surely," Mann continued, "between these extremes, there must be a medium not difficult to be found. And is not this the middle course, which all sensible and judicious men, all patriots, and all genuine republicans, must approve?—namely, that those articles in the creed of republicanism, which are accepted by all, believed in by all, and which form the common basis of our political faith, shall be taught to all." [141] Thus, such areas as the powers of government, the separation of these powers, the modes of electing and appointing officers, the duties, rights, privileges, and responsibilities of citizens, and the necessity of resort to the ballot in place of rebellion, were to be legitimate areas of common school instruction. In areas of controversy, the strictest neutrality was to be observed.[142]

> . . . when the teacher, in the course of his lessons or lectures on the fundamental law, arrives at a controverted text, he is either to read it without comment or remark; or, at most, he is only to say that the passage is the subject of disputation, and that the schoolroom is neither the tribunal to adjudicate, nor the forum to discuss it.[143]

Thus, the political influence of schoolmasters was not to concern itself with the "outbreakings of unregulated passion," [144] which were characteristic of mere party strife; but, through the exertion of their influence "upon a people and their government through

---

[139] *Ibid.*, pp. 85–90.   [140] *Ibid.*, p. 86.   [141] *Ibid.*, p. 89.

[142] Note that at all points where divisive forces threatened to wrack the curriculum, the principle of neutrality was strictly observed. This seems to strengthen the contention that the paramount value involved in the conception of the common school centered in making it available to and used by all.

[143] *Twelfth Annual Report of the Board of Education* . . . , p. 89.

[144] E. Washburn, "On the Political Influence of School-Masters," in *The Introductory Discourse and the Lectures Delivered Before the American Institute of Instruction, in Boston, August, 1835. Including the Journal of Proceedings and a List of the Officers*, p. 64.

the moral, intellectual and social condition of its citizens," it was to contribute to the general uplifting of the whole society and its institutions.[145]

VI

Note must be made at this point of the crucial role played by the above-mentioned training in moral and patriotic values in strengthening the reformers' contention that their system was uniquely capable of maintaining and perpetuating a republican society. It constituted the crux of their answer to charges from certain quarters that the system which they were proposing was strongly similar to those which had recently been instituted in certain of the despotic, monarchical governments of Europe.

These latter systems were beginning to receive increasing attention from various legislative bodies, conventions, and other groups influential in the determination of educational policy; and the decades which witnessed the development of the American common school also saw the rise of a wide interest in European educational developments. During the second quarter of the nineteenth century numerous travelers, educators, and statesmen visited the various nations of the Old World in an effort to observe the educational activities of these peoples. The more prominent of their reports came before the public with increasing interest, and the material in such publications as John Griscom's *A Year in Europe,* the translation of Victor Cousin's *Rapport sur l'état de l'instruction publique in Prusse,* Calvin Stowe's report to the Ohio legislature entitled *Elementary Public Instruction in Europe,*[146] Horace Mann's *Seventh Annual Report,* and Henry Barnard's *National Education in Europe,* exercised an important influence on the course of American educational thought.

One effect, however, was to raise several vital questions in the minds of American leaders.[147] If the system of education in Prussia, for instance, had provided for universal instruction under the aus-

---

[145] *Ibid.*

[146] See Edgar W. Knight, ed., *Reports on European Education* (McGraw-Hill, New York, 1930).

[147] *Seventh Annual Report of the Board of Education; Together with the Seventh Annual Report of the Secretary of the Board* (Dutton and Wentworth, Boston, 1844), p. 21.

pices of the state, then it was quite evident that universal education
in itself did not make for free and republican government. For
Prussia still remained a monarchy. As a matter of fact, there was
evidence in these monarchies of "a growing disregard for the *forms*
of free government, provided the *substance* be enjoyed in the security and prosperity of the people." [148] Why, then, was there such
a similarity in the proposals of the American reformers? Why was
there such a strong tendency to cite Prussian methods of support,
control, and teaching as examples to be emulated by the American
people?

In developing their response to these challenges, the reform
group frankly admitted the strong relation between these European
educational systems and despotism. Stowe said of the Prussian system:

> In every stage of instruction it is made a prominent object, and one
> which is repeatedly and strenuously insisted on in all the laws pertain-
> ing to education, to awaken a *national spirit*—to create in the youthful
> mind a warm attachment to his native land, and its institutions, and
> to fix in his affections a decided preference for the peculiarities of his
> own country. Indeed the whole plan (which is well understood to have
> originated in Prussia, when the rapid spread of republican principles
> first began to threaten the thrones of Europe,) evidently is to unite
> with the military force which always attends a despotism, a strong
> moral power over the understanding and affections of the people.[149]

Thus, the true purpose of the European monarchs in instituting
systems of universal education was to check the growing influences
of revolutionary spirit in their respective sovereignties. Education
for despotism was actually being used as the counter-revolutionary
weapon of despotism.

But proceeding from this point, the reformers provided two answers. First, they strongly maintained that the evils imputed to the
system "were easily and naturally separable from the good" which
it undoubtedly possessed.[150] Horace Mann recognized this when
he contended:

> If the Prussian schoolmaster has better methods of teaching reading,
> writing, grammar, geography, arithmetic, etc., so that, in half the time,

---

[148] Calvin E. Stowe, "Report on Elementary Public Instruction in Europe," in
Edgar W. Knight, *op. cit.*, p. 256.   [149] *Ibid.*, pp. 255–56.
[150] *Seventh Annual Report of the Board of Education* . . . , p. 22.

he produces greater and better results, surely, we may copy his modes of teaching these elements, without adopting his notions of passive obedience to government, or of blind adherence to the articles of a church.[151]

Human faculties, he held, were similar in all parts of the world; hence the best means for their cultivation and development in one place must be substantially the best for their development and growth in another.[152] On the other hand, the spirit "which shall control the action of these faculties when matured, which shall train them to self-reliance or to abject submission, which shall lead them to refer all questions to the standard of reason or to that of authority,—this spirit is wholly distinct and distinguishable from the manner in which the faculties themselves should be trained." [153] Thus, Mann held that a republican system might well profit by improved processes in the training of the faculties, without necessarily "being contaminated by the abuses which may be made to follow them." [154]

The second response, based on the first, held that if this separation could be made, then it was the responsibility of republics to develop an education peculiarly suited to the maintenance and perpetuation of their institutions. If, as Stowe maintained, republics "are considered the natural foes to monarchies," and the monarchies were seen to be strengthening themselves with universal systems of despotic education, "do not patriotism and the necessity of self-preservation, call upon us to do more and better for the education of our whole people, than any despotic sovereign can do for his?" [155] "If a moral power over the understandings and affections of the people may be turned to evil," held Mann, "may it not also be employed for good?" [156] Hence, the answer to charges against the capability of universal education to maintain and perpetuate free institutions lay in teaching Christian and republican values. Only when the influence of a community school was inclusive of these could it furnish a truly republican education.

Before leaving this section note must also be made of an implicit

---

[151] *Ibid.*   [152] *Ibid.*   [153] *Ibid.*

[154] *Seventh Annual Report of the Board of Education* . . . , p. 23. See also *Common School Advocate* (Jacksonville, Ill.), Vol. 1 (1837), pp. 17–18.

[155] Calvin Stowe, *op. cit.*, p. 256.

[156] *Seventh Annual Report of the Board of Education* . . . , p. 23.

assumption casting the school in the role of an Americanizing institution.[157] "Every body acknowledges the justness of the declaration," held Mann, "that a foreign people, born and bred and dwarfed under the despotisms of the Old World, cannot be transformed into the full stature of American citizens, merely by a voyage across the Atlantic, or by subscribing the oath of naturalization." [158] Thus, everyone who was to participate responsibly in the life of the republic needed the training of the common schools —the young of the native-born as well as both the young and old of the immigrant groups.[159] The common school, and an instrument of preparation, must be genuinely *universal* in scope.

VII

If the reformers offered the people a program of objectives for a republican common school, they also provided them with a specific program of instrumentalities. These means of achieving the broad goals of their proposed program revolved principally around modes of support and control. Two considerations entered into their determination of means—both again intimately bound up with a conception of a republican education: (1) the means had to be effective in securing the ends, and (2) the means had to be internally republican in their own right. Given these two conditions, the means could then be incorporated into the total meaning of the common school.

The basis of thought concerning means of support centered in the argument that if the state was to be dependent on common education for its very life, then it was the responsibility of the state

[157] See Benjamin Labaree, "The Education Demanded by the Peculiar Character of Our Civil Institutions," in *The Lectures Delivered Before the American Institute of Instruction, at Montpelier, Vt., August 1849; Including the Journal of Proceedings and a List of the Officers.*

[158] *Ninth Annual Report of the Board of Education, Together with the Ninth Annual Report of the Secretary of the Board* (Dutton and Wentworth, Boston, 1846), p. 95.

[159] See Benjamin Labaree, *op. cit.*, for reference to *dual* responsibility of the common school (p. 45, *ante*). It is also interesting to note the close relationship in the minds of these men of the Bible, and the training in Christian morals for which it stood, and the requisite inculcation in patriotic republican values. Through the two, the immigrant could be Americanized, at least in attitude and value. This is one of the prominent ways in which the Bible figured as a patriotic symbol during this period. See also Samuel Lewis, "Remarks on Common Schools," in Calvin Stowe, *The Prussian System of Public Instruction*, p. 98.

to provide this education for its young.[160] This contention was reinforced by the argument that if education is the immutable and irrefutable natural right of every human being, it is "the correlative duty of every government to see that the means of that education are provided for all." [161] Thus, it devolved upon the community, as "common mother" to its citizens,[162] to provide for the education of its citizens. This conception of state responsibility is clearly implicit in the Reverend Doane's "An Address to the People of New Jersey" in 1838. Viewing education as a social necessity, Doane argued:

It is in vain to say that education is a private matter, and that it is the duty of every parent to provide for the instruction of his own children. In theory, it is so. But there are some who can not, and there are more who will not, make provision. And the question then is, shall the State suffer from individual inability, or from individual neglect? When the child who has not been trained up in the way in which he ought to go, commits a crime against the State, the law, with iron hand, comes in between the parent and his offspring, and takes charge of the offender. And shall there be provision to punish only, and none to prevent? Shall the only offices in which the State is known be those of jailer and of executioner? Shall she content herself with the stern attribute of justice, and discard the gentler ministries of mercy? It was said of Draco's laws that they were writ with blood. Is it less true of any State which makes provision for the whipping-post, the penitentiary, the scaffold, and leaves the education of her children to individual effort or precarious charity? . . .

Omitting all considerations, . . . of what has been or of what may be legislative enactments on the subject, we address you as the Sovereign People, and we say that *"it is your duty and your highest interest to provide and to maintain, within the reach of every child, the means of such an education as will qualify him to discharge the duties of a citizen of the Republic;* and will enable him, by subsequent exertion, in the free exercise of the unconquerable will, to attain the highest eminence in knowledge and in power which God may place within his reach.[163]

The means by which the whole community could support education was through the appropriation of public funds. Although

[160] *Tenth Annual Report of the Board of Education* . . . , p. 112.
[161] *Ibid.*
[162] Charles Fenton Mercer, *op. cit.,* p. 58. See also *Tenth Annual Report of the Board of Education* . . . , pp. 232–33.
[163] George W. Doane, "An Address to the People of New Jersey," in *The American Journal of Education,* Vol. XV (1865), pp. 6–8.

there were several different kinds of public sources,[164] the reform group early perceived the necessity of resorting to taxation—the traditional agency through which society supported all matters of common responsibility. Education would have to stand along with the functions of law and justice as one more crucial protection to the normal functioning and perpetuation of society. Its one difference from these other instruments was that while they were corrective, education was preventive. As in so many cases, the preventive was cheaper by many times.[165] In terms of this framework, the reform group was able to construct one answer to the charge that the taxation of one man (especially a man with no children or one who provided independently for the education of his family) for the education of another's child was a wanton violation of individual rights and liberties. The reasoning on which this response is founded is well illustrated in Thaddeus Stevens' great speech to the Pennsylvania legislature in 1835—a speech which literally prevented repeal of the state's year-old common school law:

> Many complain of the school tax, not so much on account of its amount, as because it is for the benefit of others and not themselves. This is a mistake. It is *for their own* benefit, inasmuch as it perpetuates the government and ensures the due administration of the laws under which they live, and by which their lives and property are protected. Why do they not urge the same objection against all other taxes? The industrious, thrifty, rich farmer pays a heavy county tax to support criminal courts, build jails, and pay sheriffs and jail-keepers, and yet probably he never has had and never will have any direct personal use for either. He never gets the worth of his money by being tried for a crime before the court, allowed the privilege of the jail on conviction, or receiving an equivalent from the sheriff or his hangmen officers! He cheerfully pays the tax which is necessary to support and punish convicts, but loudly complains of that which goes to prevent his fellow-being from becoming a criminal, and to obviate the necessity of those humiliating instructions.[166]

[164] Other public sources, such as incomes from various permanent funds, land grants, etc., were incapable of supporting schools without the addition of tax funds. In many states, such income was negligible to the point of being inconsequential.

[165] *Tenth Annual Report of the Board of Education* . . . , p. 110.

[166] *The Famous Speech of Hon. Thaddeus Stevens of Pennsylvania in Opposition to the Repeal of the Common School Law of 1834 in the House of Representatives of Pennsylvania*, Apr. 11, 1835. (Thaddeus Stevens Memorial Association, Philadelphia, 1904), p. 5.

A second response to the resistance against being taxed for education was framed in terms of what the reformers viewed as false notions respecting rights to private property.[167] Complete freedom to dispose of property *ad libitum,* according to Mann, could exist only in a nonsocial context.[168] As soon as man lived within a society, being bound by innumerable ties, having his fortune and condition "almost predetermined and foreordained by his predecessors, and being about to exert upon his successors as commanding an influence as has been exerted upon himself," he could "no longer shrink into his individuality, and disclaim connection and relationship with the world." [169] Within a society, "successive generations of men, taken collectively, constitute one great Commonwealth," and, the property of the Commonwealth being pledged for the education of all its youth, "The successive holders of this property are trustees, bound to the faithful execution of their trust, by the most sacred obligations." [170] The withholding of funds for the fulfillment of these obligations was tantamount, Mann maintained, to "embezzlement and pillage from children." [171] Thus, by pointing out to the individual that his lot was intimately bound up with society's, the exponents of tax support sought to overcome the resistance advanced under the theory of personal property rights. In effect, they were attempting to move educational taxation within the positive tradition of support for community needs, and out of the tradition of individual rights to protection against deprivation of private property.[172]

VIII

If the role of the state as "common mother" involved community responsibility for the support of education, it similarly made it incumbent upon the community to control and supervise the facilities established.[173] The state was the only authority all-embracing enough to maintain the kind of community school which the reform group envisioned. Any lesser authority would carry the

---

[167] *Tenth Annual Report of the Board of Education . . . ,* p. 111.

[168] *Ibid.,* pp. 119–20.   [169] *Ibid.,* p. 120.   [170] *Ibid.,* p. 127.   [171] *Ibid.*

[172] This in no way precluded the attempt to assure individuals that an educated community would benefit them personally. Thus, for instance, the employer was assured that an educated employee is more efficient and valuable, etc. See Horace Mann, *Fifth Annual Report of the Board of Education.*

[173] *Common School Advocate* (Cincinnati, Ohio), Vol. 2 (1838), p. 154.

implicit danger of a curriculum that would violate the interest of one or more groups in the community, and tend to break down the all-inclusive character of the community school. The intellectual sectarianism which was potential in control by any less-inclusive body would most certainly act on segments of the school population so as to exclude.

The implications of this argument struck most powerfully, perhaps, at the conception of education supported by tax funds, but controlled by the several religious groups—each maintaining tax-supported schools for the children of its own faith. They are set forth with great clarity by the New York State superintendent of common schools in a decision in 1853. Speaking of widely advanced proposals to divide the public school funds among the various denominations according to the number of children they educated, he argued:

> To give to every sect a *pro rata* share of the school moneys, to enable it to support its own schools, and teach its own system of religious faith in them, would be, in the sparsely inhabited country districts, to divide the children within the territory convenient for attendance on a single school, and in which the support of all the inhabitants is frequently scarcely adequate, with the aid of the public moneys, to sustain a single efficient school, into a dozen or more schools. Indeed, under this arrangement a single indigent family would often be required to support its own school, to go without any, or to violate its conscience by joining with others in one in which a religious system was taught wholly at variance with its own.[174]

Thus, the values of both common education and efficient education were implicitly violated by any scheme which would pro-rate school funds among private institutions. The only authority which could preserve both was the community itself, and thus it would have to undertake the responsibility.

If one condition for the success of the common school was the maintenance of high quality instruction, another question which presented itself to the reform group was: What level of the community could best accomplish this through its control of education? In the optimum, the reformers saw this as the state. Although they

[174] *Decision of the State Superintendent of Common Schools on the Right to Compel Catholic Children to Attend Prayers, and to Read or Commit Portions of the Bible, as School Exercises* (New York, Oct. 27, 1853), p. 6. See also *Pennsylvania School Journal*, Vol. I (1852), p. 406.

urged responsibility at all levels—local through state[175]—both their writings and actions[176] indicate a vehement maintenance of the final authority of the state in educational matters. Though this probably arose from a variety of reasons, the one which seems most consistent with the total conception of common education revolved around the ability of the state, as the highest level, to compel minimum standards and to equalize opportunity. Through the exercise of its regulatory powers, the state could contribute much toward raising standards to the point where local populations would freely avail themselves of local facilities.[177] Thus, the only control pattern compatible with common education was control by the community. Final authority would rest with the states; delegated and assumed responsibilities would accrue from the local levels on up. Similarly, the only compatible pattern of support capable of maintaining these desired qualities was public community support, including taxation.[178]

I X

The conception which this reform group formulated of a school compatible with, and tending uniquely to maintain, the kind of republican society that developed in America in the early nineteenth century, emerged as a most positive educational ideal—the American common school. It was a school which was to embrace the whole community—ideally common to the young of all classes and creeds. It was a school uniquely charged with the responsi-

[175] The Federal Constitution, being an instrument of delegated powers, made no mention of education, thus leaving the states as the final possible level of community authority in education. For further reasons see Dawson Hales, "The Rise of Federal Control in American Education" (Unpublished Ph.D. thesis, Teachers College, Columbia University, 1949), Chap. II.

[176] As state officers, secretaries of state boards of instruction, etc.

[177] There is also little doubt about the influence of the Prussian school system toward establishing this end. See Calvin Stowe, "Report on Elementary Public Instruction in Europe," in Edgar Knight, ed., *Reports on European Education.*

[178] Thus the schools were government institutions. This furnished one more reason for the exclusion of sectarian religious instruction. "To introduce into them, or permit to be introduced into them, a course of religious instruction conformable to the views of any religious denomination, would be tantamount to the adoption of a government religion—a step contrary to the Constitution, and equally at variance with the policy of a free government and the wishes of the people." *Decision of the State Superintendent of Common Schools on the Right to Compel Catholic Children to Attend Prayers, and to Read or Commit Portions of the Bible, as School Exercise* (New York, Oct. 27, 1853).

bility of preparing the young of the new republic to take their places in its adult society. It was a school which was to be truly the child of the community—supported by it, controlled by it, used by it, and serving it. And it was to provide for the young that which no other institution known to the society could furnish—the experience of democratic association within a genuine miniature of a democratic society.

PART 3

THE COMMON SCHOOL

TAKES ROOT IN PRACTICE

THE essential role of tradition, wrote Ralph Barton Perry, "is to define the present. A society lives in 'the foremost files of time' by virtue of its accumulated legacy." [1] Men do not think or act outside the broad confines of their social heritage. They face their problems with the accumulation of knowledge, custom, and practice transmitted to them by their predecessors. Yet, in a sense, these form but the working endowment of a generation. There seems no limit to the infinite number of combinations, reconstructions, and innovations which men may effect in the values and practices they have learned. Tradition, then, need not be viewed as a fatally binding force upon those who live by its patterns. Rather it is, as Perry has further elaborated, "both the bed of reactionaries and the springboard of innovators. It provides a man's working capital, whether he squanders it, lives on the interest, or invests it in new enterprises." [2]

The preceding sections have sought to trace the emergence of the American common school as an educational ideal—locating its roots in the way of life it hoped to serve. This section, exploring certain representative developments among the educational institutions themselves, will attempt to consider the degree to which

[1] Ralph Barton Perry, *Puritanism and Democracy* (Vanguard Press, New York, 1944), p. 23. [2] *Ibid.*, p. 25.

this conception gained acceptance at the level of practice. Only in this way can its validity as a genuine element in the American educational tradition be adequately determined.

1. TRADITIONS OF SUPPORT

Perhaps the most pervasive educational tradition of the Colonial Period was the Protestant conception of universal education—an education which would provide each individual with the power to read and interpret the Bible for himself.[3] It expressed itself in such a variety of forms, however, reflecting always the diverse backgrounds of the colonists, that early differences in degree soon became significant differences in kind. Nurtured by ideological and environmental dissimilarities, these differences soon stood at the heart of several distinct educational traditions. In essence two patterns of support seem to represent the crux of these various forms.

The first of these might best be called the tradition of *philanthropy*. Deeply rooted in the English heritage, this tradition had been clearly embodied in the English Poor Law of 1601.[4] Essentially individualist in nature, it asserted the right and duty of individual families to provide through private means for the education of their children. The community was responsible only for the poor and indigent. Education was a private function, becoming public only in the case of persons who could not afford to provide it for themselves.

Such a tradition was vigorously reinforced by the strong individualism inherent in the agricultural and commercial patterns of colonial life. It is able to be viewed practically in its pure form in the early educational legislation of the southern colonies, particularly Virginia. Inasmuch as the colony was settled largely by Englishmen of Anglican affiliation, and in light of its decentralized agrarian economy, it is not difficult to see how such an educational pattern could easily take root. In the early laws dealing with education for religious orthodoxy, it was the *individual* responsibility

[3] For an extended treatment of this theme, see R. Freeman Butts, *A Cultural History of Education* (McGraw-Hill, New York, 1947) and Edward H. Reisner, *The Evolution of the Common School* (Macmillan, New York, 1930).

[4] A law providing for education of the poor and indigent by public taxation. 43 Eliz. Cap. II, pp. 438–42 of bound volume of Acts of Parliament (Henry VII, Henry VIII, Edward VI, Mary, and Elizabeth).

of parents and guardians to see that their children and servants were properly trained by the local minister. Thus, a law passed in 1632 required "That uppon every Sonday the mynisters shall halfe an hower or more before eveninge prayer examine, catechise, and instruct the youth and ignorant persons of his parish in the ten commandments, the articles of the beliefe and the Lords prayer." It was the responsibility of "all ffathers, mothers, maysters, and mistrisses" to cause their children to attend on penalty of censure by the courts.[5] When legislation was passed in 1645 [6] establishing limited public responsibility for education, it incorporated much the same provisions as the older English poor law—applying educational benefits only to the indigent. Aside from the occasional charitable expressions of church congregations, this kind of legislation represented the only delegation of community responsibility in the educational efforts of colonial Virginia.

The other of these basic traditions might best be called the tradition of *collectivism*. Its roots on the American scene seem definitely to have stemmed from European Calvinism;[7] and it found its earliest expression, perhaps, in the educational legislation of the Massachusetts Bay Colony. Embodied in the School Law of 1647,[8] this tradition placed on the various towns, as the agencies of civil government, the responsibility for educating the young in the rudiments of knowledge. Although a parent was still at liberty to educate his own children, the law provided for the maintenance of a public teacher who would teach all who might come to him. The town, standing in place of the collective parents, assumed the responsibility for making education available; and it was the town which the General Court fined on its failure to do so.

This tradition of collectivism was later reinforced by the humanitarian ideals of the eighteenth century. Holding that the

[5] Acts of the Grand Assembly, 1632, Act VII, quoted in William Waller Hening, *The Statutes at Large; Being a Collection of All the Laws of Virginia, from the First Session of the Legislature in the Year 1619* (R. and W. and G. Bartow, New York, 1823), Vol. 1, pp. 181–82.

[6] Acts of the Grand Assembly, 1646, Act XXVII, quoted in William Waller Hening, *op. cit.,* Vol. 1, pp. 336–37.

[7] For a good treatment of institutional antecedents in Britain, see Nelson R. Burr, *Education in New Jersey 1630–1871* (Princeton University Press, Princeton, 1942), pp. 220–24.

[8] *Records of the Governor and Company of the Massachusetts Bay in New England* (Nathaniel B. Shurtleff, ed.; William White, Boston, 1853), Vol. 2, p. 203.

individual would be raised only as the group or the society was raised, humanitarianism placed significant emphasis on collective social effort. Although its warm, idealistic, optimistic collectivism differed greatly in quality from the stern, harsh collectivism of the Calvinist, the former played an important role in reinforcing the legal precedents established under the latter.

Although the philanthropic and the collective traditions had both emerged out of the Protestant faith in education for all, each developed as a separate system reflecting the ideals of a given way of life. The former contained all the elements of the European two-track system—one track for the poor and the other for the well-to-do. Those who had the means would send their children to private tuition schools. Those who did not have the means were forced to resort to charity or to public schools for the poor. Provision for education within a given community was left to chance and individual effort. The private schools perpetuated a class which was set off, by education in addition to birth, from the class to which the philanthropic system catered. And although the system, in theory, contained the means for the education of all (those who could pay in private schools and all the remaining in public), great gaps were left by persons who proudly refused to avail themselves of public "pauper" facilities.

The collective endeavor, on the other hand, provided for a group responsibility involving, indirectly, all members of the community. Education was a public function; and the facilities established were available to all. The way was always open, of course, for those who desired to send their children to schools other than the public ones; but this in no way relieved them of their share in maintaining the latter. And there was no class of children denied an education because of any stigma of "pauperism" attached to public facilities.

I

By the end of the eighteenth century, the collective tradition was firmly rooted in New England. It had, it is true, grown out of the marriage between Calvinism and the state; but even as the forces of disestablishment became ever more powerful, the legal precedents of the old system largely remained. It was with this tradition that the New England states entered the Union in 1789. Except for Rhode Island, which did not have even a permissive school law until 1828, they generally followed the leadership of Massachusetts —authorizing taxation for education, fixing the length of the school term, prescribing the curriculum, and providing for the erection of school plant facilities. Massachusetts itself set the pace by enacting in 1789 the first general state school law in the nation.[9] This law raised to the level of state-wide requirements practices which had developed since the legislation of 1647. Every town was required to maintain an elementary school for six months out of the twelve, and towns having one hundred families or more were required to maintain one throughout the year. The law also provided for the certification of elementary school teachers, and set forth requirements for grammar schools in the larger towns. The laws of Maine,[10] Vermont,[11] New Hampshire,[12] and Connecticut[13] followed closely the pattern set by this Massachusetts legislation; and by the end of the eighteenth century, public tax support for education had firmly taken root in New England.

In general, the middle and southern states pretty well followed the philanthropic tradition. Education was considered a private function of the parent, with any state interference unjustified in terms of individual rights. The role of the state was limited to providing education for paupers and indigent children. The constitution of 1790, in Pennsylvania, directed the establishment of pauper schools at the convenience of the legislature.[14] The law of 1802 served to implement it by providing for the education of pauper children in each county.[15] New Jersey first established a school fund in 1817.[16] Delaware created a school fund in 1796,[17] but it

[9] Acts of 1789, Chap. XIX.

[10] As a district of Massachusetts from 1677; see Ava Harriet Chadbourne, *The Beginnings of Education in Maine* (Teachers College, Columbia University, New York, 1928).

[11] Constitution of 1777, Sec. XL, in Francis Newton Thorpe, *op. cit.*, Vol. 6, p. 3748.

[12] *The Laws of the State of New Hampshire* (1797), p. 306 (Law passed June 18, 1789).

[13] *The Public Records of the Colony of Connecticut* (Charles J. Hoadly, ed.; Hartford, 1868), Vol. 4, p. 331; also *Acts and Laws of the State of Connecticut*, 1796, p. 371.

[14] Constitution of 1790, Sec. 44, in Francis Newton Thorpe, *op. cit.*, p. 3091.

[15] Laws of 1801–03, Chap. XXIV.

[16] Acts of 1816–17, p. 26.

[17] Act of Feb. 9, 1796.

was not appropriated until 1817;[18] even then, it was used only to provide education in reading, writing, and arithmetic for the children of the poor. In the southern states, little was done before the nineteenth century, even in providing education for the poor. In general, a "hands off" policy on the part of government prevailed; and except in places where apprentice laws were in effect, elementary education was left to private and church groups.

Thus we see that except for the New England states, where a strong policy of collective support had taken root, education generally was the concern of the individual family. The community, acting through philanthropic agencies, religious agencies, or the state, took an interest only at points where a spirit of Christian charity impelled them to provide it for the poor.

II

One further item is worthy of note at this point—the policy of the federal government relating to the territories. Formulated in the Land Ordinances of 1785 [19] and 1787,[20] this policy was instrumental in determining the progress of education in the newer western states. Basically, it was formulated as but one aspect of the general, over-all national land policy during the period of the Confederacy.

Two principal means for disposing of public lands had been developed by the colonies before the Revolution. One had its origins in New England, and involved the carving of salable land into townships before it was offered for private purchase.[21] In general, there could be no private title to land outside a township; and town officials were responsible for boundaries and surveys. In keeping with New England tradition, grants for the support of religion and education were frequently made as part condition of the township sale.[22]

---

[18] See Laws of 1817, Vol. 5, p. 251, Chap. CXLVI.

[19] Land Ordinance of 1785, in Henry Steele Commager, ed., *Documents of American History* (Appleton-Century-Crofts, New York and London, 1948), pp. 123–24.

[20] The Northwest Ordinance, in Henry Steele Commager, ed., *op. cit.*, pp. 128–32.

[21] Payson Jackson Treat, *The National Land System* (E. G. Treat & Co., New York, 1910), p. 23.

[22] See, for instance, "Resolves, Orders, Votes, Etc. Passed at the Session Begun and Held at Boston. On the Thirty-First Day of May, A. D. 1732," Chap. 17, *The Acts and Resolves, Public and Private, of the Province of the Massachusetts Bay*, Vol. XI.

The other system for disposing of public lands had developed primarily in the South, and involved the sale of unappropriated areas in parcels varying with the individual purchase.[23] There was little definite public responsibility for the accuracy of land surveys, and consequently, gross errors in the determination of boundaries often appeared. The acquiring of land was a process by which individuals purchased tracts according to their needs and desires. Each selected the piece he desired, had it laid off by a surveyor, and claimed title on payment. He was little concerned with its relationship to surrounding or neighboring pieces of land, and the system was aptly named the system of "indiscriminate location."

In 1784, the Continental Congress, faced with an acute financial crisis, appointed a committee to draft a plan for disposing of the public lands.[24] Although a majority of this committee represented southern states, their proposals generally followed the New England plan—omitting mention of religion or education.[25] The report of the committee was tabled on presentation, however,[26] and it was not until March of 1785 that it was again taken under consideration.[27]

At that time, the report was referred to a new committee composed of one representative from each state.[28] The committee worked over the proposals for a month, and presented their report on April 14 of the same year.[29] The "township system" was retained, this time including grants for religion and education as an inducement to settlers.[30] These new proposals were under consideration by Congress for a month, the principal arguments revolving around whether the land would be sold only by townships or whether provision would be made for sale in smaller parcels. Although a compromise was worked out, the grants for education remained; and the Ordinance of 1785 carried a provision reserving

[23] Payson Jackson Treat, *op. cit.*, pp. 24–25.
[24] *Journals of the Continental Congress* (Gaillard Hunt, ed.; Government Printing Office, Washington, 1928), Vol. XXVI, p. 324. Committee members were Thomas Jefferson, Hugh Williamson, David Howell, Elbridge Gerry, and Jacob Read.
[25] *Ibid.*, Vol. XXVI, pp. 324–31 and Vol. XXVII, pp. 446–53.
[26] *Ibid.*, Vol. XXVII, p. 453.
[27] *Journals of the Continental Congress* (John C. Fitzpatrick, ed.; Government Printing Office, Washington, 1933), Vol. XXVIII, p. 114.
[28] *Ibid.*, Vol. XXVIII, p. 165.
[29] *Ibid.*, Vol. XXVIII, p. 264; draft of the report in Vol. XXVIII, pp. 251–56.
[30] *Ibid.*

the sixteenth section of each township "for the maintenance of public schools within the said township." [31]

The influence of the New England tradition in bringing about this provision for public support of schools may be gathered from the correspondence of Timothy Pickering of Massachusetts to Elbridge Gerry[32] and Rufus King[33] of the same state. Pickering's letter to King on March 8, 1785, vehemently criticized the earlier report of 1784, especially for its lack of provision for such grants. King sent a copy of the new draft to Pickering with the comment, "You will find thereby, that your ideas have had weight with the committee who reported this ordinance." [34] In general, the effect of the New England tradition in achieving the public grants for education seems strongly indicated. In any case, the policy set forth in the Ordinance of 1785 was reinforced and restated in the now famous Article 3 of the Ordinance of 1787:

Religion, morality, and knowledge, being necessary to good government and the happiness of mankind, schools and the means of education shall forever be encouraged.[35]

Summing up, then, Americans at the end of the eighteenth century possessed two traditions on which to draw in making provision for education. On the one side, they had a collective tradition of community support for schools available to all children. On the other, they had a philanthropic tradition of individual responsibility, the community taking haphazard interest only when individual means failed. The former was deeply rooted in New England and the federal territories; the latter pervaded the thinking and practice of the middle and southern states. These were the traditions which prevailed when the new demands on education were enunciated. These were the traditions which would have to provide the raw material of planning and action for those interested in securing a publicly supported common school.

[31] *Ibid.*, Vol. XXVIII, pp. 375–81.

[32] Pickering to Gerry (March 1, 1785) in Octavius Pickering, *The Life of Timothy Pickering* (Little, Brown and Co., Boston, 1867), Vol. I, pp. 504–06.

[33] Pickering to King (March 8, 1785), in Octavius Pickering, *op. cit.*, Vol. I, pp. 506–10.

[34] King to Pickering (April 15, 1785), in Octavius Pickering, *op. cit.*, Vol. I, p. 511.

[35] Art. III, The Northwest Ordinance, in Henry Steele Commager, *op. cit.*, p. 131.

2. MOVEMENT TOWARD PUBLIC SUPPORT

Given these traditions at the end of the eighteenth century, what were the dynamics involved in the various states as groups of citizens, under the leadership of the reformers, sought to realize the ideals which had been so powerfully enunciated? Analysis of the educational developments of the next half-century reveals a variety of changes in the elements of these traditions. This discussion of developments in patterns of support will attempt to trace the movement in five representative states: Massachusetts, to illustrate the strengthening of the collective tradition in New England; New York and Pennsylvania, to illustrate the movement from the philanthropic to the collective tradition in the middle states; Virginia, to illustrate the failure of attempts to move from the philanthropic to the collective tradition in the southern states; and Ohio, to illustrate the conflict of both these traditions in the western states.

I

As the seat of the collective tradition, Massachusetts had continued down through the eighteenth century its pattern of community responsibility for school support. The year 1789 witnessed a codification into one law of those practices which had become standard during this period.[36] By its provisions, towns having fifty or more families were required to furnish six months of schooling (distributed among one or more schools) during the course of the year; towns which had grown to two hundred families were also required to support a grammar school. One of the novel principles it also recognized was the district form of organization, reflecting the decentralization which had come with continued settlement of the rural areas. Although the act did not grant districts the power to tax, it did sanction the town's power to create districts. This condition continued until 1800 when the General Court, recognizing their importance, did assign them the tax prerogative.[37]

In general, then, the tradition of public tax support was clearly enunciated in Massachusetts by the beginning of the nineteenth

---

[36] Acts, 1789, Chap. XIX.
[37] An Act in Addition to an Act, entitled "An Act to provide for the Instruction of Youth, and for the Promotion of good Education," passed Feb. 28, 1800.

century. There seems little doubt that its roots were strong enough to draw approval from both the conservative and liberal camps; and the remarks of Daniel Webster in a Centennial Address at Plymouth in 1822 serve well to illustrate this broad general acceptance:

> In this particular, New England may be allowed to claim, I think, a merit of a peculiar character. She early adopted and has constantly maintained the principle, that it is the undoubted right, and the bounden duty of government, to provide for the instruction of all youth. That which is elsewhere left to chance, or to charity, we secure by law. For the purpose of public instruction, we hold every man subject to taxation in proportion to his property, and we look not to the question, whether he himself have, or have not, children to be benefited by the education for which he pays. We regard it as a wise and liberal system of police, by which property, and life, and the peace of society are secured.[38]

This approval on the part of intellectual leaders, however, in no way indicated concurrence by the whole people. Strong opposition to taxation was forthcoming, especially from the rural population and the upper classes, on the ground that taxation for education was a deprivation of personal property without just cause.[39] These negative forces, enhanced by a growing rural apathy to schooling in general,[40] led to a gradual degeneration of the public institutions—to the point where they were deserted by many who could afford private schools for their children. With little state regulation, the districts usurped much of the control of education, and in seeking to cut costs to a minimum they often compromised standards of instruction. These were the conditions which in 1825 drew the first sharp criticism from James G. Carter.

Concerning the pattern of support, Carter made vigorous use of Massachusetts' traditional collectivism as a foundation for his arguments. "The pilgrims of Plymouth," he asserted, "set the first example not only to our own country, but to the civilized world, of a system of Free Schools, . . . A system, by which the state so far assumed the education of the youth, as to make all property responsible for the support of common schools for the instruction

---

[38] *Barnard's American Journal of Education*, Vol. I (1855–56), p. 591.
[39] See Sidney Louis Jackson, *America's Struggle for Free Schools* (Washington, D. C., 1941).   [40] *Ibid.*, pp. 128–31.

of all children." [41] But crucial to his argument was his transference of collective support from an ecclesiastical to a republican context. It is not difficult to perceive the close relationship between the desirability of all children being able to read and interpret the Bible for themselves, the essence of the older Protestant tradition, and the desirability of all children being able to read in order to participate in the affairs of government. And Carter, whether unwittingly or not, effected this translation in his argument.[42] Thus he noted:

You may incorporate in your constitution, if you like, the articles, "that all men are born free and equal," and "that all are eligible to the highest offices"; but this is not freedom, while ninety-nine hundredths of the community have not the means of fitting themselves or their children, for discharging the duties of those high offices. As well might you tie the legs, and pinion the arms of a man, and tell him he has as fair a chance to win the race, as one who is free and trained to the course. *Something like this our ancestors must have felt, who established the free schools;* and something like this, their posterity must feel, if they would cherish and preserve them.[43]

Notwithstanding this translation of context, the argument was most effective in calling attention to the need for universal education; and action by the legislature was immediately forthcoming. In 1827, for the first time in the state's history, the entire support of common schools by taxation was made compulsory.[44] This pattern of public support was strengthened even further in 1834 with the establishment of a permanent school fund, the interest of which was also to apply to the maintenance of common schools.[45] However, wisely profiting from the experience of Connecticut,[46]

---

[41] James G. Carter, *Essays upon Popular Education,* pp. 19–20.

[42] Henry Barnard consciously noted this translation in citing the New England tradition as an argument to favor education in his *Connecticut Common School Journal,* Vol. II, p. 101.

[43] James G. Carter, *Essays upon Popular Education,* p. 21. (Italics added.)

[44] Laws of 1827, Chap. CXLIII.   [45] Laws of 1834, Chap. CLXIX.

[46] Connecticut, through the laws of 1750 and 1795, had created a school fund capable of making sizable contributions to local effort—a fund which had thereby created an interesting paradox. For instead of *stimulating* local initiative as originally planned, it served to cripple it. Thus, in 1821, the Law of 1700, which had required a two-mill town tax for schools, was repealed; and public support stemmed entirely from the fund. The concern of the friends of education was represented by the report of a legislative committee which asserted, concerning the Law of 1821: "The result of the experiment has decided that no appropriations of money

the framers of this enactment made participation in its benefits by the several towns contingent on two conditions: (1) the raising of at least one dollar per person of school age (four to sixteen) per year through local effort, and (2) compliance with the state requirement for tendering statistical returns.

Thus, by the 1830's, the conception of a common school entirely supported by public effort had firmly taken root in Massachusetts. Although there is occasional evidence of violations of this principle,[47] there is little doubt that they appeared to any great extent. And Horace Mann, as secretary of the Board of Education, was able validly to state in 1843:

> Our schools are perfectly free. A child would be as much astonished at being asked to pay any sum, however small, for attending our Common Schools, as he would be if payment were demanded of him for walking in the public streets, for breathing the common air, or enjoying the warmth of the unappropriable sun.[48]

Massachusetts, then, acting within a powerful tradition of community support for schools, experienced relatively little difficulty in strengthening this principle as its response to demands for universal education. As such, the primary efforts of its educational statesmen during the period from 1830 to 1850 were turned to improving the quality and effectiveness of the education they had secured.

II

Until the last two decades of the eighteenth century, the educational system of New York had remained heavily steeped in the philanthropic tradition. Within this framework, the pattern of support was largely private, supplemented by the sporadic attempts of churches and benevolent associations to educate a handful of the poor. In the years following the Revolution, however, the movement toward a state system of tax-supported schools was begun in

---

will secure the increasing prosperity of schools. They lighten the burthens of the people, but they also diminish, and for that reason perhaps, their interest in these institutions." (*American Journal of Education*, Vol. V (1858), p. 130).

[47] See, for instance, letter in the *The Common School Journal*, Vol. X, pp. 106–07, for example of an assessment upon parents as late as 1848.

[48] *Seventh Annual Report of the Board of Education; Together with the Seventh Annual Report of the Secretary of the Board* (Dutton and Wentworth, Boston, 1844), p. 68.

earnest. Influenced by migrations of New Englanders,[49] and closely connected with the New England tradition, New York rapidly moved in the direction of collective support. By 1820 the quality of her schools seriously challenged those of Massachusetts as the best of their day.

In 1784 the legislature, at the urging of Governor George Clinton,[50] created the University of the State of New York. With its administrative body, the Board of Regents, it was to be a means of facilitating the establishment of a complete educational system from the lower schools to the university.[51] One of the earliest official statements concerning the need for a system of public schools appeared in the report of a committee of the Board submitted in 1787. The report asserted:

. . . before your committee conclude, they feel themselves bound in faithfulness to add that the erecting [sic] public schools for teaching reading, writing and arithmetic is an object of very great importance, which ought not to be left to the discretion of private men, but be promoted by public authority.[52]

Both the Board of Regents and Governor Clinton continued to take strong stands in favor of a general system of schools.[53] However, indifference, the impoverishment caused by the Revolution, and the tradition of private support combined to block any action by the legislature until 1795. In that year a committee appointed to study the Governor's recommendations relating to education reported a bill which eventually became "AN ACT for the encouragement of schools." [54] The law, passed on April 9, provided for annual appropriations of twenty thousand pounds for a period of five years—which sum was to be apportioned only to those districts which maintained schools through their own efforts. Each town was required, in order to be eligible for its share of the state fund,

[49] Lois Kimball Mathews, *The Expansion of New England* (Houghton Mifflin, Boston, 1909), pp. 159–69.
[50] *Messages from the Governors* (Charles Z. Lincoln, ed.; State of New York, Albany, 1909), Vol. 2, p. 200.
[51] Laws of 1784, Chap. 51, Seventh Session.
[52] "Report of a committee of the Board of Regents, Feb. 16, 1787," quoted in Franklin B. Hough, *Historical and Statistical Record of the University of the State of New York during the Century from 1784 to 1884* (Albany, 1885), p. 52.
[53] See opening addresses of Governor Clinton, 1784, 1792, 1795, in *Messages from the Governors,* Vol. 2, pp. 220, 321, 350 respectively.
[54] Laws of 1795, Chap. 75.

to raise by local taxation a sum equal to one half of its state grant. It is interesting to note that the wording of the law in no way implies that this education is to be for the poor only. The sum is appropriated by the state for the purpose of

encouraging and maintaining schools in the several cities and towns in this State, in which the children of the inhabitants residing in this State shall be instructed in the English language or be taught English grammar arithmetic, methematics [sic] and such other branches of knowledge as are most useful and necessary to complete a good English education.[55]

It is also interesting to note that further along in the law mention is made of the schools in the City of New York. There, the state funds were released to the support of the charity schools which had been traditionally maintained in that city. In reference to this situation, the act carries the following provision:

And be it further enacted That it shall and may be lawful for the mayor aldermen and commonalty of the city of New York in common council . . . to cause as well the money so appropriated for encouraging and maintaining schools in the city and county of New York as the money to be raised in the said city and county for the same purpose by virtue of this act to be applied as well for the encouragement and maintenance of the several charity schools as of all other schools in which children shall be instructed in the English language or taught English grammar arithmetic mathematics and such other branches of knowledge as are most useful and necessary to complete a good English education. . . .[56]

Thus, whereas the rest of the state started out by appropriating money for schools free of the stigma of charity, New York City continued to apportion funds among its private and parochial institutions.

Although the Law of 1795 was a steppingstone to a general system of free schools, it was by no means either adequate or final. As a matter of fact, it was allowed to lapse at the end of its five-year period of life. Both governors' messages and the utterances of the friends of education continued to urge the enlargement, the extension, and the improvement of the precedents it had established. In 1805 a permanent school fund was set up, but no immediate provi-

[55] *Ibid.*   [56] *Ibid.*

sion for its expenditure was included.[57] Finally, in 1811, Governor Tompkins was authorized to appoint a committee to report to the next session of the legislature "a system for the organization and establishment of common schools." [58] The committee submitted its report in 1812; and both the report itself and the enactment which it secured provide an excellent enunciation of the principles of public support.

Premising its general argument on the necessity for the universal education of an electorate, the report argued that only through a combined local and state effort could this end be adequately secured. The state fund, the committee maintained, had never been meant to support education by itself. Rather, it was established to stimulate local initiative toward providing schools. As such, it was only when state moneys *supplemented* rather than *replaced* local effort that an effective school system might be secured.[59]

Accordingly, the Law of 1812 provided such a pattern for distributing the interest of the permanent state fund. Only those towns which raised an equal sum by local taxation might receive a share of this interest. Furthermore, the act provided for districting of the towns—each district being responsible, also through taxation, for the maintenance and repair of a school site and building. Thus, a pattern of support was enunciated whereby the state subsidized what was principally a local effort toward the maintenance of schools.[60]

Taken together, the laws of 1795 and 1812 laid the base of a tradition of public support for education in New York State. There was, however, a modifying element which negated much of the principle in reality; namely, the rate-bill system. According to the provisions set forth in both pieces of legislation, there were three sources of public school funds: the state, the town, and the district. According to the Law of 1812 state and town funds could only be applied to teachers' salaries.[61] The money raised by the district was for the schoolhouse, fuel, and other operating expenses. In many districts, however, a deficit appeared at the end of the year

[57] Laws of 1805, Chap. LXVI.   [58] Laws of 1811, Chap. CCXLVI, Sec. LIV.
[59] "Report of the Commissioners appointed by the Governor, pursuant to the Act passed April 9th, 1811 . . ." in Thomas E. Finegan, *Free Schools* (University of the State of New York, Albany, 1921), pp. 37–43.
[60] Laws of 1812, Chap. CCXLII.   [61] *Ibid.*, Sec. XV.

—most often in the teacher's salary. The difference between the costs of school operation and the funds secured through the above-mentioned sources was met by a tax on parents—a tax depending on the number of their children attending and the number of days of attendance. This assessment was authorized in 1814 in what was known as the rate-bill system.[62] In keeping with the philanthropic tradition, the children of the poor and indigent were excused from payment of the tax; and in their case, the burden of the extra tax was assumed by the district.[63]

Although the general base of the system was one of tax support, the small tax levied under the rate bill was enough to create the atmosphere of a pauper school. Many parents could not afford even this small assessment, and chose rather to keep their children out of the schools than to declare themselves indigent. Those who did exercise their privilege were stigmatized as relying on the public purse—and therefore not far removed from pauperism. It is evident that the kind of class distinction built up by the rate bill was the antithesis of what the laws of 1795 and 1812 were attempting to accomplish. And it was around the rate bill and its removal that a storm of controversy centered during the next few decades.

While these developments in the direction of a free school system on the state level were taking place, the City of New York continued to suffer an entirely different course. There, education yet remained a matter for the individual family, and charitable and philanthropic societies (both of a parochial and nonparochial nature) had taken over the task of educating the poor. Chief among these was the Free School Society, organized by a group of public-spirited men in 1805 for the purpose of extending "the education of such poor children as do not belong to or are not provided for by any religious society." [64] Although the function of conducting public education in the city gradually shifted into the hands of this group, the pattern as late as 1850 was still associated with public support to diverse religious and secular organizations.

By a law passed on April 11, 1842,[65] the schools managed by the Society, together with the schools of the several other charitable

---

[62] Laws of 1814 (Thirty-seventh Session), Chap. CXCII, Sec. XIII, XIX.
[63] Ibid.   [64] Laws of 1805, Chap. CVIII.   [65] Laws of 1842, Chap. 150.

organizations dependent partially on the public purse, were placed under the supervision of an elected board of education. Eleven years later, in 1853, the Public School Society passed on its real and personal property, valued at close to half a million dollars,[66] to the New York City Board of Education. It is only at this point that the educational facilities of New York City were integrated into the general system which had concurrently been developing in the state as a whole.

Meanwhile, on the state level, the forces for and against the extension of the public system had been marshalling their respective strengths. The first major encounter was experienced during the constitutional convention of 1846, where a conflict developed over a provision sanctioning free schools supported by a tax on property. The proposed controversial section read as follows:

> The legislature shall, at its first session after the adoption of this Constitution, and from time to time thereafter, as shall be necessary, provide by law for the free education and instruction of every child between the ages of four and sixteen years, whose parents, guardians, or employers shall be residents of the State, in the Common Schools now established, or which shall hereafter be established therein. The expense of such education and instruction, after applying the public funds as above provided, shall be defrayed by taxation at the same time and in the same manner as may be provided by law for the liquidation of town and county charges.[67]

The proposition, advanced by Henry Nicholl, chairman of the Committee on "education common schools and the appropriate funds," [68] was to be submitted separately to a referendum of the people. It was, however, part of a general article providing for the inviolability and appropriation of the school fund. A motion, carrying the proposed article *in toto,* was reported out of this committee on July 23, 1846.[69] It received a good deal of mention in the press during the following weeks—the positive comments citing the grave necessity of universal education in a republic, the

[66] "Report of the Committee of Transfer" (July 29, 1853), in William Oland Bourne, *History of the Public School Society of the City of New York* (William Wood & Co., New York, 1870), pp. 587–93.
[67] *Report of the Debates and Proceedings of the Convention for the Revision of the Constitution of the State of New-York, 1846* (Reported by William G. Bishop and William H. Attree; Office of the Evening Atlas, Albany, 1846), p. 388.
[68] *Ibid.,* p. 91.   [69] *Ibid.,* p. 388.

negative ones citing principally the infringement of taxation for education on individual rights. The press in general seemed largely in favor of the provision. The *New-York Weekly Tribune,* powerful because of its circulation in the rural upstate districts, reported the following remarks editorially concerning the proposed provision:

—Here is a section reported by the Committee on Education, to be submitted separately to the People for their approval or rejection, which we trust will receive a hearty "Yes!" from three-fourths of our voters. Remember, lovers of Justice and Intelligence! that a section providing for at least the nominal Education of every Child reared in the State, and making the support of such Education a part of the annual tax-bill, so that every common school shall be truly a FREE SCHOOL, is to come before you. Do not forget to vote "Yes!" upon it! [70]

Illustrative of the argument that the state had no right to tax one man for the education of another's son is the following extract from an anonymous letter in the *Newburgh Telegraph* on August 6, 1846. Commenting on the controversial provision, the letter remarks:

This proposition contemplates the taxation of the community for the education of the children of those who are rich and able to educate their own children, as well as the education of the poor. The people have never expressed their dissent to being taxed for the purpose of educating the poor. They know that the permanency of our institutions depends upon the intelligence of the masses, and they willingly contribute to the expense of securing such intelligence under the idea that it is a simple performance of duty which every citizen owes to his country, and which is necessary for its long standing; and it is upon this principle only that the people of a free country can be taxed even for the education of the poor. It is to advance their own interest by securing the country from that most formidable danger to Republics, the ignorance and consequent turbulence of the masses. Thus far and no farther can the principle be tolerated. There is no danger that the children of the rich will grow up in ignorance, and therefore the people cannot be called upon to provide for their education. . . . Our present constitution recognizes this principle by expressly providing that the property of the individual cannot be taken away from him without his consent, except for public purposes, and then only by giving an adequate compensation. To allow the majority to say that the minority shall part with their property in the shape of taxes to defray the expense

[70] *New-York Weekly Tribune,* Vol. 5, No. 47, Aug. 1, 1846, p. 5, col. 1–2.

of the education of the children of others, who are able to bear such expense, is a palpable blow at this well recognized principle, and is not the less odious because being submitted to the people it should meet the approval of a majority of them. . . .

There is no subject in government more disagreeable than that of the call of the tax-gatherer; and care should be taken that all who are made to contribute should feel the justice of their contribution. In any other event hard feelings and dissatisfaction are engendered against the laws, and the happiness of society deeply affected.[71]

The proposed constitutional section came before the convention on October 8, 1846, and although the article as a whole passed, the controversial provision was stricken out on the afternoon of the discussions. Thus the motion was passed without the provision directing the legislature to take action in the direction of making the schools entirely free.[72]

The agitation toward passage of a new, more comprehensive school law continued. In the first months of 1849, the legislature again began consideration of legislation extending the principle of free, tax-supported schools. The usual interests for and against passage of the bill became vocal in the press and through petitions and memorials. Finally, on March 26, 1849, "AN ACT Establishing free schools throughout the state" was passed. Section 1 of this bill contained the following provision:

Common schools in the several school districts in this state shall be free to all persons residing in the district, over five, and under twenty-one years of age. Persons not residents of a district may be admitted into the schools kept therein, with the approbation, in writing, of the trustees thereof, or a majority of them.[73]

Section 2 carried provision for compulsory taxation for school support, while Section 7 provided for "free and gratuitous education" in the common, public, ward, and district schools of the cities. The act depended for final approval, though, on an affirmative vote of the people at the next annual election. This approval was secured by a majority in excess of 150,000.[74]

Notwithstanding the magnitude of popular sanction, the forces opposed to the legislation, reinforcing their traditional arguments

---

[71] *Newburgh Telegraph*, Aug. 6, 1846; letter signed "One of the People."

[72] *Report of the Debates and Proceedings of the Convention for the Revision of the Constitution of the State of New-York, 1846*, pp. 1074–76.

[73] Laws of 1849, Chap. 140.   [74] Thomas E. Finegan, *op. cit.*, pp. 197–98.

with the contention that the Law of 1849 was unconstitutional,[75] procured passage on April 10, 1850 of a law calling for the resubmission of the issue to the people.[76] They failed, though, to obtain the required vote, and the legislation stayed by a popular mandate which, though considerably smaller than the former, was yet a healthy one.[77] Pressing their victory, the free school forces on April 12, 1851 put through another act to establish free schools.[78] This law provided for an annual property tax of $800,000. Together with other state moneys accruing to education, it would be apportioned so that one third went to the school districts, and two thirds to the counties, cities, and towns according to the legislative provisions apportioning the school fund. Section 6 of the bill still provided, though, that any balance required by the districts for the payment of teachers' salaries be raised by rate bill—thus maintaining this system of invidious distinctions.

It was around the removal of these rate-bill provisions that the forces of the pro-school camp directed their major efforts in the next years. In the early 1860's, the subject came more and more before the public eye. Superintendent H. H. Van Dyck, in his seventh annual report of January 31, 1861, made the following comment concerning the rate bill as a means of securing free education:

There are other incongruities to the act, not amongst the least of which is that which admits of the imposition of a rate bill upon the pupils. A *free* school supported by rate bills, is such an anomaly as could be found sanctioned nowhere else save in the "Code of Public Instruction" in the State of New York.[79]

The reports of the state superintendent in 1864, 1865, 1866, and 1867 pressed the same argument. Local superintendents concurred.[80] Finally, on April 16, 1867, the legislature passed an act abolishing the rate-bill authorization which had been in effect since 1814.[81] This stood as the final step in making the schools

---

[75] It was finally declared unconstitutional in Barto *v.* Hemrod 8 N. Y. 483 by the Court of Appeals on the premise that the legislature cannot delegate powers.

[76] Laws of 1850, Chap. 378.

[77] Thomas E. Finegan, *op. cit.*, p. 415 (majority of 25,038).

[78] Laws of 1851, Chap. 151.

[79] Thomas E. Finegan, *op. cit.*, p. 493.

[80] *Ibid.*, p. 537.   [81] Acts of 1867, Chap. 406.

free to all children. Discussing the abolition of the rate bill in his special report of 1867, Superintendent Rice outlined the remaining sources of income for common schools: income from the common school fund; the amount that the legislature would annually set apart from the income of the United States deposit fund; the general state tax; district, village, and city taxation; and the income from local funds.[82] Thus New York State completed its establishment of a publicly supported school system available at no cost to its entire population.

III

The movement toward public support in Pennsylvania, and the struggle associated with this movement, is indicative of the dynamics in many areas where the tradition of publicly supported "pauper" education had taken root. This latter pattern was firmly established in Pennsylvania by the first decade of the nineteenth century. While the provisional constitution of 1776, for instance, had contained the following provision respecting education:

A school or schools shall be established in each county by the legislature, for the convenient instruction of youth, with such salaries to the masters paid by the public, as may enable them to instruct youth at low prices: And all useful learning shall be duly encouraged and promoted in one or more universities . . . ,[83]

it was amended by the constitutional convention of 1789–90 to read:

The legislature shall, as soon as conveniently may be, provide, by law, for the establishment of schools throughout the State, in such manner that the poor may be taught gratis.[84]

Legislation implementing this directive was passed in 1802,[85] 1804,[86] and 1809.[87] These laws strictly limited public support to education of the poor and indigent. However, the forces looking to the extension of tax support for general education were active contemporarily with the passage of these acts. Wickersham has

---

[82] Thomas E. Finegan, *op. cit.*, p. 556.

[83] Constitution of Pennsylvania (1776), Sec. 44, in Francis Newton Thorpe, *op. cit.*, Vol. V, p. 3091.

[84] Constitution of Pennsylvania (1790), Art. VII, Sec. 1, in Francis Newton Thorpe, *op. cit.*, Vol. V, p. 3099.   [85] Laws of 1801–03, Chap. XXIV.

[86] Laws of 1803–04, Chap. LXV.   [87] Acts of 1808, Chap. CXIV.

observed that not one of the governors during the time that the
Law of 1809 remained in force was satisfied that it fulfilled the
constitutional provision respecting education.[88] Illustrative is a
statement of Governor Shulze in 1823:

The object of the convention seems to have been, to diffuse the means
of rudimental education so extensively, that they should be completely
within the reach of all—the poor who could not pay for them, as well
as the rich who could. Convinced that even liberty without knowledge,
is but a precarious blessing, I cannot therefore too strongly recommend
this subject to your consideration.[89]

In response to such urgings, a new law was passed in 1824, repealing the Act of 1809 and providing "more effectually for the
education of the poor gratis, and for laying the foundation of a
general system of education throughout the Commonwealth." [90]
It directed the citizens of the several towns, wards, and boroughs
to vote on whether they desired a system of public education in
their communities, and granted them the power to vote a school
tax if an affirmative was given on the first question. The law met
with violent opposition, though, and was repealed in 1826 with a
restoration of the Act of 1809.[91]

In 1830, Governor George Wolf again voiced the necessity of
making the public schools extensive enough to embrace children
of all classes. His first annual message to the legislature announced
in clear and forceful terms his position regarding the extension of
the free school system:

Of the various projects which present themselves, as tending to contribute most essentially to the welfare and happiness of a people, and
which come within the scope of legislative action, and require legislative aid, there is none which gives more ample promise of success, than
that of a liberal and enlightened system of education, by means of
which, the light of knowledge will be diffused throughout the whole
community, and imparted to every individual susceptible of partaking
of its blessings; to the poor as well as to the rich, so that all may be
fitted to participate in, and to fulfil all the duties which each one owes
to himself, to his God, and to his country. The constitution of

[88] James Pyle Wickersham, *A History of Education in Pennsylvania* (Inquirer
Publishing Company, Lancaster, 1886), p. 269.
[89] Inaugural address, *Journal of the Thirty Fourth House of Representatives,*
1823–24, pp. 151–52.
[90] Acts of 1823, Chap. LXXXVIII.   [91] Acts of 1825, Chap. XIII.

Pennsylvania, imperatively enjoins the establishment of such a system. Public opinion demands it. The state of public morals calls for it; and the security and stability of the invaluable privileges which we have inherited from our ancestors, require our immediate attention to it.[92]

There was an increasing number of friends of education at this time, and public sentiment had voiced a strong desire for educational improvement. The efforts of the workingmen's organizations, the memorials of the Pennsylvania Society for the Promotion of Public Schools, and numerous petitions to both houses of the legislature constituted a strong and vocal public movement in favor of revising the school system. The legislature appointed committees to study the situation, and the report of the house committee, chaired by N. P. Fetterman of Bedford, is indicative of the sentiment in favor of change. Speaking of the evils of the pauper system which then prevailed in the state, the report noted:

To remedy these evils, the unremitted attention of your committee has been directed to the labour of compiling the details of a system of common schools, in which eventually all the children of our commonwealth may at least be instructed in reading, and a knowledge of the English language, in writing, arithmetic and geography—subjecting them to such regulations as may best promote their future usefulness—securing competent and able teachers, and providing for their support; . . .[93]

Accompanying this report, as with the report of the senate committee, was a bill establishing a general system of education. However, the forces in favor of common, publicly supported schools had not yet gained the strength required to push through such a measure, and their efforts resulted in April in the partial success of a measure creating a school fund.[94] Hardly satisfied with this victory, they continued with unrelenting effort their pressures on the legislature. During the session of 1832–33, though, a conservative senate refused to take action on educational measures. The house, though considering in committee and on the floor a number of bills, also failed to act; and the culmination of the pro-school efforts was left to the session of 1833–34.

The forces in favor of free school legislation had increased in

---

[92] Governor's Message (1830–31), in *Register of Pennsylvania*, Vol. VI (1830), p. 386.
[93] "Report of the Committee on Education," in *Register of Pennsylvania*, Vol. VII (1831), p. 93.   [94] Laws of 1830–31, No. 181.

both houses, and Governor Wolf earnestly discussed the subject at length in his annual message.[95] Mr. Samuel Breck, senator from Philadelphia, was appointed chairman of a Joint Committee on Education established for the express purpose of "digesting a system of general education." [96] Breck was a New England man who had come to Pennsylvania from Massachusetts to use "his best efforts to secure the establishment of a system of common schools in the State." [97] The report of the committee clearly demonstrates the liberal position of its members on the subject at hand:

> A radical defect in our laws upon the subject of education, is that the public aid now given, and imperfectly given, is confined *to the poor.* Aware of this, your committee have taken care to exclude the word *poor,* from the bill which will accompany this report, meaning to make the system *general,* that is to say, to form an educational association between the rich, the comparatively rich, and the destitute. Let them all fare alike in the primary schools; receive the same elementary instruction; imbibe the same republican spirit, and be animated by a feeling of perfect equality.[98]

Along with its report, the committee forwarded a proposed bill, which was passed on April 1 as "AN ACT to establish a General System of Education by Common Schools." [99] This law allotted a share of the common school fund to counties voting to tax themselves toward the maintenance of schools. Its provision for using state moneys only as *supplementary* to local funds strongly resembled New York's legislation of 1812. Each county, to participate in the benefits of the state fund, was required to raise through local effort a sum not less than twice the amount received from the state. Counties which elected not to participate in the program were left to continue under the Law of 1809, providing only for public education of the poor. The law passed both houses of the legislature with near unanimity, but, as the coming year was destined to reveal, a unanimity which signified a general dissatisfaction with the provisions of the Law of 1809 rather than a positive support of the newer legislation.

[95] Governor's Message (1833–34), in *Register of Pennsylvania,* Vol. XII, pp. 369–73.
[96] *Register of Pennsylvania,* Vol. XIII (1834), p. 97.
[97] James Pyle Wickersham, *op. cit.,* p. 309.
[98] "Report of the Joint Committee of the two Houses of the Pennsylvania Legislature, on the subject of a System of General Education . . . ," in *Register of Pennsylvania,* Vol. XIII (1834), p. 97.   [99] Laws of 1833–34, No. 102.

There were three groups principally responsible for the vocal opposition to the legislation of 1834. The first was a group which, as has been mentioned above, continued to oppose such legislation in every state of the Union: the upper classes. First, they were not willing to be taxed to educate other men's children; and second, they could not see their children attending the same schools as the children of the poor. The remarks of the editor of the *National Gazette* of Philadelphia, on a workingmen's resolution favoring a tax-supported system, are illustrative of the position taken by these interests. Commenting on the resolution, the editorial states:

Authority—that is, the State—is to force the more eligibly situated citizens to contribute a part (which might be very considerable) of their means, for the accommodation of the rest; and this is equivalent to the idea of an actual, compulsory partition of their substance. . . .

We have no confidence in any compulsory equalizations; it has been well observed that they pull down what is above, but never much raise what is below, and often "depress high and low together beneath the level of what was originally the lowest." [100]

The propertied interests, maintaining their idea of a class-stratified society, could see their way clear to public support of education for the poor and indigent. This was compatible with the philosophy of Christian charity. But they could not at all see their way clear to supporting an extensive system of publicly supported common schools for the education of all comers.

Also prominent among the interests opposed to the legislation of 1834 were several firmly entrenched religious bodies. Such groups as the Friends, the Lutherans, the Reformed, and the Mennonites, though strongly in favor of education and the dissemination of knowledge, had long maintained religious schools for the children of their congregations. These schools taught not only the fundamentals of secular instruction but also the basic doctrines advocated by their respective churches. The whole educational enterprise, of course, was carried on under the immediate direction of the church authorities, and these authorities naturally exercised the function of selecting the teachers. To the congregations supporting these schools, the arguments advanced by those in favor of

---

[100] *The National Gazette and Literary Register* (Philadelphia) (Daily), Vol. X, No. 2965, Aug. 19, 1830, p. 2, col. 2.

a state system carried little weight. It did not seem logical to withdraw support from these institutions only to pay taxes for the support of others—schools which did not bear the same intimate relationships to their lives and their religious beliefs.

A third group which threw its weight behind the efforts to prevent establishment of a general free school system was the large number of Germans residing in the state. They saw, in the establishment of a general system, the replacement of the German language, traditionally the medium of instruction in their local schools, with English; and in their steady adherence to their mother tongue, this group consistently opposed the provisions of a state system of free education.

These groups, aided by other diverse conservative forces, united during the next session of the legislature in an attempt to repeal the legislation of 1834. Petitions demanding its withdrawal were presented from thirty-eight out of fifty-one counties. The legislature, in its early days, was literally flooded with such petitions and memorials. The situation was so unusual that a special committee was appointed in the house of representatives "to ascertain the number of Petitions in each county of the Commonwealth praying for the repeal or modification of the School Law; and the number remonstrating against said repeal." [101] The majority report of this committee, though it found 558 petitions (carrying 31,988 signatures) praying for repeal of the law, 50 petitions (2,084 signatures) for modification, and only 49 petitions (2,575 signatures) against repeal, yet felt that the number opposed to the law was "but a small minority of the whole number of voters in the Commonwealth." The high proportion of Germans among the opposition is amply reflected in the committee's inability to decipher over 90 per cent of the signatures. This, the committee noted, afforded "the strongest evidence of the deplorable disregard so long paid by the Legislature to the constitutional injunction, to establish a general system of education." [102]

---

[101] "Report of the Committee appointed to ascertain the number of Petitions in each county of the Commonwealth praying for the repeal or modification of the School Law; and the number remonstrating against said repeal, &c.," in *Hazard's Register of Pennsylvania*, Vol. XV (1835), p. 205.

[102] It is interesting to note that although one member of the committee, in a dissenting minority report, noted the cause of this illegibility as the German character

The legislature of 1834–35 became the scene of a terrific struggle over the school issue; and it seems doubtful that the tide of repeal would have been stemmed had it not been for the tireless efforts of the reform group. Perhaps the central figure in the eventual victory was Thaddeus Stevens, a New Englander who had come to Pennsylvania in 1815. His speech in favor of public education was a rousing enunciation of the principles for which the reform group stood:

> If an elective republic is to endure for any great length of time, *every* elector must have sufficient information, not only to accumulate wealth, and take care of his pecuniary concerns, but to direct wisely the legislatures, the ambassadors, and the executive of the nation—for *some* part of all these things, *some* agency in approving or disapproving of them, falls to every freeman. If then, the permanency of our government depends upon such knowledge, it is the duty of government to see that the means of information be diffused to every citizen. This is a sufficient answer to those who deem education a private and not a public duty—who argue that they are willing to educate their *own* children, but not their *neighbor's* children.[103]

The forces favoring free schools were marshaled and were able to achieve their aims. The bill which eventually emerged out of their efforts not only reaffirmed the course taken during the previous session, but strengthened and streamlined its operation and administration.[104]

Although the Law of 1834, now continuing in force, remained permissive in its stipulations regarding taxation, its provisions in a few years embraced the majority of the counties. Spurred by legislation in 1836 allowing districts which had accepted taxation to repeal it on reconsideration every third year,[105] many districts joined the system. By the time of the Third Annual Report of the superintendent of common schools in 1837, 742 out of 987 districts of the state had accepted the pattern of tax support.[106] An ever-

---

of the script, the majority report used it, in addition to the fact that sixty-six petitioners for repeal had signed "by making their marks" as a slur against the character of the whole opposition group. See *Hazard's Register of Pennsylvania,* Vol. XV (1835), pp. 205–06.

[103] Thaddeus Stevens in the House of Representatives, quoted in *Hazard's Register of Pennsylvania,* Vol. XV, p. 284.

[104] Laws of 1834–35, No. 176.   [105] Laws of 1835–36, No. 166.

[106] Third Annual Report, in *Pennsylvania School Journal,* Vol. XVI (1867–68), p. 155.

growing number during the following years brought the principle increasingly nearer to universal acceptance.[107] This essentially remained the situation in Pennsylvania until mid-century. In effect, the pauper school conception had been reconstructed, and the principle of tax support for common schools largely accepted in most parts of the state.

IV

The development of the support pattern in Virginia before the Civil War represents an excellent example of educational movement in the South. Prominent in the history of Virginia's early efforts to establish a public school system was the plan set forth by Thomas Jefferson in his "Bill for the More General Diffusion of Knowledge." It was proposed by the Committee of Revisors of the state code[108] in 1776 and reported to the General Assembly on July 18, 1779. The preamble to the bill aptly describes its general aim:

. . . whence it becomes expedient for promoting the publick happiness that those persons, whom nature hath endowed with genius and virtue, should be rendered by liberal education worthy to receive, and able to guard the sacred deposit of the rights and liberties of their fellow citizens, and that they should be called to that charge without regard to wealth, birth or other accidental condition or circumstance; but the indigence of the greater number disabling them from so educating, at their own expence, those of their children whom nature hath fitly formed and disposed to become useful instruments for the public, it is better that such should be sought for and educated at the common expence of all, then that the happiness of all should be confined to the weak or wicked.[109]

The object of the bill, then, was "to diffuse knowledge more generally through the mass of the people." [110] The proposed system was a vertical one, running from the primary school up through the College of William and Mary. Its most universally applicable aspect centered in a series of schools for teaching reading, writing,

---

[107] Fifth Annual Report, in *Pennsylvania School Journal*, Vol. XVI (1867–68), p. 265.

[108] Thomas Jefferson, Edmund Pendleton, and George Wythe; see *The Writings of Thomas Jefferson* (Paul Leicester Ford, ed.; G. P. Putnam's Sons, New York and London, 1893), Vol. II, p. 195.

[109] "A Bill for the More General Diffusion of Knowledge," in *The Writings of Thomas Jefferson*, Vol. II, p. 221.

[110] Thomas Jefferson, "Notes on the State of Virginia," in *The Writings of Thomas Jefferson*, Vol. III, p. 251.

and arithmetic established in districts five or six miles square—schools in which children might receive up to three years of elementary instruction without cost. The bill also provided for a continuing selection of youths in these lower schools to go on without cost to middle schools, and then, on further selection, to the college.[111] In this way, Jefferson hoped "to avail the state of those talents which nature has sown as liberally among the poor as the rich, but which perish without use, if not sought for and cultivated." [112]

Although much of the general report of which this plan was a part was eventually accepted and written into the state code, the provisions on education were rejected. Even in the face of their rejection, Jefferson felt that the legislature had been favorable to the plan embodied in his proposals. In a letter to George Washington in 1786 he said concerning its reception: "I never saw one received with more enthusiasm than that was, in the year 1778, by the House of Delegates, who ordered it printed. And it seemed afterwards, that nothing but the extreme distress of our resources prevented its being carried into execution, even during the war." [113] The failure to take root, however, of a similar piece of legislation passed in 1796 illustrates the opposition, at least at the local level, to the institution of a comprehensive tax-supported system.[114] Perhaps it also points to a degree of over-optimism in Jefferson's statement. The individualist, laissez-faire tradition in education was still far too pervasive to secure widespread acceptance of any such act by those who would inevitably bear the burden of its support.

During the first decade of the nineteenth century, the words

[111] *Ibid.*, pp. 251–54.

[112] *Ibid.*, p. 254.

[113] John C. Henderson, *Thomas Jefferson's Views on Public Education* (G. P. Putnam's Sons, New York and London, 1890), pp. v–vi.

[114] A. J. Morrison, *The Beginnings of Public Education in Virginia, 1776–1860* (Richmond, 1917), pp. 22–23. Although this act carried permissive provisions for a comprehensive system of elementary training, its adoption and operation remained contingent on initiation by the several county courts. The latter, inevitably controlled by the more well-to-do members of the community, would be prone to inertia. When this was reinforced by the laissez-faire tradition, sparsity of population, and general opposition to taxation, it is not difficult to see how the permissive nature of the law rendered it ineffective. See also William Arthur Maddox, *The Free School Idea in Virginia Before the Civil War* (Teachers College, Columbia University, New York, 1918), pp. 15–16.

public schools, free schools, and *education* were commonly heard in the proceedings of the General Assembly; but no bills for the establishment of public schools emerged. Although small, local communities here and there had employed the direct tax on property to support schools,[115] these instances apparently proved the exception rather than the rule. In general, the wide diversity of private educational enterprise, when taken together with the various charitable enterprises which were evidenced, presented a rather unorganized picture. It must be noted, also, that demands in favor of education during this period were not by any means limited to the lower levels of schools. The support of higher education and the establishment of new academies partially aided by public funds were certainly subjects of widespread concern.

Taken together, these demands led eventually to a bill enacted on February 2, 1810.[116] It provided that all escheats, confiscations, penalties, and forfeitures, and all rights in personal property found derelict should be appropriated to the encouragement of learning. The Auditor of Public Accounts was directed to open an account to be designated as the Literary Fund. The act provided that the fund be "divided and appropriated as to the next legislature shall seem best adapted to the promotion of literature: *Provided always,* That the aforesaid fund shall be appropriated to the sole benefit of a school or schools, to be kept in each and every county . . . subject to such orders and regulations as the general assembly shall hereafter direct." [117]

The direction for the expenditure of the Literary Fund was incorporated the next year into "An Act to Provide for the Education of the Poor," passed on February 12, 1811.[118] The act indicated a solemn protest against any money from the Literary Fund being appropriated by future legislation to purposes other than the "education of the poor"—"an object equally humane, just and necessary, involving alike the interests of humanity and the preservation of the constitution, laws and liberty of the good people of this commonwealth." [119] To manage the fund the act provided

[115] An instance is the town of Charlottesville in 1806; see *The Statutes at Large of Virginia (from October Session 1792, to December Session 1806, inclusive),* New Series, Vol. 3, pp. 254–55. (Chap. 65; passed Jan. 25, 1806).

[116] Acts of 1809, Chap. XIV, p. 15.

[117] *Ibid.*   [118] Acts of 1810, Chap. VIII.   [119] *Ibid.,* Sec. 5.

for a board [120] who were required to establish "as soon as a sufficient fund shall be provided for the purpose, . . . a school or schools for the education of the poor in each and every county of the commonwealth." [121]

On February 24, 1816 the Literary Fund was suddenly augmented to the point where it could become an effective source for the support of education. This was accomplished through legislation adding to the fund moneys which the federal government had tendered in payment of a debt contracted in 1812.[122] By this action the Literary Fund immediately leaped from the comparatively low point at which it had stood after several years of operation to a size sufficient to provide adequate support for a number of plans hitherto incapable of implementation.[123] In view of the extreme hostility to any plan involving local taxation for education, the Literary Fund had become the last recourse of those who desired public support for their plans. Now that it had been augmented, the latitude of the legislature was greatly broadened; and friends of a primary school system, supporters of increased aid to secondary schools, and those who desired state aid to a proposed university system[124] all saw in the fund the means of effecting their aims.

Within the framework of these efforts, a bill "providing for the establishment of primary schools, academies, colleges, and an university" was introduced into the house of delegates in February of 1817.[125] The bill provided for the establishment, through money from the fund, of primary schools, academies, colleges, and a university. The coordinating agency was to be a Board of Public Instruction provided for in the first sections of the bill. This board was directed to institute "as many primary schools as shall tend to

---

[120] *Ibid.,* Sec. 1—composed of the governor, lieutenant governor, treasurer, attorney general, and president of the Court of Appeals.

[121] *Ibid.,* Sec. 4.   [122] Acts of 1815, Chap. II, Sec. 5.

[123] See *Journal of the House of Delegates of Virginia,* 1815–16, p. 181.

[124] The leader of these forces was Thomas Jefferson, now retired from the Presidency at Monticello. In a letter to Peter Carr, president of the Board of Trustees of the Albermarle Academy, on September 7, 1814, he evidenced his interest in higher education. "I have long entertained," he wrote, "the hope that this, our native State, would take up the subject of education, and make an establishment, either with or without incorporation into that of William and Mary, where every branch of science, deemed useful at this day, should be taught in its highest degree." Quoted in A. J. Morrison, *op. cit.,* p. 25.

[125] Quoted in A. J. Morrison, *op. cit.,* pp. 32–34.

promote the easy diffusion of knowledge among the youth of all classes of society." [126] It was also directed to divide the state into forty-eight academical districts, and to establish academies in those districts which did not have them.[127] And finally, it was directed to establish three new colleges, and to fix, as soon as possible, a site for the university.[128] The bill was passed in the house of delegates on February 18,[129] but defeated in the senate two days later.[130] A substitute bill was introduced a year later, providing for the education of the poor, with the revenue of the fund paying for tuition, books, and materials. This bill was approved on February 21, 1818.[131] Thus, what might have been an opportunity for changing the older philanthropic tradition into one of collective responsibility was used merely to reaffirm and strengthen the older tradition; and public funds were still used to educate only the children of the poor rather than the children of all classes.[132]

The victory of the conservatives in 1817 by no means implied that there were no powerful liberal forces in the state. The population of the western sections had increased tremendously in the first decades of the nineteenth century, and there was in evidence a growing sectionalism based on the conflicting interests of the two groups. At the heart of the conflict was the disparity between those who were rapidly gaining political power, and those who held the property.[133] It was within the framework of this disparity that the conflicts over education were set.

The men of the eastern sections—the men who owned the property and would have to bear the brunt of any taxation for educa-

[126] *Ibid.*, pp. 32–33.   [127] *Ibid.*, p. 33.   [128] *Ibid.*, pp. 33–34.

[129] *Journal of the House of Delegates of the Commonwealth of Virginia*, 1816–17, pp. 214–15.

[130] *Journal of the Senate of the Commonwealth of Virginia*, 1816, p. 67.

[131] Acts of 1817, Chap. XI.

[132] The arguments pro and con the use of public funds for the education of children of all classes are much the same in this case as in the other instances that have been discussed. An excellent illustration of the reasoning advanced by the conservative interests hoping to maintain the individualist traditions in the face of efforts to establish a tax-supported system is provided by a series of letters by "A Constituent" published in the *Richmond Enquirer* early in 1818. See *Richmond Enquirer*, Jan. 8, 1818 (Vol. 4, No. 75), p. 4; Jan. 15, 1818 (Vol. 14, No. 78), pp. 2–3; Jan. 20, 1818 (Vol. 14, No. 80), p. 3; Jan. 22, 1818 (Vol. 14, No. 81), p. 3; and Jan. 31, 1818 (Vol. 14, No. 88), p. 3.

[133] See *Proceedings and Debates of the Virginia State Convention, of 1829–30* (Ritchie and Cook, Richmond, 1830) for an excellent example of this kind of conflict.

tion—saw any movement toward a public system more comprehensive than one for the poor as an infringement of their rights.
They saw in the tax-supported programs of the newly enfranchised
voters the very despotism of the mass which the older republicans
had feared. "It is the very essence of property," said John Randolph before the constitutional convention of 1829, "that none
shall tax it but the owner himself, or one who has a common feeling and interest with him." [134] The efforts, therefore, of the western sections to secure a broad system of tax-supported primary
schools were in direct violation of this principle. The western
forces responded, on the other hand, with arguments that a general
system of education would benefit the whole, that it would be
cheaper than the decentralized, localized system which then existed,
and that sectional issues were being unduly stressed. Thus,
Charles Fenton Mercer, in the same convention, stated:

And is the education of the people, who are every where in America,
the acknowledged guardians of their own rights, the source of all political power, a subject of mere Eastern or Western interest, in Virginia?
Who are the people of the West? Are they not our fellow-citizens, our
friends and brothers? Whence did they spring? From the East? Have
they forgot their common origin? [135,136]

The next significant piece of educational legislation, the act of
February 26, 1829, was framed and debated in light of the above
controversy. The basic provisions of this act made it possible for
any district which so desired to use its portion of the Literary Fund
to provide a "free school for the instruction, without fee or reward,
of every white child within said district." Such schools were to be
"subject to the controul and direction of three trustees, two to be
appointed by the annual contributors within the district, and one
by the School Commissioners for the county." [137] Unfortunately,
the operation of the law left the establishment of such schools at
the discretion of the individual districts—and in doing so relied
on the operation of two factors which had not yet gained maturity
in the state: (1) the initiative of local political democracy, and (2)

[134] *Ibid.*, p. 318.   [135] *Ibid.*, p. 202.
[136] This does not mean that there were no liberal elements in the East, or conservative in the West. Much influential discussion in favor of liberal reform came
from the eastern sections—particularly the cities.
[137] Acts of 1828, Chap. 14.

the willingness of local interests to levy taxes for education. Furthermore, its chances of working effectively were decreased even further by the sparsity of population in the rural areas.

The effect of these forces, when reinforced by public indifference, was enough to nullify the potentialities of the bill. Maddox reports that even the western sections of the state failed to avail themselves of its provisions.[138] In general, notwithstanding passage of the Act of 1829, the philanthropic tradition of private support continued in force. Publicly supported education was still only for the poor and indigent. Tax-supported education was sporadic at best. The forces which favored it, though vocal, were not yet able to change a tradition which was far more compatible with thought and life in Virginia than the one which they advocated.

During the next two decades, Virginia definitely felt the effect of the nation-wide agitation in behalf of tax-supported common schools. Educational conventions met in many parts of the state,[139] and periodical literature showed ample evidence of wide discussion from all camps.[140] Such organs as the *Richmond Enquirer* and the *Southern Literary Messenger* opened their columns to debates, and vigorously championed the cause of public education. This heightened interest could not help but bring pressure on the legislature; and the year 1846 saw three new attempts deal with the question.

The ground for this legislation had been paved in Governor McDowell's message to the legislature on December 2, 1845. In his address, the governor posed clearly and laconically the alternatives which confronted the legislature. Speaking of education in the state, the governor remarked:

. . . it is obviously important that the legislature should settle definitely upon the ground on which this subject is to be treated—whether

[138] William Arthur Maddox, *op. cit.*, p. 103.

[139] Clarksburg (1841), Lexington (1841), Richmond (1841), and Richmond (1845). Also numerous such meetings were held on the local level with smaller communities in Tidewater and Piedmont areas (1839–41).

[140] For instance, the *Richmond Enquirer* under the editorship of Thomas Ritchie, the *Evangelical and Literary Magazine* under the editorship of John Holt Rice, the *Southern Literary Messenger*, and the *Richmond Whig* (political opponent of the *Enquirer*), etc. Beginning in 1840, the *Southern Literary Messenger* excluded all convention and lyceum addresses in order to preserve its purely literary character, but in February of 1842, the address on *Popular Education* of James Mercer Garnett was published, by unanimous vote of the first Richmond convention in December, 1841.

as a private affair or as a state affair. If, in its judgment, it should be
. . . left, like the acquirement of property, to every man's separate exertions—those to receive much who have the means to procure it with,
and those nothing, who are without the means—and it determines in
consequence to add nothing to the provision already allowed for its
benefit—if this is its judgment, it is highly proper that it should be
made known, that the necessary steps might be taken by the people
themselves, either to reverse it or to carry it into effect. If, on the other
hand, the sounder judgment is entertained, that education is a public
as well as private concern; that, unlike the acquirement of property,
which can be pursued by each one for himself, without dependence
upon others, its only permanent success depends upon the effectiveness
of the co-operation with which it is conducted; that this co-operation
can be more fitly settled by public authority than by casual and voluntary arrangement; and further, that education is too sacred an element
in the well-being and safety of a state, governed like ours, to be left to
the hazards of unorganized, individual combination;—if this is its
opinion, it follows, that the public aid which it recognizes as a legitimate aid in the case, should be extended to every grade of education,
and every description of learner.[141]

When the legislation was passed, however, it still failed to take a
definite stand on the crucial question of taxation—all three acts
being permissive rather than compulsory as far as the tax question
was concerned.

Two of the acts were passed on March 5, 1846. The first, "An
ACT amending the present primary school system," [142] made
obligatory the establishment of county boards of school commissioners. These would supervise the finances and attendance at the
district schools for the poor—schools which were under the supervision of local trustees. The act also included a permissive section
holding that on action by one fourth of the local voters in any
county an election might be called on the question of adopting a
system of *district free schools*. If two thirds of the voters of a given
district were in favor of establishing a tax for the maintenance of
such schools, the tax would be "binding in all respects on such
county." [143] The second piece of legislation, "An ACT for the
establishment of a district public school system," [144] carried provisions making its proposals optional with the several counties. In
counties where its provisions were adopted the act provided that

[141] *Journal of the House of Delegates of Virginia*, Doc. No. 1, p. 3.
[142] Acts of 1845–46, Chap. 40.   [143] *Ibid.*, Séc. 7.   [144] Acts of 1845–46, Chap. 41.

"all the white children, male and female . . . resident with the respective districts, shall be entitled to receive tuition at said schools free of charge." [145]

A third act, a special act which was passed prior to the others on February 25, 1846,[146] contained provisions pertaining only to counties whose voters had established themselves as favorable to the principle of tax support. The school reports by 1860, however, show that only three counties actually had adopted free schools under its provisions, although permission to incorporate such systems was given, in the course of the years, to many more.[147]

The legislation of 1846 represented Virginia's last major attempt before the Civil War to push through a system involving tax support for education. The response to its permissive clauses clearly demonstrated that the older philanthropic tradition, deeply ingrained in Virginia's heritage, had remained dominant. The cultural patterns of the South had suffered few of the profound changes of the North. A "Greek Democracy" could well afford to leave education to the private efforts of its citizens, and provide publicly, in a spirit of Christian philanthropy, for the education of its poor. The sweeping demands for change which vehemently struck at the educational systems of Pennsylvania and New York failed to strike the system of Virginia with similarly compelling force. Thus Virginia, in its failure to move from its older philanthropic tradition to one of general public support for common schools, stands as an example of the pattern largely followed by the South.

V

Up to this point, this section has treated only the educational developments of the older, settled regions of the nation. It remains, however, to consider similar developments in the West. The emergence of education in the state of Ohio during the first half of the nineteenth century—the first fifty years of Ohio's statehood —will serve as an excellent illustration of the growth of educational support patterns in that section.

[145] *Ibid.*, Sec. 5.
[146] Acts of 1845–46, Chap. 42.
[147] William Arthur Maddox, *op. cit.*, p. 158.

Basic to any consideration of the roots of educational policy in a new state such as Ohio were two items: first, the kind of policy laid down in the organic laws which governed it before, during, and immediately following its inception as a state; and, second, the traditions which settlers entering the new state brought from the societies they had left. Both of these taken together constituted the limited tradition available to a new area in meeting its educational problems and issues.

With respect to the first item, Ohio came strongly within the scope of the federal policy embodied in the Land Ordinances of 1785 and 1787. Consistent with this policy, the federal government provided in the Enabling Acts of most states entering the Union after 1800 provisions for educational support through gifts of federal lands. Basically, three kinds of grants were involved in these Enabling Acts. The first was a grant going directly "to the inhabitants of such townships, for the use of schools." [148] Ohio was the first state to enter with this kind of grant provided in its Enabling Act. The second was a grant going "to the state for the use of the inhabitants of such townships, for the use of schools." [149] And the third was a grant going "to the state for the support of common schools." [150] Regardless of the specific nature of the grant, and its quantity, every one of the new states included was immediately provided with some legal precedent of public support for education. Thus, when Ohio entered the Union in 1802, it had already come under the provisions of the Northwest Ordinance and an Enabling Act ceding the sixteenth section of every township to the support of education.

With respect to the cultural backgrounds of its settlers, Ohio, by the nature of its location, was provided with two distinct traditions. The northern section of the state was called the Connecticut

---

[148] Ohio, Louisiana, Indiana, Mississippi, and Alabama were granted the sixteenth section in every township under this provision.

[149] Illinois, Missouri, Arkansas, and Florida were granted the sixteenth section in every township under this provision.

[150] Michigan, Iowa, and Wisconsin were granted the sixteenth section of every township; and California, Minnesota, Oregon, Kansas, Nevada, Nebraska, Colorado, Montana, North Dakota, South Dakota, Washington, Wyoming, and Idaho were granted the sixteenth and thirty-second section of every township under this provision.

Reserve, and was settled principally by New Englanders.[151] The southern sections were settled by people from the middle and southern states—with Pennsylvania, New Jersey, Delaware, and Virginia represented.[152] There seems little doubt that these people carried with them the educational support traditions of their respective states. Foote, an early historian of Ohio, made the following comments regarding this phenomenon:

> The early immigrants to Ohio from New England, considered schools and churches as among their *first* wants—those from Pennsylvania considered them the *last*—while those from New Jersey, and the few from Maryland, Virginia, and the other southern States, had their views of education fixed upon so high a scale that nothing less than colleges, or seminaries of the highest class, could claim much of their attention, or seem to require any extraordinary efforts for their establishment.[153]

The New Englanders, though they had migrated, brought with them the traditions of educational support in which they had grown up—the traditions of collectivism and taxation. The Pennsylvanians, and other immigrants from the middle states and the upper South, brought with them their traditions—of individual support, of private schools, and of public facilities for the poor. Thus, in the backgrounds of its people, Ohio had the elements of two traditions which were destined inevitably to come into conflict.

When set against the practical necessities of western life, the Pennsylvania and upper South traditions stood as a powerful barrier to the establishment of schools. The rigors of life on the frontier, coupled with the relative isolation and sparsity of population, were far from conducive to education. As Foote said of the Pennsylvanians in Ohio:

> the doctrine of the necessity of a most rigid social and family economy was so practical a belief, that any doctrine of political economy which appeared to interfere with it made no converts . . . . and to oppose Satan by the diffusion of knowledge did not seem to them, by any means, so important as to oppose the Indians, who were considered his representatives, by the rifle.[154]

Reinforcing this feeling was the spirit of western anti-intellectualism. Inherent in the equality of the frontier, this spirit reflected

[151] See Lois Kimball Mathews, *The Expansion of New England;* and John P. Foote, *The Schools of Cincinnati, and Its Vicinity* (C. F. Bradley, Cincinnati, 1855), p. 35.   [152] John P. Foote, *op. cit.*, p. 35.   [153] *Ibid.*   [154] *Ibid.*, pp. 35–36.

but one of many attempts to throw off the marks of eastern social stratification. Knowledge was a mark of privilege, a sign of aristocracy. It was something to beware of lest a man use it for unscrupulous ends.[155] Thus, when the older individualist traditions were set within the rigors of frontier life and western anti-intellectualism, they constituted an unfavorable pattern which enthusiasts of education had continually to face in their efforts to obtain support for their proposals.[156]

But if the equality of the West gave birth to an anti-intellectualism hindering efforts on behalf of education, it also bore another factor which equally facilitated their efforts. In its vigorous assertion of the basic equality of all individuals, and its rejection of social stratification, this spirit largely precluded the establishment of pauper systems. The ambivalent assertion of this equality, then, was that education wasn't necessary—that it was a mark of social distinction; but if available, it should be available to all.[157] Thus, the first Ohio constitution in 1802 declared:

[155] Baynard Rush Hall, *The New Purchase*, pp. 175–76.

[156] The poverty of the early migrants to the West, as well as the traditions which they brought with them, were instrumental in determining their attitudes toward taxation for educational support. Burns, in his discussion of the early history of education in Ohio, notes vividly the primacy of urgently practical activity in the interests of the people. Thus, "The early settlers of Ohio, as a rule, were too busy in erecting rude habitations, felling trees, burning off the heavy timber, fencing the clearings, guiding the plow through rooty ground, and making passable highways to mill and market, to allow them to devote any attention to any other interest less pressing, and that could be deferred to a more convenient season. Hence it is not strange that school interests were often neglected." See James J. Burns, *Educational History of Ohio* (Historical Publishing Co., Columbus, 1905), p. 21. Miller, in his analysis, points out another aspect of this problem: "Ohio in its early statehood was a frontier community, settled by a class of people that in the very nature of the case were compelled largely to be self-reliant and to solve their own problems, educational as well as other. It was a heavily timbered area. Means of communication were difficult. It would have been a hard matter to establish any general system of control or supervision in the early period, and when means of communication had become simplified, through a system of state roads and canals, the people had become habituated to attending to their own educational needs." See Edward Alanson Miller, *The History of Educational Legislation in Ohio from 1803 to 1850* (University of Chicago, Chicago, 1920), p. 2.

[157] An excellent illustration is provided by Baynard Rush Hall, *The New Purchase*, p. 321: "Be it remembered . . . that Uncle Sam is an undoubted friend of *public* education, and that, although so sadly deficient in his own; and hence, in the liberal distribution of other folk's land, he bestowed on us several entire townships for a college or university. It was, therefore, democratically believed, and loudly insisted on, that as the State had freely received, it should freely give; and that 'larnin, even the most powerfullest highest larnin,' should at once be bestowed on every body!"

That no law shall be passed to prevent the poor in the several counties and townships within this State, from an equal participation in the schools, academies, colleges, and universities within this State, which are endowed, in whole or in part, from the revenues arising from the donations made by the United States for the support of schools and colleges; and the doors of the said schools, academies, and universities shall be open for the reception of scholars, students, and teachers of every grade, without any distinction or preference whatever, contrary to the intent for which the said donations were made.[158]

During its early years of statehood, Ohio came to depend largely on income from the school lands, and fees in the form of rate bills, for its schools. In keeping with the cultural backgrounds of the inhabitants, it is likely that these years saw a good deal of school-keeping in the southeastern and northeastern portions of the state —areas which had been settled by persons immigrating from New England and New York. In other localities, where the population had been drawn largely from the middle and upper southern states, there was considerably less of such activity in evidence.[159] The first constitution had provided that the encouragement of schools and the means of education (required by the Ordinance of 1787) would take place "by legislative provision"; so it was to the legislature that those in favor of a general tax-supported system had to look. From 1802 to 1821, though, no such legislation authorizing general or local taxation was forthcoming. What laws were passed during this period dealt principally with the use of funds obtained through the federal land grants.

The first legislative mention of tax support appeared in the Law of 1821—the first general school law enacted.[160] By its provisions the property of all residents of school districts which had previously been liable to taxation for state and county purposes was rendered liable to taxation for school purposes. The law, however, made such taxation permissive rather than compulsory, and therefore still allowed indifference to prevent the fulfillment of its purposes. Specifically, it authorized the householders in any school district, by a two-thirds vote, to levy a tax to build a schoolhouse and pay

---

[158] Constitution of 1802, Sec. 25, in Francis Newton Thorpe, *op. cit.*, Vol. V, pp. 2911–12.

[159] A. D. Mayo, "The Development of the Common School in the Western States from 1830 to 1865," *United States Commissioner of Education Report*, 1898–99, Vol. 1, p. 358.   [160] Acts of Ohio, 1820, Chap. XXXIV.

the tuition of indigent school children. The tax, however, was not
to exceed one half the amount that might be levied for state and
county taxes during the same year. It is interesting to note that
the four men principally responsible for the passage of this statute
were all born in Massachusetts;[161] and their interest in tax support
bears out the assertion that the New England tradition was an
important factor in the educational history of Ohio. This role of
the New England tradition was also prominent in the legislature,
where, as Foote has remarked:

A majority of the legislators . . . were, a few years before the establishment of our school system, natives, or descendents from natives, of
New England, and in due time, they gave efficient aid to the enactment
of the school law.[162]

The fact that the Act of 1821 was merely permissive in its principles caused the friends of education to pursue their aims with
unrelenting zeal. Although there was still a good deal of opposition to tax support, the people in 1824 sent to the legislature a
majority favoring the cause of public schools.[163] The addresses of
Governor Morrow had evidenced deep insight into the acute problems inherent in Ohio's conflicting educational traditions:

In this state there are causes extrinsic in their nature for difference of
opinion on the subject. The population composed principally of emigrants from the different states of the union: With habits and modes
of thinking on the subject, as different as are the regulations of the
states from whence they came.[164]

Speaking of the legislation of 1821, the governor had pointed to
the inadequacy of permissive legislation. "Was this act made positive," he noted, "and in some other respects modified, we should
have a system in force perhaps not perfect, for the regulation of
common schools, which could be further improved as experience
under it would point out its defects." [165] His address of 1824 referred to this former address, and reaffirmed his position.[166] A joint

[161] Ephraim Cutler, Caleb Atwater, Nathan Guilford, and Samuel Lewis.
[162] John P. Foote, *op. cit.*, p. 35.
[163] Edward Alanson Miller, *op. cit.*, pp. 9–10.
[164] *Journal of the House of Representatives*, 1823, p. 19 (numbered 13 in the copy
consulted).
[165] *Ibid.*, pp. 19 (13)–20.
[166] *Journal of the House of Representatives*, 1824, p. 15.

committee[167] was appointed to study the situation, their efforts culminating in the educational legislation of 1825.[168]

This law provided that a school tax be levied by the several counties in the amount of one-half mill. It directed the trustees of the various townships to lay them off into one or more school districts. The penalty for refusing to carry out the districting provisions of the act was loss of the township's share of this tax after five years. Although this attempt to encourage the townships to proceed with districting was not universally successful, the townships generally seem to have availed themselves of the act. As a matter of fact, the act stands as the beginning point of the principle of tax support for schools—a principle which continued from that time forward. The tax was steadily raised until 1838,[169] when the required county tax was two mills. However, in 1839 this law was amended to allow the county commissioners to reduce the county tax to any sum not less than one mill;[170] and the continuing sentiment in opposition to taxation mounted to the point where in 1847 the county commissioners were forbidden to levy any tax amounting to more than two fifths of a mill.[171] Even during this period of educational reaction, though, the principle of taxation was maintained throughout. It is interesting to note that the legislation of 1838 also contained optional provisions for a township tax not to exceed an additional two mills, and a variable state tax to bring the revenue from the permanent school fund to a total of $200,000 annually.

Although the principle of tax support was firmly enunciated in the legislation of 1825, a fee system, closely resembling the New York rate-bill system, was also maintained.[172] This principle of

[167] *Ibid.*, p. 70. It is interesting to note that Nathan Guilford, one of the New Englanders who had been instrumental in effecting passage of the legislation of 1821, was a principal figure in securing the enactment of the law of 1825. As chairman of this committee, he and Ephraim Cutler (also of New England) were active in securing passage of the act in the legislature by effecting a coalition with legislators who were working in the interests of internal improvements. See William G. W. Lewis, *Biography of Samuel Lewis*, pp. 102–03.

[168] Acts of 1824, Vol. XXIII, p. 36.   [169] Acts of 1837, Vol. XXXVI, p. 21.

[170] Acts of 1838, Vol. XXXVII, p. 61.   [171] Acts of 1846, Vol. XLV, p. 60.

[172] During the years of his superintendency from 1837 to 1840, Samuel Lewis singled out the rate bill as one of the items contributing most to the ineffectiveness of the common school system. Thus in his first Annual Report he noted:

"Another and much larger number of the districts, adopt a practice of which the following is an example.

applying money received from fees to the school budget was recognized in the educational legislation of 1821,[173] 1829,[174] 1831,[175] 1834,[176] and 1836.[177] The system of rate bills was maintained until the legislation of March 14, 1853 finally made the schools entirely free to all children of the commonwealth.[178]

Thus in Ohio, as in many of the western states, the institution of a pattern of public support became a function of three things. First, the peculiar conditions of western life and thought—the concern for urgently practical activity coupled with opposition to "booklearning"—were almost inevitably a hindrance to genuine interest in schooling. These unfavorable factors were reinforced by the conditions of poor communication, and therefore decentralized ways of coping with problems. This last detail leads to the second item on which education depended—the traditions of the people who settled the land. In this respect, we have noted the importance, in Ohio's case, of the traditions carried by the New Englanders in securing publicly supported schools; and conversely, the role of the emigrants from the middle and southern states in breeding apathy and resistance to taxation. The third item centered in that aspect of the New England tradition indirectly bequeathed to all states except five entering the Union after the original thirteen colonies.[179] In the legal precedents associated with the federal land grants for education, every one of these new states was provided with a tradition favoring public support for common schools. It remained, then, for the interplay of these factors in each of the western states to determine its peculiar course of movement regarding the patterns and principles of school support.

"The district has funds which would pay a teacher one quarter or less; but in order to keep up a school as long as possible, it is divided between two or more quarters; the teacher makes his estimate of the amount, besides public money, that must be paid by each scholar, and gets his subscription accordingly. Here none send but those who can pay the balance; of course, the children of the poor, the very intemperate and careless, with sometimes the inordinate lovers of money, are left at home." See *First Annual Report of the Superintendent of Common Schools*, 36th Ohio General Assembly, Jan. 1838, Doc. No. 17.

[173] Acts of 1820, Vol. XIX, p. 51.
[174] Acts of 1828, Vol. XXVII, p. 72.
[175] Acts of 1830, Vol. XXIX, p. 414.
[176] Acts of 1833, Vol. XXXII, p. 25.
[177] Acts of 1835, Vol. XXXIV, p. 19.
[178] Acts of 1852, Vol. LI, p. 429.
[179] Maine, West Virginia, Kentucky, Vermont, and Texas.

3. The Principle of Public Support Established

By 1850, through the dynamics outlined above, the principles and precedents of public support for common schools may be said in varying degrees to have taken root throughout the Union. In general, the pattern had assumed two basic aspects, and within both there were tremendous differences in the case of individual states. The first of these was the permanent school fund, the interest of which was devoted to common schools; the second was taxation for a similar purpose.

By mid-century, every single state had established some form of permanent school fund.[180] Just what purposes had stimulated their institution in every case was not always clear. In some states, such as Connecticut or Arkansas, it seems likely that its role was clearly to supplant or obviate taxation. In others, like Massachusetts where it was established only after the acceptance of complete support by taxation, it was more likely adopted to alleviate part of the tax burden on the citizenry. And in still others, like New York, it was adopted as an encouragement to local initiative. It is quite possible, moreover, that states adopting such a fund as an encouragement might soon allow it to lapse, out of intensive opposition to taxation, into a role where it would carry the whole burden. With such a number of conflicting purposes it is clear that a variety of causal factors were instrumental in securing such funds. It is important to note also in the institution of these funds the importance both of the federal grants for education, and the distribution of the surplus federal revenues in 1837. The land grants, in every case having been legally reserved for education, automatically constituted such a fund; while the surplus revenues were applied to education by sixteen of the twenty-seven states participating in the distribution.[181] There is little doubt concerning the stimulation which these two actions of the national government provided in the establishment of these funds.

[180] Fletcher Harper Swift, *A History of Public Permanent Common School Funds in the United States, 1795–1905* (Henry Holt and Co., New York, 1911), Table XVI, pp. 98–99.

[181] Frank Wilson Blackmar, *The History of Federal and State Aid to Higher Education in the United States* (Government Printing Office, Washington, 1890), United States Bureau of Education Circulars of Information, 1890, No. 1, pp. 46–47.

Gradually, though, it became increasingly obvious to the educational reform group that the interest from these school funds alone could not possibly secure the kind of school they envisioned; and their efforts turned more and more to securing taxation for their cause. It was at this point that they encountered their most vehement and bitter opposition; for it was here that the burden of school support was reduced to individual terms. But the groups favoring education worked long and arduously in changing this notion from a violation of individual rights into a necessity for ✓ the welfare of the community. Their efforts did not go unrewarded. By 1850, every state in the Union except Arkansas had experimented in one way or another with permissive tax legislation;[182] and although a few such enactments, violently opposed, had suffered repeal a short time after passage, the great majority remained on the statute books. Some, to be sure, were seldom taken advantage of by local communities—becoming mere "dead letters" accomplishing nothing. Others became the instruments of building more or less comprehensive state-wide systems. Still others had soon become obsolete—serving only as stepping stones to unified systems of compulsory taxation. And if it would be unwise to conclude from this that school taxation itself had gained anything approaching cheerful universal acceptance by 1850, yet it is evident that the legal precedents had been generally established—such acceptance awaiting only the emergence into active

[182] Alabama (Laws of 1825, An Act Establishing Schools in the County of Mobile, Jan. 10, 1826); California (Constitution of 1850, Art. XX); Connecticut (Acts and Laws of the State of Connecticut, 1796, p. 371); Delaware (Laws of 1829, An Act for the Establishment of Free Schools passed Feb. 12, 1829); Florida (Laws of 1848–49, Chap. 229); Georgia (Acts of 1838, p. 257, Acts of 1843, p. 43); Illinois (Laws of 1824–25, p. 21); Indiana (Laws of 1848, Chap. CXVI); Iowa (Constitution of 1846, Art. 9); Kentucky (Session Acts, 1837–38, Chap. 898, p. 274); Louisiana (Laws of 1847, No. 225); Maine (Laws of 1821, Chap. CXVII); Maryland (Laws of 1825, Chap. 162); Massachusetts (Laws of 1827, Chap. 143); Michigan (Laws of 1837, Chap. LXIII); Mississippi (Laws of 1846, Chap. 2); Missouri (An Act to provide for the organization, support and government of common schools, Feb. 9, 1839); New Jersey (An Act to establish public schools, Mar. 1, 1838); New Hampshire (Laws, 1789, An Act for the better regulation of Schools within this State, and for repealing the laws now in force respecting them, June 18, 1789); New York (Acts of 1849, Chap. 140); North Carolina (Laws, 1840–41, Chap. VII); Ohio (Laws of 1824, Vol. XXIII, p. 36); Pennsylvania (Laws of 1834, No. 102); Rhode Island (Laws of 1839, An Act to revise and amend the several Acts relating to Public Schools); South Carolina (Laws of 1811, p. 27); Tennessee (Laws of 1832, Chap. XXXVIII); Texas (Constitution of 1845, Art. X); Virginia (Acts of 1828–29, Chap. XII); Vermont (Acts of 1850, No. 44); Wisconsin (Constitution of 1840, Art. X, Sec. 4).

citizenry of a generation who had enjoyed the first fruits of a common school education.

By mid-century, then, within these two patterns—of the permanent school fund and of taxation for education—the conception of public, community support for the common school had taken root. The principles and precedents having been established, it remained only for the people to decide how good and how universal a common school education they desired for their young. This eventually would decide the extent to which they drew on their newly established tradition.

4. Traditions of Control

Within the two colonial traditions described above, one may also discern the seeds of two distinct patterns of educational support. The collective tradition, enunciating community responsibility for the maintenance of schools for all, inevitably involved some measure of community control—even if this often entailed merely the hiring of a teacher. Within the philanthropic tradition, precedents of an entirely different kind emerged. In this case, the indigent children for whom the community assumed responsibility were educated in one of two ways: (1) as charity cases in private facilities maintained principally by tuition rates; or (2) by benevolent organizations (parochial or non-parochial in nature) in schools established especially for the poor. More often than not, the community exercised little control over such facilities, allowing them to remain largely in the hands of their respective nonpublic managements.

Any treatment, then, of the movement toward community control of publicly supported schools divides itself into two aspects. The first involves the emergence of control machinery in systems where from the beginning, community control came as a concomitant of community support. Such a movement is well illustrated by the development of educational control in Massachusetts. The second aspect involves the development of control machinery in systems where varying degrees of public support were given to schools under private or parochial sponsorship. In this case, the movement would necessarily include two phases: (1) the efforts of communities to gain control of institutions largely or totally supported by public funds; and (2) the efforts of communities to withdraw public support from institutions which they did not control. Such a development is well illustrated by New York City's fight to wrest control of its schools from the Public School Society and the other private and church organizations which shared its public funds at the beginning of the nineteenth century.

5. Movement Toward Public Control

I

In the early years of Massachusetts' settlement, the management of schools probably implied little more than hiring a teacher and securing a place where school might be held.[183] The Law of 1647 assigned these function to the towns;[184] and they in turn exercised them through the town meeting—an agency whereby the whole community governed itself.[185] In the next fifty years, however, with the growing complexity of town affairs, the powers of the town meeting came gradually to be delegated to representatives—or selectmen; and in 1692, the General Court recognized this development by granting to "the selectmen and inhabitants of such towns," the power to "take effectual care and make due provision for the settlement and maintenance of such school-master and masters." [186] Even this assignment, however, did not solve the increasing demands of education. The selection of teachers and the supervision of schools were continuing problems, and being such, they demanded continuing attention.[187] Thus even greater specialization was required. Charged with the many responsibilities of town administration, the selectmen began to delegate their educational powers to special committees—first made up of their own personnel, and later of separate personnel. This was the final step in the

---

[183] Henry Suzzallo, *The Rise of Local School Supervision in Massachusetts* (Teachers College, Columbia University, 1906), p. 1.

[184] *Records of the Governor and Company of the Massachusetts Bay in New England*, Vol. 2, p. 203.

[185] *The Body of Liberties* granted to "the Freemen of every Towneship . . . power to make such by laws and constitutions as may concerne the well-fare of their Towne," in *The Colonial Laws of Massachusetts* (William H. Whitmore, ed., Boston, 1889), p. 47.

[186] *The Acts and Resolves, Public and Private, of the Province of the Massachusetts Bay* (Boston, 1869), Vol. 1, p. 63.

[187] Henry Suzzallo, *op. cit.*, pp. 76–77.

evolution of an official group charged solely with the responsibility of maintaining and regulating local school effort.

One interesting phase between the latter two steps in this evolution is worthy of note—the utilization of town ministers as school supervisors. Within the framework of an established religion, the minister was a public servant. It is understandable that a community would attempt to draw on existing facilities in its first efforts to cope with local problems. Considering the place of the minister in the public affairs of colonial Massachusetts, the early attempts to use him as a school supervisor are not at all surprising.[188]

As has been stated above, the Law of 1789 codified many of the practices which had emerged in the state's century and a half of educational development. As such, it gave important attention to matters of control and supervision. The law delegated to the ministers and selectmen the responsibility of inspecting the schools and using their influence to encourage attendance by the youth. Concerning this function, the act directed:

And it shall be the duty of the minister or ministers of the gospel and the Selectmen (or such other persons as shall be specially chosen by each town or district for that purpose) of the several towns or districts, to use their influence and best endeavours, that the youth of their respective towns and districts, do regularly attend the schools appointed and supported as aforesaid, for their instruction; and once in every six months at least, and as much oftener as they shall determine it necessary, to visit and inspect the several schools in their respective towns and districts, and shall enquire into the regulation and discipline thereof, and the proficiency of the scholars therein, giving reasonable notice of the time of their visitation.[189]

When authorized by the town or district, it was also the duty of the selectmen or school committee to hire the teacher. Whereas previously the town ministers had been responsible for the educational and moral qualifications of secondary teachers,[190] and the selectmen for the elementary,[191] the certification of teachers on both levels now fell to the selectmen.[192] The ministers retained some degree of control, however, through a requirement that they attest to the moral character of all teachers.

[188] Ibid., pp. 44–45.   [189] Acts of 1789, Chap. XIX.
[190] The Acts and Resolves, Public and Private, of the Province of the Massachusetts Bay, Vol. I, p. 470.
[191] Ibid., Vol. I, pp. 681–82.   [192] Acts of 1789, Chap. XIX.

Of great importance are the three levels of educational authority involved in the Law of 1789: the state, the town, and the district. As this phenomenon was paralleled in almost every other state, this seems an excellent opportunity to discuss the relationship which existed among them.

The state, as the agency of the largest community involved, was represented by the General Court which passed the bill. Historians of the Massachusetts school system are virtually agreed that in matters of school support and control, each town proceeded pretty much along its own individual course. In emphasizing this comparatively independent development, however, the effect of the over-all authority of the General Court must not be ignored. Although as a rule it acted only to compel certain towns to institute advances which had become fairly well accepted throughout the colony, its legislation setting up and enforcing standards definitely established it as the ultimate authority in educational affairs.[193]

This authority of the community on the state level was secured by the United States Constitution in the Bill of Rights. The Tenth Amendment, recognizing the federal government as an agency existing through delegated powers, reserved all "powers not delegated to the United States by the Constitution, nor prohibited by it to the States" to the several states respectively, or to the people.[194] Inasmuch as education is nowhere mentioned in the Constitution, the state was to have final authority in matters of educational concern.

The town, represented by its selectmen, ministers, or school committee, is the second level of community organization represented in the Law of 1789. The Body of Liberties had originally granted to the freemen of every township the power to legislate concerning the welfare of their town. In 1641 a law authorized the townspeople to "choose yearly or for lesse time out of themselves a convenient number of fitt men to order the planting or prudentiall occasions of that Town, according to Instructions given them in

---

[193] See Henry Suzzallo, *op. cit.*; Harlan Updegraff, *The Origin of the Moving School in Massachusetts* (Teachers College, Columbia University, New York, 1908); and George H. Martin, *Evolution of the Massachusetts School System* (D. Appleton and Company, New York, 1908). It is interesting to note that this tendency to delegate its authority to the small units eventually resulted in a challenge by the smaller units when the state tried to reclaim its authority in the interests of efficiency and equalization throughout the area involved in its jurisdiction.

[194] *Constitution of the United States*, Amendments, Art. X.

writeing, *Provided nothing be done by them contrary to the publique laws and orders of the Countrie. . . .*" [195] Thus the town was granted an independence in the management of its own affairs limited only by conformance to the laws of the general commonwealth. In this way, allowances were made for differences in local conditions and initiative.

The district, through its representatives, is the third level of community organization referred to in the Act of 1789. The story of the development of the district in Massachusetts is one intimately bound up with certain basic forces in the later seventeenth and eighteenth centuries. Perhaps the most important of these is the development of a decentralized pattern of living in place of the older and closer pattern of town settlement. By 1700 many forces which had formerly acted to stimulate close settlement in towns were on the wane. The necessity of universal attendance at church exercises, the fear of Indians, and other physical factors demanding cooperation and group effort, had led the early leaders of Massachusetts to enact legislation providing that no dwelling should be built more than one-half mile from any town meeting house.[196] However, it is doubtful that this ruling was ever strictly observed, and modification was early in evidence.[197] By the end of the seventeenth century, the impact of these forces had declined appreciably. There was a pronounced movement toward the separation of civil authority from church authority—thus removing the legal basis of requirements for church attendance. The danger of attack by the Indians had fairly well subsided; and the removal of these two stimuli greatly weakened the arguments favoring close settlement. Gradually, then, families began to settle in the rural areas of townships; and the older, tightly knit communities dispersed over the countryside.

This decentralization of population posed a difficult problem for town authorities. Large distances, coupled with poor communication facilities, made it virtually impossible for rural children to attend the town school. This in turn led to two difficulties: first, getting a tax voted for the support of town schools, and second,

[195] *The Colonial Laws of Massachusetts*, p. 49. (Italics mine)
[196] *Records of the Governor and Company of the Massachusetts Bay in New England*, Vol. 1, pp. 157, 181.
[197] *Ibid.*, Vol. 1, p. 291. (Repealed in 1640)

obtaining sufficient attendance to justify their maintenance. The result was a significant falling off in compliance with the compulsory education requirements of the colony—a situation which prevailed until the General Court raised the fine for noncompliance to a point where it was equally profitable for a town to maintain a school or to pay the fine.[198] Even at this point, however, residents in the outlying districts were reticent to support education. They wanted somewhat more benefit from it than they could see accruing from the traditional town schools. It was in response to these demands that the school district emerged.

The initial response to dissatisfaction in the outlying districts was the moving school—a process whereby the teacher moved for limited periods of the year to the various sections of the township.[199] In general, this phenomenon was characteristic of the first quarter of the eighteenth century. It was during the next fifty years that the school district developed—a response which went one step beyond the moving school and actually saw the establishment of schools in the rural areas. During this period, many towns informally divided their areas into sections, and the people in these sections were given their share of the town funds to do with as they pleased. This action was *de facto* rather than *de jure,* however, in that no legal provision had been made recognizing such division. It was the Law of 1789 which actually represented the first official sanctioning of the process. While this legislation gave no actual powers to the district (i.e., district authorities could not tax, hire teachers, etc.), its permissive provisions paved the way for the growth of the practice throughout the state.

Thus the Law of 1789 in Massachusetts dealt in principle with two realms of school control: (1) it delineated, either through implication or direct statement, three levels of community organization involved in the exercise of control and supervision of education, and (2) it gave legal recognition to the school committee as an agent in implementing this control and supervision. The conception of "committee" held by the framers of the law is adequately implied in the description of its functions: namely, in the two areas

---

[198] *The Acts and Resolves, Public and Private, of the Province of the Massachusetts Bay,* Vol. 1, p. 470.

[199] Harlan Updegraff, *op. cit.,* p. 172.

which had emerged as continuing problems of selectmen—the hiring of a teacher and the visitation of schools.[200]

The evolution of school control involved two continuous trends during the next three decades. One was a decline in the power of the minister; the other was an extension of the power of the local school district. Concerning the former, the Law of 1789 probably represented the zenith of the clergy's influence on the Massachusetts school system. Although ministers had been prohibited by earlier legislation from holding posts as teachers in the community,[201] yet, as has been mentioned above, they were called upon as public servants to participate in the management and supervision of schools.[202] Suzzallo has observed that prior to 1789 ministers did not appear on most of the town committees charged with the selection of teachers.[203] They had, on the other hand, been used extensively as school visitors. The suggestion of the Law of 1789, however, was for many towns which had not done so a sufficiently powerful incentive now to include the minister in the general control of school affairs.[204]

The subsequent rise of the school committee became a primary factor in the curtailment of the minister's power; and the committee itself was probably the principal agency in bringing about his eventual removal from school affairs. Thus in 1822, when Boston was organized as a city, its laws provided that a school committee, one member elected from each ward, should "jointly with the Mayor and Aldermen, constitute the School Committee for the said city, and have the care and superintandence [sic] of the public schools." [205] No mention of ministers was made in the provisions. This pattern was applied to the whole state by the Act of 1826,[206] when the maintenance of school committees was made compulsory for all towns. The powers formerly held jointly by the ministers and the school committees were now vested entirely in the school committees. The Law of 1827 [207] reaffirmed this principle, and left to the ministers only the task of using their best endeavors

---

[200] Acts of 1789, Chap. XIX.

[201] *The Acts and Resolves, Public and Private, of the Province of the Massachusetts Bay,* Vol. 1, p. 470.

[202] Probably out of their qualification to pass on two criteria: academic training and religious orthodoxy.   [203] Henry Suzzallo, *op. cit.,* p. 56.

[204] *Ibid.,* pp. 56, 58.   [205] Laws of 1822, Chap. CX.

[206] Laws of 1826, Chap. CLXX.   [207] Laws of 1827, Chap. CXLIII.

"that the youth of their respective towns, and districts, do regularly attend the Schools established . . . for their instruction." [208] Henceforth the minister, though a force in the encouragement of education, was no longer officially connected with its control or supervision. The rising support of the principle of separation of church and state—the principle of differentiation of function—prevailed. The control of education thus fell entirely to the civil authorities, and the common schools became schools controlled and supervised by the civil community which supported them.

After gaining *de jure* recognition in the legislation of 1789, the school district came into increasing use by the townships. The towns rapidly took to laying them out according to the permissive sections of this act. Having no legal power early districts were confined to voluntary subscription in raising money to supplement their share of town school funds. By legislation passed in 1800, however, the power to tax was conferred upon them; and the people of these units were authorized to hold meetings, to choose clerks, and to raise money for schoolhouses and their maintenance.[209] The tendency toward district organization, necessitated by the changing character of the population distribution, continued. In 1827, legislation required those towns which had districts to choose for each district a prudential committeeman, whose duties would involve the care of the school property in his district and the selection and employment of teachers.[210] The limitation of this latter function, of course, was that the district could employ only those teachers who held certificates of qualification from the town school committee. Thus it became the responsibility of the district prudential "committee" to hire a certified teacher, and the responsibility of the town committee to visit and inspect the work of the several district schools under its jurisdiction.[211]

The definite acceptance of the school committee by the Act of 1826 as the agency of school control and supervision throws interesting light on its character at that time. The exact provision establishing the committee as a permanent part of the Massachusetts school system read as follows:

[208] *Ibid.*, Sec. 3.
[209] An Act in Addition to an Act, entitled "An Act to provide for the Instruction of Youth, and for the Promotion of good Education," passed Feb. 28, 1800.
[210] Laws of 1827, Chap. CXLIII, Sec. 6.   [211] *Ibid.*, Sec. 5.

That each town in this Commonwealth, shall, at the annual March or April meeting, choose a School Committee, consisting of not less than five persons, who shall have the general charge and superintendence of all the public schools in said town; and it shall be the duty of said committee, to visit the schools in said town, which are kept through the year, at least once a quarter, for the purpose of making a careful examination of the same, and to see that the scholars are properly supplied with books; also, to inquire into the regulation and discipline of such schools, and the proficiency of the scholars therein; and it shall also be the duty of said committee to visit each of the district schools in said town, for the purposes aforesaid, on some day during the first week of the commencement thereof, and also on some day during the last two weeks of the same; and it shall further be the duty of one or more of said committee to visit all the schools in the town, at least once a month, for the purposes aforementioned, without giving previous notice thereof to the instructors. And it is hereby further made the duty of said committee, to require full and satisfactory evidence of the good character and qualifications of said instructors, conformably to the laws now in force relating to the subject; or to require them to furnish such other evidence of character and qualifications, as shall be equally satisfactory to said committee; and no instructor shall be entitled to receive any compensation for his service, who shall teach any of the schools aforesaid, without first obtaining from said committee a certificate of his fitness to instruct.[212]

It is interesting to note, first, that neither ministers nor selectmen were designated members of the school committee by virtue of their official positions.[213] Thus the committees were *lay*, or *civil* boards—representatives of the civil rather than ecclesiastical authority of the town. Second, they were an entity apart from the actual governmental machinery of the town. It is true that they originally evolved out of a specialization of function which demanded their appointment as subcommittees of the town government. But when the Law of 1826 required the town to choose a committee who would specifically concern themselves with education, it was requiring a controlling agency which, though related to the actual government of the town, was actually something dif-

---

[212] Acts of 1826, Chap. CLXX, Sec. 1.

[213] It is true that as late as 1846 nearly half the school committeemen in Massachusetts were clergymen, but not by virtue of their official ministerial titles. See Horace Mann, *Sequal to the So Called Correspondence Between the Rev. M. H. Smith and Horace Mann, Surreptitiously Published by Mr. Smith; Containing a Letter from Mr. Mann, Suppressed by Mr. Smith, with the Reply Therein Promised* (William B. Fowle, Boston, 1847), p. 19.

ferent and apart from it. Third, the law nowhere mentioned professional qualifications or educational standards for membership on the committee, so that again the committees were lay representatives of the community rather than professional representatives, educationally speaking. Thus this legislation early established a tradition that the public agencies of school control were to be lay, civil committees with a specialized function peculiar unto themselves.

By the end of the second decade of the nineteenth century, then, Massachusetts had virtually accepted the principle of community control for publicly supported common schools. A decade later, when Theodore Edson delivered a lecture "On Private and Public Schools" before the annual meeting of the American Institute of Instruction, he made this factor the essence of his conception of a public, or common, school. "Public schools," he said, "are those by law established among us, the common free schools of New England, such as we actually observe them, scattered through the towns and villages of our own commonwealth, . . ." [214] Concerning these schools, he went on to say:

Over these the law provides for each town a superintending committee, having general charge of all the town schools, empowered to prescribe the books and direct the exercises. In the cities and some of the larger towns this committee supersedes the district prudential committee, and is entrusted with the duties of employing, paying, and, if need be, of removing the teachers. . . .
An obvious feature of distinction between public and private schools, as I have now classed them, is that the former are under the supervision of selected men, responsible more or less directly to the community. The private schools have no supervision, or only that of the parents.[215]

Reflecting on the various evils connected with private institutions lacking adequate supervision, Edson saw in the system of public superintendence a means of exercising a stabilizing influence on education:

[214] Theodore Edson, "On the Comparative Merits of Private and Public Schools," in *The Introductory Discourse, and the Lectures Delivered Before the American Institute of Instruction, at Worcester (Mass.) August, 1837. Including the Journal of Proceedings, and a List of the Officers* (James Munroe & Company, Boston, 1838), p. 93.
[215] *Ibid.*, pp. 93–94.

No better remedy can be devised for these evils, than that provided by our common school system, where the entire direction of the studies and exercises is put into the hands of a committee, acting under a sense of responsibility, and which should consist of the most intelligent and best qualified of the community.[216]

Though the principle of public control had been clearly enunciated in Massachusetts by 1827, men of vision saw in this control the potentialities of both an adequate and an inadequate system. If it was the community's privilege to control these institutions, it was also its responsibility to make them as attractive as possible. Having enunciated the principle of public schools, and having provided them, it became incumbent on the community which controlled them to inquire into their quality and efficiency. It was at this point that educational leaders saw the shortcoming of the Massachusetts system. Public apathy and indifference, the poverty caused by the Revolution, and the ever more powerful individualism of the period had led to a decline of community interest in education. Although there was a degree of compliance with the legislation which has been mentioned, the decentralized local control of the district system had subjected the schools to petty local interests. Tremendous inequalities had sprung up over the state,[217] and in many cases public education had largely lost the faith of the community.[218] It was the improvement of these conditions that consumed a large share of the energies of the Massachusetts reform group. Having secured their system of public control, they looked

---

[216] *Ibid.*, p. 99.

[217] In his *Eighth Annual Report,* Horace Mann sought to examine the various modes by which the towns apportioned funds for school support to the districts. Nowhere is the individuality of the various towns more apparent. Inasmuch as the state had never prescribed any specific means of apportionment, the practices of the towns ranged all the way from apportionment according to houses, or population, or school-age children to equal distribution in proportion to taxes paid. It is obvious that tremendous inequalities could and did easily result out of this diversity of practice.

[218] See, for instance, an article in the *U. S. Review* offering the following impression of a district school:

"Let any body go into one of these, and mark the uninteresting discipline of the master, the listless languor and weary indifference which every where reigns, the unmeaning gaze with which the pupils pore over and recite their lessons, and the joy, or rather the bounding exultation, with which they greet even a momentary respite from what they think their slavish toils." *Remarks upon Mr. Carter's Outline of an Institution for the Education of Teachers* (Bowles and Dearborn, Boston, 1827), p. 12.

next to the adequacy of the product. Illustrative of their attempts is the work of James G. Carter, pioneer among the New England educational reform group.

Carter's first publications on behalf of public education appeared in the Boston newspapers of 1821. They continued there until 1824, when he published a more extended treatment of his ideas called *Letters to the Hon. William Prescott, LL.D. on the Free Schools of New England, with Remarks on the Principles of Instruction.*[219] In tracing the history of legislative efforts to establish and maintain a system of free schools, Carter forcefully decried the falling off of efforts to maintain a high level of education in the state. He pointed to the relaxation of the requirements for the maintenance of grammar schools, and showed how the rise and expansion of private academies had created invidious distinctions between those able and those unable to pay their tuition. Finally, he put his finger on the major inadequacies he saw in the schools:

Two principal causes have operated from the first establishment of the free schools, to impair and pervert their influence. 1st, Incompetent instructors; 2d, Bad school books. It is not a little surprising, that a public so deeply impressed with the importance of the system of schools, and so resolved to carry it into full operation, by liberal appropriations, should stop short of their purpose, and stop precisely at that point, where the greatest attention and vigilance were essential, to give efficacy to the whole. I do not mean that much good has not been realized; on the contrary, as has been repeatedly remarked, the success of the free school system is just cause of congratulation; but I mean, that their influence has not been the greatest and the best which the *same means,* under better management, might produce.[220]

In the winter of 1824–25, Carter followed up his initial observations with a series of "Essays upon Popular Education" in the *Boston Patriot.*[221] These were reprinted in pamphlet form in 1826.[222] Reviewing the imperfections he had pointed out in his earlier pamphlet, Carter launched a plea that the state reaffirm its authority over public education:

[219] James G. Carter, *Letters to the Hon. William Prescott, LL.D. on the Free Schools of New England, with Remarks upon the Principles of Instruction* (Cummings, Hilliard and Co., Boston, 1824).
[220] *Ibid.,* p. 55.
[221] *Barnard's American Journal of Education,* Vol. V (1858), p. 412.
[222] James G. Carter, *Essays upon Popular Education.*

If the policy of the legislature, in regard to free schools, for the last twenty years be not changed, the institution, which had been the glory of New England will, in twenty years more, be extinct. If the State continue to relieve themselves of the trouble of providing for the instruction of the whole people, and to shift the responsibility upon the towns, and the towns upon the districts, and the districts upon individuals, each will take care of himself and his own family as he is able, and as he appreciates the blessing of a good education. The rich will, as a class, have much better instruction than they now have, while the poor will have much worse or none at all. The academies and private schools will be carried to much greater perfection than they have been, while the public free schools will become stationary or retrograde; till at length, they will be thrown for support upon the gratuitous, and of course capricious and uncertain efforts of individuals . . .[223]

Tying together his two recommendations—improvement in the agencies of control (mentioned in the *Essays*) and in the schools themselves (mentioned in the *Letters*)—Carter proposed the establishment of an institution to train competent teachers for the public schools. "Our ancestors ventured," he proposed, "to do what the world has never done before, in so perfect a manner, when they established the free schools. Let us also do what they have never so well done yet, and establish an institution for the exclusive purpose of preparing instructors for them. This is only a second part, a developement or consummation of the plan of our fathers." [224]

Carter envisioned the institution as both literary and scientific in character. One of its unique tasks would rest in the formulation of a body of principles dealing with the development of the intellect and the communication of knowledge.[225] Professionally, he saw the institution contributing not only to better schools but also to the development of a professional spirit among teachers which would have a positive effect in all aspects of their work.[226] Vitally important was the role of community control and sponsorship which Carter recognized. Starting with the premise that "free governments are the proprietors of all literary and scientific institutions so far as they have the tendency to diffuse knowledge generally among the people," [227] he advanced the following arguments in favor of state control:

[223] *Ibid.*, p. 41.   [224] *Ibid.*, p. 46.   [225] *Ibid.*, p. 47.   [226] *Ibid.*   [227] *Ibid.*, p. 49.

An institution for the education of teachers, as has been before intimated, would form a part, and a very important part of the free school system. It would be, moreover, precisely that portion of the system, which should be under the direction of the State whether the others are or not. Because we should thus secure at once, an uniform, intelligent and independent tribunal for decisions on the qualifications of teachers. Because we should thus relieve the clergy of an invidious task, and ensure to the public competent teachers, if such could be found or prepared. An institution for this purpose would become by its influence on society, and particularly on the young, an engine to sway the public sentiment, the public morals, and the public religion, more powerful than any other in the possession of government. It should, therefore, be responsible immediately to them. And they should, carefully, overlook it; and prevent its being perverted to other purposes, directly or indirectly, than those for which it is designed. It should be emphatically the State's institution. . . . The Legislature of the State should, therefore, establish and build it up, without waiting for individuals at great private sacrifices to accomplish the work. . . . If it be not undertaken by the public and for public purposes, it will be undertaken by individuals for private purposes.[228]

There seems little doubt but that much of the school legislation in 1826 and 1827 stemmed directly from the efforts of Carter. The strengthening of the superintendence and certification powers of the town school committees was one attempt to remedy some of the inequalities of the district system. More than this, however, the efforts of Carter presaged two lines of development which were destined to dominate Massachusetts' educational scene for a quarter of a century: the establishment of the State Board of Education, and the establishment of state normal schools.

The establishment of the Massachusetts Board of Education in 1837 represented the effort to achieve the state supervision which Carter had so forcefully recommended in his early writings. In February 1836, the American Institute of Instruction petitioned the General Court for the appointment of a superintendent of common schools. Their memorial held that such an official might aid common schools by improving the quality of their teachers, their instruction, and their plant facilities.[229] In his address to the

---

[228] *Ibid.*, pp. 49–50.
[229] "Memorial of the American Institute of Instruction, Praying for the Appointment of a Superintendent of the Common Schools," House of Representatives, Document No. 27, 1836.

legislature in 1837, Governor Edward Everett also strongly recommended legislation creating a Board of Education as a means of furthering the educational interests of the state.[230] Such urgings finally bore fruit in 1837.[231] A Board of eight members was created, appointed by the governor and the council, with the governor and lieutenant-governor as ex-officio members. The Board was given no direct authority—only the function of enlightenment through its abstracts of school returns[232] and an annual report to the legislature on the condition and efficacy of the school system. The legislation also provided for the appointment of a secretary whose duties were to:

collect information of the actual condition and efficiency of the common schools and other means of popular education; and diffuse as widely as possible throughout every part of the Commonwealth, information of the most approved and successful methods of arranging the studies and conducting the education of the young, to the end that all children in this Commonwealth, who depend upon common schools for instruction, may have the best education which those schools can be made to impart.[233]

Though many of the friends of education had expected Carter to fill the secretaryship, the Board at its first meeting on June 29, 1837 chose Horace Mann for this post. On June 30 he accepted the appointment, writing in his journal that evening: "Henceforth, so long as I hold this office, I devote myself to the supremest welfare of mankind upon earth." [234] During the twelve years in which Mann served in this capacity, he never deviated from this driving commitment to the people. In his attempts to carry out the Board's responsibilities Mann resorted, generally, to four agencies: public meetings, county institutes of teachers, the annual reports required by the original legislation, and a biweekly publication he edited called the *Common School Journal*. Through these four media, he hoped to reach the groups on which the quality of education would

---

[230] "Address of His Excellency Edward Everett, to the Two Branches of the Legislature, on the Organization of the Government, for the Political Year Commencing January 4, 1837," Senate, Document No. 1, 1837, p. 17.

[231] Laws of 1837, Chap. CCXLI.

[232] The Law of 1834, establishing a school fund, provided that towns receiving such aid must make periodical statistical returns to the state.

[233] Laws of 1837, Chap. CCXLI, Sec. 2.

[234] *Life of Horace Mann by His Wife* (Lee and Shepard, Boston, 1891), p. 80.

largely depend—the public, the school committees, and the teachers.

The Board, though, was not without its adversaries—political, religious, and economic. The most serious opposition, perhaps, resided (1) in the more conservative groups in the legislature, (2) in certain religious interests, and (3) oddly enough, in certain elements of the educational profession itself. The opposing elements in the legislature gained ascendancy in the state election of 1839, and a Democratic governor, Marcus Morton, replaced the Whig candidate. In his inaugural address, the governor strongly emphasized the democracy involved in decentralized control and administration, and suggested that control and supervision of common schools be left to the town or district meeting.[235] The matter was referred to the Committee on Education, which published a report embodying both a majority decision advocating abolition of the Board, and a minority decision advocating its retention.[236]

The majority decision indicted the Board on several counts. Maintaining that "If . . . the board has any actual power, it is a dangerous power, trenching directly upon the rights and duties of the Legislature;" and then asking "if it has no power, why continue its existence, at an annual expense to the Commonwealth?" [237] the report made little of the Board's function as an organ for the collection and diffusion of educational information. Even if its task were one of enlightenment, stated the report, it still remained without justification in view of the superior facilities of the several voluntary teachers' associations already in existence.[238] Furthermore, such a Board was a centralization of authority contrary to the American conception of democratic government.[239] Citing Tocqueville's comments on the basis of New England democracy, the report further stated:

This system of local authority, is as beneficial to the schools, as to any thing else. It interests a vast number of people in their welfare, whose zeal and activity, if they find themselves likely to be overshadowed by

[235] *Address of His Excellency Marcus Morton, to the Two branches of the Legislature, on the organization of the Government for the political year commencing January 1, 1840* (Published by Bay State Democrat, Boston, 1840), p. 11.
[236] House of Representatives, Documents No. 49 and 53, 1840.
[237] House of Representatives, Document No. 49, 1840, p. 3.   [238] *Ibid.*
[239] The allusion to centralization as an imitation of the despotic monarchical system of Prussia is made here.

the controlling power of a Central Board, will be apt to grow faint. Improvements, which a teacher or school committee have themselves hit upon, will be likely to be pushed with much more spirit, than those which are suggested, or, as it were, commanded, by a foreign and distant power.[240]

The report ended on a note of decentralization which seemed to be its main argument throughout. "In conclusion," it read, "the idea of the State controlling Education, whether by establishing a Central Board, by allowing that Board to sanction a particular library, or by organizing Normal Schools, seems to your Committee a great departure from the uniform spirit of our institutions,—a dangerous precedent and an interference with a matter more properly belonging to those hands, to which our ancestors wisely entrusted it." [241] The report was accompanied by an act to abolish the Board of Education.[242]

The minority report,[243] concurred in by two members of the committee, John A. Shaw and Thomas A. Greene, ably countered every one of the arguments in the majority statement. In answer to the principal accusations of the latter centering in the alleged attempt of the Board to Prussianize the Massachusetts school system, the minority charged that not a single specific instance was cited in which the Board had "attempted to control, or in any way to interfere with the rights of towns or school districts." [244] They thus labeled the charges of the majority report as *imaginary* evils." "If every institution," it continued, "is to be abolished, which it is possible to pervert to some evil purpose, we beg leave to ask, what one would be left?" Citing further the diverse political and religious creeds represented on the Board, the minority report noted:

Entire unanimity exists among them but upon one point, that of the welfare of the rising generation, through the improvement of our public schools. If these men are worthy of confidence as individuals, much more so are they, when taken collectively; for, when acting together as a Board they are a mutual watch and check upon each other's sectarian or party preferences. This very organization of the Board, is the surest defence that can be devised against such dangerous tendencies, as seem to alarm a majority of our committee.[245]

---

[240] House of Representatives, Document No. 49, 1840, p. 5.   [241] *Ibid.*, p. 11.
[242] *Ibid.*, pp. 13–14.   [243] House of Representatives, Document No. 53, 1840.
[244] *Ibid.*, p. 2.   [245] *Ibid.*, pp. 2–3.

In answer to further majority charges that the Board constituted an authoritarian means of educational control, the minority cited instances in which, as a consequence of the Board's diffusion of information, many districts had voluntarily effected constructive changes. Thus, as George Combe noted in his journal, the Board "By the wisdom of its suggestions and the character of its members . . . may exercise a *moral power* which may prove highly beneficial, while it does not, and cannot, trench on the rights and duties of the Legislature." [246] The influence of this minority report on the Legislature cannot be underestimated. Through its cogent remonstrance to the arguments of the majority, it was able to sway a majority of the House, and the forces in favor of abolition were defeated. The ability of the Board and its supporters to meet this challenge was not only a victory which confined itself to Massachusetts. In its effect on the friends of education in Connecticut and New York, it assumed a regional influence.

The second group of forces which marshaled its strength against the Board and its secretary was made up of the more conservative religious sects. Bitterly opposed both to the Unitarianism of Mann and to the Board's policy of excluding sectarianism from the schools, these forces allied themselves with the other conservative elements seeking to abolish the Board. In 1844, from the pen of Reverend Edward A. Newton, Episcopalian minister and former member of the Board, [247] and in 1846, from the pen of Reverend Matthew Hale Smith, [248] came vigorous attacks on Mann and the Board. They were pointedly accused of excluding religion, the Bible, and consequently, morality, from the common schools— thus allowing them to become "Godless schools." Heated controversy flared in both cases, more so in the latter for the unreserved fury of Smith's attack. Generally, in both instances, public sentiment and editorial opinion seemed definitely favorable to Mann

---

[246] George Combe, *Notes on the United States of North America*, Vol. III, pp. 310–11.

[247] See *The Common School Controversy; Consisting of Three Letters of the Secretary of the Board of Education, of the State of Massachusetts, in Reply to Charges Preferred Against the Board, by the Editor of the Christian Witness and by Edward A. Newton Esq. of Pittsfield, Once a Member of the Board; to Which are Added Extracts from the Daily Press, in Regard to the Controversy* (Boston, 1844).

[248] *The Bible, the Rod, and Religion, in Common Schools* (Boston, 1847).

and the Board. And in his inaugural address of 1847, Governor Briggs, an ardent Baptist, commended the work of Mann as a service that would "earn for him the lasting gratitude of the generation to which he belongs." [249]

The final group of antagonists to the Board and its secretary came from the ranks of the profession itself. The specific incident which brought about their attack was the publication of Mann's *Seventh Annual Report*. The controversy at hand revolved around the antipathy aroused by Mann's remarks concerning the degeneration of the common schools, the poor teaching which transpired there, and the necessity for broad and basic reforms. When Mann incorporated recommendations growing out of the Prussian system, it was enough to start the fires of the controversy. Thirty-one of the Boston schoolmasters organized a Principals' Association, appointed a committee to prepare a defense against his charges, and issued a report [250] which sought to "correct erroneous views and impressions" and to recapture the faith of the public in the schools of Massachusetts. [251]

The report proceeded from the assumptions that education had been progressing steadily since its inception in the early colonial period, and that it was *"never more prosperous than at the time the Board of Education was formed."* [252] Based on these assumptions, it conceived the role of the Board as *improvement,* rather than *revolution,* of the common school system. [253] The report was generally critical of Mann's recommendations concerning methods of teaching and the whole problem of discipline.

Two months after the *Remarks* of the schoolmasters appeared, Mann issued a *Reply* [254] in answer to its accusations. Although his document was sufficiently well done to enlist strong support among persons interested in the controversy, it was curiously vindictive and lacking in discretion at many points. It thus laid him open to criticism which was not long in coming. In December 1844, the Association appointed a committee to answer the *Reply,* and in a

[249] Acts and Resolves of 1847, pp. 576–78.

[250] *Remarks on the Seventh Annual Report of the Hon. Horace Mann, Secretary of the Massachusetts Board of Education* (Charles C. Little and James Brown, Boston, 1844).   [251] *Ibid.,* p. 3.   [252] *Ibid.,* p. 6.   [253] *Ibid.*

[254] Horace Mann, *Reply to the "Remarks" of Thirty-One Boston Schoolmasters on the Seventh Annual Report of the Secretary of the Massachusetts Board of Education* (Wm. B. Fowle and Nahum Capen, Boston, 1844).

short time a *Rejoinder*[255] was issued, restating, perhaps in a somewhat milder tone, many of the points taken in the original *Remarks*.
It is interesting to note that two of the original thirty-one schoolmasters had dropped out of the controversy, so that the latter report
was signed by only twenty-nine persons. In August of 1845, Mann
published his *Answer to the Rejoinder*,[256] which was the final document relating to the controversy. The results of the controversy,
rather than being detrimental to the cause of the Board, were quite
favorable in the public attention they inspired. Perhaps Professor
Hinsdale, one of Horace Mann's earlier biographers, best summed
up the general impression on the public when he stated: "The
champion of the new régime had met the champions of the old and
overthrown them in the arena of public debate." [257]

When Horace Mann resigned the secretaryship of the Board in
April 1848 (in order to take the Congressional seat of the late John
Quincy Adams), it had become an established institution in the life
of the Massachusetts public school system. In slightly more than a
decade, through his tireless efforts this agency had more than vin-
dicated itself in the eyes of the people. The Massachusetts Board
of Education was a reality in the supervisory services of the state.
It had functioned in the face of a loosely construed grant of authority so as to reassert the educational authority of the state. And although this authority by 1850 remained principally in the form
of powers delegated to the towns and districts, two of the principles
had been reasonably well enunciated: (1) that the people of the
state would control their agencies of public education, and (2) that
it was the state's duty to see to the efficiency and quality of these
institutions.

If the Board of Education was the first line of response to the
demands for better schools, the second was the establishment of
teacher training as a function of state supervision. Carter's efforts

[255] *Rejoinder to the "Reply" of the Hon. Horace Mann, Secretary of the Massachusetts Board of Education, to the "Remarks" of the Association of Boston Masters,
upon his Seventh Annual Report* (Charles C. Little and James Brown, Boston,
1845).
[256] Horace Mann, *Answer to the "Rejoinder" of Twenty-Nine Boston Schoolmasters, Part of the "Thirty-One" Who Published "Remarks" on the Seventh Annual
Report of the Secretary of the Massachusetts Board of Education* (Wm. B. Fowle
and Nahum Capen, Boston, 1845).
[257] B. A. Hinsdale, *Horace Mann and the Common School Revival in the United
States* (Charles Scribner's Sons, New York, 1898), p. 199.

to secure a normal school followed closely on the heels of his publications in 1824–25. In 1827, he presented a memorial to the legislature requesting the establishment of a seminary for the education of teachers.[258] His memorial was favorably reported on by a committee, but it missed passage in the senate by one vote.[259] During the same year, however, the people of Lancaster appropriated a section of land and the use of an academy building to aid him in carrying out his projected plans. He purchased further plant facilities, hired the necessary personnel, and started the establishment on a semi-private basis. Within a few months of its institution, though, difficulties arose out of hostility manifested by the townspeople and the growing burden of expenses which Carter was privately bearing. He was soon forced to abandon the project as a quasi-public function; but he continued to give private instruction in the principles of pedagogy for many years thereafter.

In 1830, Carter was one of the figures instrumental in organizing the American Institute of Instruction. This group was influential in pressing the legislature for the establishment of a normal school. In 1837, he made an unsuccessful attempt to secure the appropriation of one half of the surplus revenue fund for teacher training. The first report of the Board of Education at the end of the decade devoted substantial attention to the problems involved and to suggestions for the establishment of such institutions.[260] The governor endorsed the plan in his inaugural address;[261] and, finally in 1838, Edmund Dwight, a member of the Board of Education, offered to donate ten thousand dollars for such an establishment if the legislature would appropriate an equal amount.[262] On April 19, 1838, the legislature passed resolutions accepting Dwight's offer and appropriating an additional ten thousand dollars to be expended by the Board of Education for the training of teachers.[263] The Board decided to use the funds in establishing three schools for a period

[258] Barnard's American Journal of Education, Vol. V (1858), p. 415.
[259] Ibid.
[260] First Annual Report of the Board of Education (Dutton and Wentworth, Boston, 1838).
[261] "Address of His Excellency Edward Everett, to the Two Branches of the Legislature, on the Organization of the Government, for the Political Year Commencing January 3, 1838," House of Representatives, Document No. 3, 1838, p. 25.
[262] Barnard's American Journal of Education, Vol. IV (1857), pp. 1–22.
[263] Resolves of 1838, Chap. LXX.

of three years.[264] The first school was opened at Lexington on July 3 and the second at Barre on September 4, 1839.[265]

It was in March of the next year that the Committee on Education of the legislature presented its report concerning the move to abolish the Board. Part of the majority report consisted of a condemnation of the two public normal schools established by the Board. As far as the majority was concerned, the two schools presented no "peculiar or distinguishing advantages" [266] when compared with the academies and high schools which had, until the establishment of the first public normal school, been charged with the responsibility of preparing teachers. "Academies and High Schools," wrote the committee, "cost the Commonwealth nothing, and they are fully adequate, in the opinion of your Committee, to furnish a competent supply of teachers." [267] They were more than adequate, in the opinion of the committee, to carry on the work of teacher training for the community.[268]

In answer to these arguments, the minority report cited the obligations which several towns of the commonwealth had undertaken to assist in the establishment of the three schools, and proposed the following:

Whatever objection any one might have had to the establishment of the Board and the Normal Schools originally, yet since they have been created and organized, it seems but right that they should have a fair trial. Let the experiment be tried, and not broken off as soon as begun.[269]

As has been stated before, the minority report carried, and the provisions for the establishment of the normal schools were thereby continued. The third school was opened at Bridgewater on Sep-

[264] *Second Annual Report of the Board of Education. Together with the Second Annual Report of the Secretary of the Board* (Dutton and Wentworth, Boston, 1839), p. 10.

[265] *Third Annual Report of the Board of Education. Together with the Third Annual Report of the Secretary of the Board* (Dutton and Wentworth, Boston, 1840), pp. 5–6. See also *Fourth Annual Report of the Board of Education, Together with the Fourth Annual Report of the Secretary of the Board* (Dutton and Wentworth, Boston, 1841), p. 4.

[266] House of Representatives, Document No. 49, 1840, p. 9.

[267] *Ibid.*

[268] See the bill which the committee reported providing for the refunding of Dwight's money, in House of Representatives, Document No. 49, 1840, Sec. 6, p. 14.

[269] House of Representatives, Document No. 53, 1840, p. 12.

tember 10, 1840.[270] When the tentative three-year period had expired, the schools had been sufficiently successful in the eyes of the legislature to warrant continued operation—their total financial burden being assumed by the state.[271]

Finally, in connection with teacher training, brief mention must be made of the establishment of teachers' institutes. These have already been cited as one of the media through which Mann hoped to reach the teachers of the state. He saw in them a chance for professional gatherings that would have a salutary effect on school affairs in every local community. It was Edmund Dwight who again offered the initial funds—tendering one thousand dollars to enable Mann to attempt the experiment.[272] This too was so successful during its first year that the next legislature appropriated public funds to defray its complete expense; and the institutes became a permanent part of the state's educational function.[273]

By 1850, then, Massachusetts had clearly enunciated certain principles concerning common school control. Generally, it had been decided that the people would control the schools they supported; and certain institutional forms had emerged through which such control might be effectively exercised. For the most part, legal theory and practice held that ultimate responsibility for education rested with the people of the state, and the struggle clearly to establish this responsibility was one characteristic of the period. Although there had been considerable legal precedent for state control in the seventeenth and eighteenth centuries, the decentralization of rural life had rendered education largely a local affair. The conflict between state and locality for the control of education remained the essence of much early nineteenth century conflict over this issue.

The resolution of these seemingly antithetical patterns, however, was accomplished only through extensive delegation of authority from the state down to the several towns and districts. If the practical demands of life had made education a local affair, the authority of the larger community was clearly evidenced in cases where

---

[270] *Fourth Annual Report of the Board of Education,* p. 5.
[271] Acts and Resolves of 1842, Resolves, Chap. 74.
[272] *Ninth Annual Report of the Board of Education, Together with the Ninth Annual Report of the Secretary of the Board* (Boston, 1846), p. 45.
[273] Acts of 1846, Chap. 99.

inequalities and shortcomings were in evidence. Thus, the delegation of authority carried to a point at which the smaller community
remained competent to handle its responsibility. In cases where it
failed, the larger community interceded—with aid or compulsion.
Through these patterns the people were able to control, maintain,
and supervise the schools for which they had provided the support.

II

Thus far, discussion has centered in the emergence of patterns
of control in areas where public supervision emerged from the beginning as a concomitant of public support. The strengthening
and extension of such agencies, however, represented only one aspect of the movement toward community control. The other was
the struggle (1) to secure public control and supervision of private
facilities largely or totally supported by public funds; and (2) to
withdraw public support from institutions which refused to subject
themselves to public control. Though this struggle might have
been observed in many kinds of community, the cities perhaps provide the best examples of the dynamics involved. It was the city,
with its new industry and commerce, which experienced the need
for skilled personnel. And it was also the city that bred some of
the greatest social and economic inequities. Against such a background, it was the urban populations who sought to provide out of
a spirit of Christian charity for the education of their poor and
indigent young.

The agencies which arose were of two kinds: the nonchurch-
related school, usually conducted by a benevolent society; and the
church-related school, usually organized by a religious congregation. Rapidly perceiving the value of such agencies, legislatures
began to encourage their endeavors by grants of public funds. But
their sectarian, nonpublic character soon led to violent challenges
from many groups. Perhaps the best illustration of such a situation
is provided in the history of the early nineteenth century struggle
to control the rapidly growing public school system of New York
City.

The New York Act of 1795, for the encouragement of schools,
provided that in the City and County of New York funds might be
applied "for the encouragement and maintenance of the several

charity schools as of all other schools." [274] There were several schools known as "charity schools" in operation at the time, most of which were under denominational control.[275] Generally, however, such facilities were hopelessly inadequate;[276] and their principal function, perhaps, was as an indication of the pressing need for further institutions in this sphere.

The extension of educational opportunity to children not provided for by available religious or benevolent associations, came increasingly to the attention of citizens in the city; and on February 19, 1805, a meeting was called to discuss the possibility of concerted action in this direction.[277] A committee was appointed to frame a course of action; and at a second meeting a few days later, a memorial was prepared and submitted to the legislature.[278] Accordingly, an enactment was secured, designating a group of prominent citizens[279] as a body corporate under the title of "The Society for establishing a free school in the city of New-York, for the education of such poor children as do not belong to or are not provided for by any religious society." [280] The act also called for the annual election of thirteen members of the corporation as trustees, and designated the mayor, recorder, alderman, and assistants of the City of New York as ex-officio members of the corporation. The first school sponsored by the Society was opened on May 19, 1806—a school to be conducted according to the principles of Lancasterian instruction.[281]

[274] Laws of 1795, Chap. 75.

[275] See, for instance, *Laws of the State of New York* (Albany, 1807), Vol. 2, Chap. CLXXXIX. An interesting departure from denomination control was the African Free School, organized in 1787. See Charles C. Andrews, *The History of the New-York African Free-Schools, From Their Establishment in 1787, to the Present Time; Embracing a Period of More Than Forty Years: Also a Brief Account of the Successful Labors, of the New-York Manumission Society: With an Appendix* (Mahlon Day, New York, 1830).

[276] Andrews sets the average number of scholars in attendance between 1790 and 1809, when the Lancasterian system was introduced, at between forty and sixty. See *op. cit.*, p. 17.

[277] *An Account of the Free-School Society of New-York* (Collins and Co., New York, 1814), p. 3.   [278] *Ibid.*, p. 4.

[279] It is to be noted that prominent persons in public and private life, representing a wide range of religious affiliation, were included.

[280] *Laws of the State of New York* (Albany, 1806), Vol. 4, Chap. CVIII.

[281] *An Account of the Free-School Society of New-York*, p. 8. The Lancasterian, or Monitorial, system of instruction was a system by which the master taught directly several of the older children and these, in turn, taught the others—thus enabling one teacher to provide for many more children than he could normally handle.

In January 1807, the trustees, anxious to expand the now successful activities of the Society, petitioned the legislature for further public aid.[282] Their request fell on favorable ears, and on February 27 an Act for the encouragement of Free-Schools in the City of New York provided four thousand dollars for the erection of a "suitable building or buildings, for the instruction of poor children," and one thousand dollars annually "for the purposes of promoting the benevolent objects of the said corporation." [283] The act was passed, significantly, by the unanimous vote of both houses of the legislature.[284] Encouraged by continued success, the trustees of the Society obtained in April of 1808, permission to extend their facilities to "all children, who are the proper objects of a gratuitous education," rather than only those children who were not members of any religious sect. This legislation also changed the Society's name to the Free School Society, replacing its older and rather encumbering title.[285]

The next few years may be described as ones of continuing expansion and success. In November 1811, through the efforts of a new subscription drive and with the assistance of another public grant of four thousand dollars, School No. 2 was opened with accommodations for over four hundred children.[286] By this time the organization had successfully taken root as a philanthropic society, supported partially through tax funds, and controlled by a body which, though private, represented public men of all denominations.[287] Thus, the Society might well be termed a quasi-public organization at this stage of its development. In this capacity, it continued its expansion, opening a third school on May 25, 1818, and a fourth in May 1819. During the year between these two dates, there had been an average of 1,449 students in attendance;

[282] *An Account of the Free-School Society of New-York,* p. 9.
[283] Laws of 1807, Chap. XX.
[284] *An Account of the Free-School Society of New-York,* p. 10.
[285] Laws of 1808, Chap. XCIX.
[286] *An Account of the Free-School Society of New-York,* pp. 15–16. For a description of these schools and their auspices see De Witt Clinton, *An Address to the Benefactors and Friends of the Free School Society of New-York, Delivered on the Opening of that Institution, in their New and Spacious Building on the Eleventh of the Twelfth Month (December) 1809* (New York, 1810).
[287] It might well be regarded, for this fact, as *quasi-public* at this stage of its development.

and during the next year the attendance rapidly increased to 2,145.[288]

It must be noted that in these latter years, the Society was sharing with other philanthropic organizations the funds provided by the state. Legislation passed on March 12, 1813, had provided that New York City's share of the common school fund be apportioned and paid to the trustees of the Free School Society, the trustees or treasurers of the Orphan Asylum Society, the Society of the Economical School in the City of New York, the African Free School, and "such incorporated religious societies in said city as now support or hereafter shall establish charity schools within the said city, who may apply for the same."[289] The funds paid under these provisions were to be used only toward payment of teachers' salaries.[290] It was out of these provisions that the first struggle over the use of tax funds in the city arose.

In 1820, the trustees of the Bethel Baptist Church opened a school in the basement of their church for the reception of poor children of every denomination.[291] During the next year they received an appropriation from the common school fund under the provisions of the legislation of 1813.[292] In 1822, however, the trustees obtained passage of a special law granting them permission to employ any public funds remaining after teachers' salaries had been paid toward "the instruction of schoolmasters, to the erection of buildings for schools, and to all other needful purposes of a common school education, but to no other purpose whatever."[293] It was this provision that the Society saw as a potential threat to the inviolability of the school fund. Around it revolved the "Bethel Baptist Controversy."

On August 2, 1822, the trustees of the Society adopted a resolution holding that the above-mentioned legislation was "calculated to divert a large portion of the common school fund from the great

---

[288] See *Nineteenth Annual Report of the Trustees of the Free-School Society of New-York* (New-York, 1824), p. 63.

[289] Laws of 1812, Chap. LII, Sec. IV. (This Session began November 1812 and continued through April 1813.)   [290] *Ibid.*, Sec. VI.

[291] *Memorials, Presented to the Legislature in the Session of 1823, Praying the Repeal of the Section of a Law Granting Peculiar Privileges to the Trustees of the Bethel Baptist Church, in the Appropriation of the Common School Fund. Together with Introductory Observations and Facts* [Board of Trustees of the Free School Society of New-York (New York, 1823)], p. 8.

[292] *Ibid.*   [293] Laws of 1822, Chap. XXIV.

and beneficial object for which it is established, and apply the same for the promotion of private and sectarian interests." It stated that they would use every means within their power to obtain the repeal of the objectionable clause.[294] Several months later, the Board prepared a memorial to the legislature outlining the dangers they saw implicit in the legislation. Speaking of the uses of surplus funds permitted by the Act of 1822, the memorial held:

As the sum drawn from the common School Fund for each scholar, is more than is requisite to pay the salaries of teachers, on the Lancasterian plan of education, when the number of scholars is large, a very considerable surplus may remain. This surplus may, by said law, be devoted, in the opinion of your Memorialists, to the purchase of real estate, or to the erection of buildings which belong not to the public— not in fact to the poor of the City of New-York, but to the Baptist Bethel Church. In this religious society, the fee will permanently vest, and the estate and property thus created, may be sold, and the fee be conveyed to others. There is no limit to the number of Scholars which may be instructed under the direction of this Church, and the sum drawn from the commissioners of the School Fund, must conform to the returns made to them by this religious denomination. Teachers may be employed at low salaries, to increase this surplus, who are incompetent to the faithful discharge of their duty; and there is nothing to prevent the conversion of the monies drawn by the Trustees of this Church, to the education of children *who do not belong* to that poor and needy class of scholars, who should be peculiar objects of instruction in the expenditure of the School Fund in this city.[295]

On the basis of this primary argument, the Society urged the repeal of the objectionable clause. Although the question was pressed earnestly upon the legislature in the session of 1823,[296] and the Society's position was endorsed favorably in the Corporation of the City of New York,[297] no action was taken at this time.

While these proceedings were taking place, the Bethel Church had been steadily extending its educational effort. Three schools had been opened, two of which had come into conflict with the

---

[294] William Oland Bourne, *History of the Public School Society of the City of New York* (Wm. Wood and Co., New York, 1870), p. 51.

[295] *Memorials Presented to the Legislature in the Session of 1823, Praying the Repeal of the Section of a Law Granting Peculiar Privileges to the Trustees of the Bethel Baptist Church, in the Appropriation of the Common School Fund,* pp. 28–29.

[296] *Ibid.*

[297] *Ibid.,* pp. 23–25.

Society's schools.[298] But the drawing away of scholars and funds from the efforts of the Society was not the only source of conflict. Several other denominations, seeing the success of the Bethel Church, had established schools of their own, adapting them to the wants of the public by receiving children of all denominations.[299]

Viewing this development with alarm, the Society in 1824 continued with renewed vigor its efforts to limit religious societies to schools for their own congregations. The Board took action in this direction through two means: a memorial by the New York City Common Council to the legislature endorsing their position,[300] and their own memorial to this body.[301] Both requested that the original spirit of the law be restored; namely, the granting of aid to denominational charity schools teaching only the poor of their own respective faiths. The memorial of the Society was endorsed by a number of prominent religious bodies in the city.[302]

Both memorials and their endorsements were submitted to the

[298] The second school established by the Bethel Church was in the same vicinity as School No. 5 of the Society, the latter having been contemplated previous to the former (see *Nineteenth Annual Report of the Trustees of the Free-School Society in New-York*, pp. 12–13); the third school of the church was opened in the vicinity of the Society's School No. 3 (*ibid.*, p. 13). The immediate effect of the last-named conflict was the withdrawal of three hundred children from the Society's school to the Bethel school. The report, however, maintains that some returned after withdrawing.

[299] One school was opened in Grace Church; another, for females, by the Congregational Church on Chambers Street; and a third, by the Dutch Reform Church at the corner of Williams and Duane Streets. With respect to the efforts of these denominations to establish schools for the children of the poor of all sects, the Common Council included the following in their memorial to the legislature of 1824 concerning the controversial fourth section of the Act of 1813: "Your memorialists respectfully conceive, that at the passage of the section last referred to, it was not contemplated by the Legislature, that the respective religious societies provided for in the section, would engage in the business of educating poor children generally, but that, if any availed themselves of the privilege granted them, they would do so in the establishment of schools for the education of the poor of their respective congregations." (*Nineteenth Annual Report of the Trustees of the Free-School Society of New-York*, p. 42).   [300] *Ibid.*   [301] *Ibid.*, pp. 46–48.

[302] The following groups and individuals sent letters of endorsement to the Committee on Colleges, Academies, and Common Schools: Trustees of the Methodist Episcopal School; Pastor of the Baptist Church on Mulberry-Street; Pastor of the Baptist Church on Oliver-Street; President and Secretary of the Reformed Dutch Church on Market-Street; Pastor and President of the Board of Trustees of Rutgers-Street Church; Pastor and Trustees of the Bowery Presbyterian Church; Pastor and Chairman of the Board of Trustees of Central Presbyterian Church, Broome-Street; Pastor, President, and Clerk of the Board of Trustees of the Brick Presbyterian Church. See *Nineteenth Annual Report of the Trustees of the Free-School Society in New-York*, pp. 48–49.

Committee on Colleges, Academies, and Common Schools of the legislature. This group reported back a short time later, tendering along with its report a draft of a proposed bill embodying the proposals of the Society. The section of the committee's report bearing on control of tax-supported institutions by private bodies is worthy of note at this point:

It appears that the city of New-York, is the only part of the State where the School Fund is at all subject to the control of Religious Societies. This fund is considered by your committee, purely of a civil character, and therefore it never ought, in their opinion, to pass into the hands of any corporation or set of men, who are not directly amenable to the constituted civil authorities of the government, and bound to report their proceedings to the public. Your committee forbear in this place, to enter fully into this branch of the subject, but they respectfully submit whether it is not a violation of a fundamental principle of our Legislation, to allow the funds of the State, raised by a tax on the citizens, designed for civil purposes, to be subject to the control of any religious corporation.[303]

Though no action was taken by the legislature before adjournment,[304] the committee had stated clearly and forcefully the incompatibility of private control and public support. The Free School Society, a quasi-public group, was considered to be a controlling body above narrow, private, or sectarian interests; and of the contending elements it was, perhaps, the closest approximation to representative community control. Thus the committee, having examined the performance of the Society's task to date,[305] saw fit to vest such control in this body. The report did state that the memorialists had not asked for the complete exclusion of religious corporations from the fund, nor, perhaps, did they think it expedient to effect such an exclusion at that time. The principle as outlined above, though, had been clearly enunciated and adopted by this body.

When the legislature reconvened for an extra session on November 2, 1824, it passed legislation directing the Common Council to

---

[303] "Report of the Committee of the Assembly," *ibid.*, p. 51.
[304] Bourne attributes this to the nature of the questions involved, and to "the high respectability of the influence brought to bear in favor of a continuance of the privilege granted to the Bethel Schools." See *op. cit.*, p. 72.
[305] *Nineteenth Annual Report of the Trustees of the Free-School Society of New-York*, p. 51.

designate at least once every three years, the schools to participate in the school fund.[306] Final action on the question came on April 28, 1825, when the Common Council complied with this law.[307] The institutions designated were the Free School Society of New York, the Mechanics' Society, the Orphan Asylum Society, and the trustees of the African Free Schools. An amendment to include the trustees "of such incorporated religious societies in said Cities as support, or shall establish Charity Schools" was voted down 13 to 3.[308] "The grounds on which the restriction was advocated," stated the Society's report of 1842, "were, that the intention of the law of 1813, granting the church schools a portion of the funds was solely for the education of *their own poor,* never contemplating an extension of their schools that would at all interfere with those of the Free School Society, the design of which was solely the extension of *common* schools, and especially for the poor. It was considered further that the principles that had heretofore guided all legislation on this subject were infringed, and a fund designed for civil purposes, diverted to the support of religious institutions, contrary to the spirit of the acknowledged principles of our government,—which has ever left religion to be sustained by voluntary contributions, and the individual effort and patronage of its own votaries." [309] The Society felt, "After so full and mature a consideration of the subject; and the unanimous decision which designated these institutions as the channels of distribution of the school fund; the clearness of the principles on which such decision was founded . . . that the result had given strength and permanency to their institution." [310]

The reflection of this "strength and permanency" appeared in the annual report in 1825. ". . . still it is to be lamented," stated the report, "that a description of public school is wanting amongst us, where the rich and the poor may meet together; where the wall of partition, which seems now to be raised between them, may be removed." [311] A committee appointed in December of the

[306] Laws of 1824, Chap. CCLXXVI.
[307] *Minutes of the Common Council of the City of New York, 1784–1831,* Vol. XIV, p. 498.　[308] *Ibid.,* Vol. XIV, p. 499.
[309] *Thirty-Seventh Annual Report of the Trustees of the Public School Society of New-York* (New-York, 1842), p. 23.　[310] *Ibid.,* p. 24.
[311] *Twentieth Annual Report of the Trustees of the Free-School Society of New-York* (New-York, 1825), p. 7.

preceding year to report on plans for improving the system of educational organization in the city, also presented its report in January of 1825.[312] The crux of its recommendations centers in this problem of changing the nature of the Society's schools. Its basic conclusion was:

On a review of the whole subject, the conclusion to which the committee have arrived, is the proposition that the *Free School Society be changed into a Public School Society,* and that children of *all classes* be admitted into the schools, paying therefor such compensation as may be within their pecuniary ability, and that, for the extension and support of these public schools, *the whole of the common school fund* be paid annually to said Society.[313]

The Society's efforts yielded results in the legislation of January 28, 1826, changing its name to the Public School Society and embodying the following provisions:

That it shall be the duty of said society to provide, so far as their means may extend, for the education of all children in the city of New-York, not otherwise provided for, whether such children be or be not the proper objects of gratuitous education, and without regard to the religious sect or denomination to which such children or their parents may belong.

. . . That it shall be lawful for the trustees to require of the pupils received into the schools under their charge, a moderate compensation, adapted to the ability of the parents of such pupils, to be applied to the erection of school-houses, the payment of the teachers' salaries, and to the defraying of such other expenses as may be incident to the education of children:[314] . . . And provided further, . . . That no child shall be denied the benefits of the said institution, merely on the ground of inability to pay for the same, but shall at all times be freely received, and educated by the said trustees.[315]

Under this new organization, the Society continued to flourish. The report of 1831, five years after the change in the organization's character showed twenty-three schools in twelve buildings, and

[312] See *Report of a Committee of the Trustees of the Free-School Society, on the Distribution of the Common School Fund* (New York, 1825).   [313] *Ibid.,* p. 12.

[314] It is interesting to note that the charges were introduced not only to help defray expenses, but to remove the stigma of pauperism attached to attendance at gratuitous instruction. Thus the Society hoped to attract those who did not have the means for attending a private school, and who had hitherto shunned the free instruction offered. The pay plan was unsuccessful, and was abolished on February 3, 1832.   [315] Laws of 1825, Chap. 25.

6,323 pupils under instruction.[316]   The report asserted rather pointedly the Society's continuing policy on the disposal of public funds. "The Trustees," it stated, "have endeavored to keep in view the great object of the Society—the general diffusion of education, without regard to political or religious distinctions;—composed of persons of various opinions, they have permitted neither party, nor sectarian feelings to mingle in their deliberations, or influence their conclusions. Hence it may be safely inferred, arises the confidence which the community repose in the Society, and its Board of Trustees." [317]

The year 1831, however, brought to the educational scene another struggle over the disposal of tax funds and the control of the facilities which enjoyed their benefit. Early in the year, on March 7, the directors and friends of the Roman Catholic Orphan Asylum on Prince Street, feeling that the association had been unjustly discriminated against, applied to the Common Council for public support. If the Orphan Asylum Society enjoyed public support, they argued, so should their institution. On the 21st of the same month, the Methodist Charity School, convinced that they too were entitled to funds, submitted their petition to this same body.[318] Both petitions were referred to the Committee on Common Schools. Sensing a new threat to quasi-public control, similar to the challenge in 1822, the trustees of the Public School Society prepared a remonstrance and presented it to the Council on May 2.[319] Feeling the import of the situation, they also adopted on May 6 an address to the public[320] offering their reasons for opposing the request of the two religious societies. Again they stated their basic contention that the intent of the common school fund was to support schools supported and controlled by the community:

Let us now look to the language of our State Constitution. It is thereby declared, "that the proceeds of certain public lands belonging to the State, together with the Fund denominated the 'Common School Fund,'

---

[316] *Twenty-Sixth Annual Report of the Trustees of the Public School Society of New-York* (New-York, 1831), pp. 1, 4.   [317] *Ibid.*, pp. 2–3.

[318] Board of Assistants, Document No. LXXVIII, 1832, pp. 312–14.

[319] *Minutes of the Common Council of the City of New York, 1784–1831*, Vol. XIX, p. 692.

[320] *Reasons of the Trustees of the Public School Society, for their Remonstrances against the Petition of the Roman Catholic Benevolent Society, to be Admitted to a Common Participation in the School Fund* (New York, 1831).

shall be and remain a perpetual Fund, the interest of which shall be inviolably appropriated to the support of *Common Schools* throughout the State."

It is well known that our Common Schools are supported by the joint funds derived from taxes, and from the said School fund, so that no part of the money distributed by the Corporation, can be diverted from the support of Common Schools without a violation of the Constitution.

What are Common Schools?—This phrase cannot possibly mean any thing else than those Schools, which are commonly known by that name, and have been so called, because they are Common, that is, open to all. Those cannot be Common Schools which are the property of a particular Corporation, and from which all persons may be lawfully excluded, who do not belong to a particular sect.[321]

On August 3 of the same year the Board of Aldermen undertook consideration of an ordinance approved by the Board of Assistants on July 18. It merely extended the provisions of former ordinances, granting aid only to the four nonparochial institutions which had enjoyed it since 1825. The aldermen attached an amendment adding the New York Catholic Benevolent Society—the agency directing the Catholic Orphan Asylum—to the schools enjoying such aid, and returned it to the Board of Assistants.[322] The latter, after some postponement,[323] referred the whole question to the Law Committee of the Board of Assistants.[324] The Law Committee returned its report at the meeting held on September 19,[325] a report which is monumental in its definition of the role of common education.[326]

Holding that a common school, in order to be common, must be "open to all . . ." the committee argued: "If religion be taught in a school it strips it of one of the characteristics of a Common School, . . . No school can be common unless parents of all religious sects, Mohammedans and Jews, as well as Christians, can send their children to it, to receive the benefits of an education without doing violence to their religious belief." [327] In terms of this, the committee defined a common school as "a school in which nothing but the rudiments of an English education are taught to all who are

---

[321] *Ibid.*, p. 6.
[322] *Proceedings of the Board of Aldermen*, Vol. 1, pp. 255–56.
[323] *Proceedings of the Boards of Assistants*, Vol. 1, p. 154.
[324] *Ibid.*, Vol. 1, p. 160.   [325] *Ibid.*, Vol. 1, p. 178.
[326] Board of Assistants, Document No. XXI, 1831, pp. 67–79.   [327] *Ibid.*, p. 69.

admitted into it, which is open to every child that applies for admission, and into which all can be admitted without doing violence to their religious opinions, or those of their parents or guardians." [328] Holding further that the principle of separation of church and state was involved in the use of public funds for sectarian education, the report inquired:

The question is this—Can we, without violating the Constitution, appropriate any of the Public Funds to the support of those schools or institutions in which children are taught the doctrines and tenets of religious sectarianism? The Constitution of this State declares that the free exercise and enjoyment of religious professions and worship, without discrimination or preference, shall forever be allowed in this State to all mankind. This article of the Constitution recognizes not only religious toleration but perfect religious freedom so long as that freedom is exercised in a manner not inconsistent with the peace and safety of the State. Each individual in religious matters is left to pursue the bent of his own inclination, and to follow the dictates of his own conscience.

If an effort should be made to raise a fund by taxation, for the support of a particular sect or every sect of christians, it would unhesitatingly be declared an infringement of the Constitution, and a violation of our chartered rights. Your Committee, however, cannot perceive any marked difference in principle, whether a fund be raised for the support of a particular church, or whether it be raised for the support of a school in which the doctrines of that church are taught as a part of the system of education.

In the one case, an ordained and regularly constituted ministry are paid for delivering their lessons from the pulpit; and in the other, a more humble though not less useful class of teachers are paid for giving the same instruction in a different manner. Both tend to the same end, and both designedly promote the growth and extension of sectarianism. The one act will be as great a violation of the Constitutional rights and conscientious scruples of the people as the other. Jews, Christians of every denomination, Deists, and Unbelievers of every description, contribute their due portion to the School Fund, and it ought to be so distributed and disposed of, that all may participate in the benefits flowing from it, without doing violence to their consciences. It would be but a poor consolation to an individual to know that he may entertain whatever religious opinions he pleases, and attend any church he may select, and at the time be legally compelled to contribute a portion of his property to the support of a school in which religious doctrines, diametrically opposed to those he entertains, are taught. Any legisla-

[328] *Ibid.*

tion sanctioning such a principle, would meet with the decided disapprobation of this community.

So thoroughly were the founders of our State convinced that religion in every shape should be untouched by legislative acts that they urged, and procured the adoption of an article of the Constitution disqualifying Ministers of the Gospel, and Priests of every denomination, from holding any Civil or Military office, or place, within this State. The duties of a spiritual guide and religious instructor were considered as incompatible with those of a Civil or Military station. It would be a virtual violation of this article of the Constitution, to appropriate a fund purely civil in its character and object, to the support of religious schools, and would not be sanctioned by a people ardently and devotedly attached to the maintenance of Civil and Religious Liberty.

Your Committee are of the opinion, that if the two Asylums are admitted to accept a portion of the School Fund, it will open the door for the admission of every school or institution in which children are taught gratuitously, notwithstanding it may be sectarian to the fullest extent.

Methodist, Episcopalian, Baptist, and other sectarian school, must come in for a share of this fund. And the Common Council cannot stop here. If Charity Schools are founded in which the doctrine of an Owen and a Wright are taught, or in which the "Age of Reason" or the Khoran is adopted as a standard work, they will stand on the same footing as other religious schools.

Should such a course be pursued it will be a violation of the liberal principle established by the Common Council in 1825, of denying admission to all schools and institutions which were considered as sectarian. A departure from this salutary precedent will be productive of incalculable mischief. If all sectarian schools be admitted to the receipt of a portion of a fund sacredly appropriated to the support of Common Schools, it will give rise to a religious and anti-religious party, which will call into active exercise the passions and prejudices of men. A fierce and uncompromising hostility will ensue, which will pave the way for the predominance of religion in political contests. The unnatural union of Church and State will then be easily accomplished, an union destructive of human happiness, and subversive of Civil Liberty.[329]

In spite of the fact that the report of the Law Committee explicitly applied these principles to the Roman Catholic Benevolent Society, the Board of Assistants chose to disregard its admonitions. Thus it concurred with the amendment to admit the Catholic

---

[329] *Ibid.*, pp. 76–78. This splitting, ad infinitum, was also an effective answer to the Catholic argument that a school fund which was raised equally ought to be distributed equally, implying pro rata allotments to the various religious sects.

Orphan Asylum to participation in the school fund, as passed earlier by the Board of Aldermen.[330] In doing so, it is probable that both boards had chosen to admit the orphanage because of the nature of its service, rather than to modify in any way the "cardinal principles" of 1825 which had denied church schools the right to public funds.[331]

Consideration of the request of the Methodist Society came up late in 1831, and carried on well into the following year. On May 7, 1832, the Committee on Arts and Sciences of the Board of Assistants, which now held the petition of the Society, recommended the granting of funds to the Methodists.[332] No action, however, was taken on its report.[333] In the other house, the petition had also been referred to the Committee on Arts, Sciences, and Schools in 1831; and this committee, on March 12, 1832, also recommended the granting of the application.[334] On the 26th of March, the Public School Society tendered the Board a remonstrance against the granting of said funds,[335] and the matter was referred back to the committee for consideration at the following meeting.[336] At that time, the committee again urged the granting of funds to the Methodist Society. At the Board's meeting on May 7, however, the question came up for the last time. Receiving the favorable report of the Committee on Arts, Sciences, and Schools, the Board went into a Committee of the Whole, and disagreed with the report of its committee. The report of the Committee of the Whole, refusing the application of the Methodists, was finally accepted by a vote of 8 to 3.[337] With this action, the agitation over the question ceased, and the Methodist Society abandoned its claim.

The Public School Society, having again had its position affirmed by the Common Council, proceeded to expand its facilities. Through legislative action in 1834, the schools of the Manumission

---

[330] See *Proceedings of the Board of Assistants,* Vol. 1, p. 254; and *Proceedings of the Boards of Aldermen and Assistant Aldermen, and Approved by the Mayor,* Vol. 1, p. 93.

[331] See *Thirty-Seventh Annual Report of the Trustees of the Public School Society of New-York* (New-York, 1842), p. 31; and Arthur Jackson Hall, *Religious Education in the Public Schools of the State and City of New York* (University of Chicago Press, Chicago, 1914), p. 52.

[332] Board of Assistants, Document No. LXXVIII, 1832, p. 312.

[333] *Proceedings of the Board of Assistants,* Vol. 1, p. 431.

[334] *Proceedings of the Board of Aldermen,* Vol. 2, pp. 255–56.

[335] *Ibid.,* p. 292.   [336] *Ibid.*   [337] *Ibid.,* Vol. 2, pp. 435–36.

Society and its proportional share in the school fund were transferred to the Society; and the steady progress of the 30's is reflected in the statistics for 1840, which showed a total of 18,583 children on the Society's registers on May 1 of that year.[338]

In 1840, however, another controversy beset the city in the struggle over public funds. This last, and perhaps greatest, struggle in the Society's career was precipitated by the inaugural message of Governor Seward in that year. Remarking on the great number of children who were not yet enjoying the benefits of education, the governor made the following statement:

The children of foreigners, found in great numbers in our populous cities and towns, and in the vicinity of our public works, are too often deprived of the advantages of our system of public education, in consequence of prejudices arising from difference of language or religion. It ought never to be forgotten that the public welfare is as deeply concerned in their education as in that of our own children. I do not hesitate, therefore, to recommend the establishment of schools in which they may be instructed by teachers speaking the same language with themselves and professing the same faith. There would be no inequality in such a measure, since it happens from the force of circumstances, if not from choice, that the responsibilities of education are in most instances confided by us to native citizens, and occasions seldom offer for a trial of our magnanimity by committing that trust to persons differing from ourselves in the language or religion.[339]

Encouraged by the governor's message, the trustees and members of a number of the Catholic churches which maintained free schools in the city submitted to the Common Council in February applications for a portion of the school fund.[340] At the end of the same month, the trustees of the Society presented to the Common Council a remonstrance against the granting of such funds, citing much the same kind of argument as they had in the controversy of 1831.[341] They also offered in support of their position the precedents which had been established by prior actions of the Council. After the Society had communicated with the Board of Commis-

[338] *Thirty-Fifth Annual Report of the Trustees of the Public School Society, of New-York* (New-York, 1840), p. 13.

[339] *Messages from the Governor*, Vol. 3, p. 768.

[340] See "Report of the Committee on Arts and Sciences and Schools of the Board of Assistants, on the Subject of Appropriating a Portion of the School Money to Religious Societies, for the Support of Schools," New York City Board of Assistants, Document No. 80, 1840, pp. 356–62.   [341] *Ibid.*, pp. 366–76.

sioners of School Money concerning the matter, this latter group met on February 29 and also adopted a resolution holding "that schools created and directed by any particular religious society, should derive no aid from a fund designed for the common benefit of *all* the youth of this city, without religious distinction or preference." [342]

The controversy having thus been opened, adherents of both sides began to marshal their forces. During the early months of 1840, the Catholics organized an association designed to take whatever measures were deemed wise in furtherance of their claims.[343] They also established the *New York Freeman's Journal*, a weekly newspaper (the first number of which appeared on July 4, 1840) having as one major purpose the pressing of their claims on the public.[344] Several preliminary meetings were held, and on September 21, 1840, a "great and important meeting of the Catholics" at St. James Church drew up and adopted a petition to the Board of Aldermen, stating their case in applying for a share in the school fund.[345] Basically, they argued that common school education in the city had been denied to them "except on conditions with which their conscience, and, as they believe, their duty to God, did not, and does not leave them at liberty to comply." [346] The schools of the Public School Society, the petition further stated, were propounding a sectarianism as biased as that of any religious institution; for in the reading of the Protestant version of the Bible in the schools, and in the objectionable remarks directed toward Catholics in the textbooks used by the Society, the Catholics found a situation in which their rights of conscience were being "wantonly violated." This situation having become unbearable, the Catholics felt it within their rights to request, *as citizens* rather than as Catholics, a share of the school fund. "The

[342] *Ibid.*, p. 377.

[343] See reports in the *New-York Freeman's Journal, passim* (e.g., Vol. 1, No. 5, Aug. 1, 1840, p. 36, col. 3; pp. 37–38).

[344] *Ibid.*, Vol. 1, No. 1, July 4, 1840, p. 4, col. 2; p. 5, col. 2–3.

[345] *Ibid.*, Vol. 1, No. 13, Sept. 26, 1840, p. 101, col. 2.

[346] "Petition to the Honorable the Board of Aldermen of the City of New York," in *The Important and Interesting Debate, on the Claim of the Catholics to a Portion of the Common School Fund; With the Arguments of Counsel, Before the Board of Aldermen of the City of New-York, on Thursday and Friday, the 29th and 30th of October, 1840* (Second Edition, published by the proprietor of the *New-York Freeman's Journal*, New York, 1840), p. 5.

members of that Society," concluded the argument, "who have shown themselves so impressed with the importance of conveying *their* notions of 'early religious instruction' to the 'susceptible minds' of Catholic children, can have no objection that the parents of the children, and teachers in whom the parents have confidence, should do the same, provided no law is violated thereby, and no disposition evinced to bring the children of other denominations within its influence." [347]

Action by the Common Council set October 29, 1840 as the date when that body would assemble to hear the arguments of the petitioners and the remonstrants.[348] Bishop Hughes, who had now taken over the leadership of the Catholic cause, presented at length the position of his group. His arguments tended to center, with many specific examples, largely in points involving the sectarian nature of the Society's schools. Catholics, he maintained, were absolutely unable to allow their children to attend without violation of their rights of conscience.[349] Theodore Sedgwick[350] and Hiram Ketchum[351] spoke on behalf of the Society's trustees. Basing their arguments on the history and work of the Society, they founded their case on three points: (1) the Society's conception of common education as embracing only those elements of moral and religious training common to all sects and denominations; (2) the Society's efforts through expurgation to meet the justifiable objections of the Catholics to certain passages in textbooks; and (3) the inviolability of public funds from sectarian use or control. Other speakers from Protestant denominations largely supported the arguments of Sedgwick and Ketchum.[352] A committee of the Board, which had been charged with the responsibility of inquiring into the situation, tendered its report on January 11, 1841. The essence of its point of view is embodied in the concluding paragraphs of this document:

The unwillingness of the petitioners to agree to any terms which did not recognize the distinctive character of their schools as Catholic

[347] *Ibid.,* p. 6.

[348] It is interesting to note that the Methodist Episcopal Church, which had been one petitioner for funds in the controversy of 1831, was now actively opposed to the Catholic request.

[349] See *The Important and Interesting Debate, on the Claim of the Catholics . . . , op. cit.,* pp. 7–22.   [350] *Ibid.,* p. 23. (Paging becomes irregular).

[351] *Ibid.*   [352] *Ibid.*

schools, or which would exclude sectarian supervision from them entirely, was the obstacle to a compromise, which could not be overcome. However much we may lament the consequences, we are not disposed to question the right of our Catholic fellow citizens to keep their children separated from intercourse with other children, but we do not believe the Common Council would be justified in FACILITATING such an object; they have an unquestionable right to pursue such a course, if the dictates of conscience demand it of them; and they have a just claim to be sustained by the Common Council in the exercise of that right, but they cannot justly claim public *aid* to carry out such intentions, unless they can show that the public good would be promoted by it, and that such public aid can be extended to them without trespassing upon the conscientious rights of others; but if any religious society, or sect, should be allowed the exclusive right to select the books, appoint or nominate the teachers, or introduce sectarian peculiarities of any kind into a public school, the exercise of such a right, in any one particular, would very clearly constitute such school a sectarian school, and its support at the public expense would, in the opinion of the Committee, be a tresspass upon the conscientious rights of every taxpayer who disapproved of the religion inculcated by the sect to which such school might be attached; because they would be paying taxes for the support of a religion which they disapproved. Your Committee are, therefore, fully of the opinion, that the granting of the prayer of the petitioners, or conforming to the terms of the proposals submitted by the Committee who represented them, would render the school system liable to the charge of violating the rights of conscience, a charge which would be fatal to the system, because it would invalidate its just claim to public patronage.[353]

The report was adopted by a vote of 15 to 1, and the application of the Roman Catholics for a share of the school fund was thus disapproved.[354]

Having been defeated in the Common Council, the Catholic organization saw fit in the early months of 1841 to continue its efforts, now addressing its claims to the legislature.[355] Securing a number of petitions requesting revision of the school laws, the organization presented them to the legislature. Together with a remonstrance from citizens protesting any diversion of the school

---

[353] Board of Aldermen, Document No. 40, 1841, pp. 567–68. See also, for the concurrent point of view among a committee of the Assistants, Board of Assistants, 1840, Document No. 80.

[354] Board of Aldermen, Document No. 40, 1841, p. 557.

[355] *New-York Freeman's Journal and Catholic Register*, Vol. 1, No. 33, Feb. 13, 1841, p. 260, col. 1.

fund from its legitimate objects, they were referred to the Honorable John Spencer, who, in his office as secretary of state, was ex-officio superintendent of common schools.[356] On April 26, 1841, his report was read to the senate and referred to the committee on literature.[357]

Spencer's analysis of the situation stood as the initial step in the final stages of securing public control for the tax-supported schools of the city. Referring to the objection embodied in some of the memorials, to the effect that "the existing system in New-York devolves upon a private corporation the discharge of an important function of government, without a direct and immediate responsibility to the people," the secretary emphatically stated:

> However acceptable the services of such a society may have been in the first imperfect effort to establish common schools; however willing the people may have been to submit to an institution which promised immediate benefit; and however praiseworthy and successful may have been its efforts—yet it involves a principle so hostile to the whole spirit of our institutions, that it is impossible it should be long sustained, amid the increased intelligence which its own exertions have contributed to produce, especially when other and more congenial means of attaining the same objects have been pointed out, and when therefore, the necessity which called it into existence, has ceased.[358]

Together with this report, the secretary submitted a plan calling for the election of a Board of Commissioners representing the people of each ward in the city. This Board was to have full control of the public school moneys as well as the schools supported thereby. In essence it involved, with certain modifications, the extension of the school laws of the state to the city.[359]

On the 21st of May, the trustees of the Society submitted a memorial and remonstrance taking issue with the proposals of the superintendent. Basically, they saw three evils inherent in the system outlined in Spencer's report: (1) the tendency of such a board to associate itself with party politics, (2) the want of uniformity in curricular materials, and (3) incapacity to remove the deficiencies in the system cited in Spencer's report.[360] No action, however, was taken by the legislature, and the senate postponed

[356] *Journal of the Senate of the State of New-York,* 1841, pp. 147, 244.
[357] *Ibid.,* 1841, pp. 358–59.   [358] Senate, Document No. 86, 1841, p. 15.
[359] *Ibid.,* pp. 21–22.   [360] Senate, Document No. 97, 1841.

further consideration until the next January. This course allowed an election to intercede before the matter was again raised for consideration.

The interest of a great number of people was now aroused, and the school question became one of paramount interest during the election of 1841. The Catholics decided to work for the achievement of their aims through an independent organization, and to nominate a school ticket favorable to their cause. Accordingly, the candidates of both the Democratic and the Whig parties were canvassed regarding their views on the school controversy, and a ticket was nominated presenting "friends we could find already before the public, and those whom not being so prominently before the public, we have found for ourselves." [361] The *Freeman's Journal* of October 23 carried a notice of a meeting to be held three days[362] later at Carroll Hall of "THE FRIENDS OF CIVIL AND RELIGIOUS FREEDOM, in favor of extending the benefits of a Common School Education to the neglected and indigent children of this city." [363] The principal speaker at this meeting was Bishop Hughes,[364] who gave his endorsement to the candidates which the Catholic organization had selected. His remarks are significant:

We heve [sic] uniformly avoided all questions of a political character, and I have more than once expressed publicly, as I do now, my determination to retire from such meetings the moment any political question was introduced. It is not my province to mingle in politics. The course which I have pursued hitherto in this regard I shall not abandon now, and I have therefore to request that you shall not look for forms here which may be usual iu [sic] meetings of a political character, but to which I am a stranger, and which I do not desire to see introduced for the accomplishment of the object which we have in view.[365]

As a closing note of the meeting, the Bishop made the following request:

I ask then, once for all—and with the answer let the meeting close— will this meeting pledge its honor, as the representative of that oppressed portion of our community, for whom I have so often pleaded, here as well as elsewhere—will it pledge its honor that it will stand by

---

[361] *New-York Freeman's Journal and Catholic Register*, Vol. 2, No. 19, Nov. 6, 1841, p. 149, col. 3.   [362] The meeting was finally held on October 29.
[363] *Ibid.*, Vol. 2, No. 17, Oct. 23, 1841, p. 132, col. 1.
[364] *Ibid.*, Extra, Oct. 30, 1841.   [365] *Ibid.*, p. 1, col. 1.

these candidates whose names have been read, and that no man com-
posing this vast audience will ever vote for any one pledged to oppose
our just claims and incontrovertible rights? [366]

In the election which followed, ten of the thirteen candidates on
this Carroll Hall ticket were successful; but it is significant that
they included only the ten nominees of the *regular parties* to whom
the Catholics had given endorsement. Those who had been proposed by the Carroll Hall organization alone suffered defeat.[367]

The question of school reform continued to occupy the legislature when it returned for its January session. The Democratic
party had won a majority of seats in both houses, and upon them
fell the responsibility of working out a solution to the question.
Though there was much interest in the matter, it was admitted
that a great deal hinged on the manner in which Governor Seward's
almost inevitable presentation of the subject was framed. And
when the governor did present his message, the course of future
legislation was definitely foreshadowed. Largely reaffirming the
stand which Secretary Spencer had taken some months before, the
governor re-emphasized the necessity for public control of tax-
supported education.[368] Speaking of the work of the Public School
Society in this respect, he stated that their "philanthropy and
patriotism . . . and their efficiency in imparting instruction, are
cheerfully and gratefully admitted." [369] "It is only insisted," he
continued, "that the institution, after a fair and sufficient trial, has
failed to gain that broad confidence reposed in the general system
of the State, and indispensable to every scheme of universal education. No plan for that purpose can be defended, except on the
ground that public instruction is one of the responsibilities of the
government." [370] In light of this position, the governor proposed
vesting the control of the common schools in the hands of a public
agency responsible entirely to the citizenry:

I submit, therefore, with entire willingness to approve whatever adequate remedy you may propose, the expediency of restoring to the
people of the city of New York—what I am sure the people of no other

---

[366] *Ibid.*, p. 2, col. 1–2.
[367] See *Journal of the Assembly of the State of New-York*, 1842, p. 5; and *Journal
of the Senate of the State of New-York*, 1842, p. 3.
[368] *Messages from the Governors*, Vol. 3, pp. 947–51.
[369] *Ibid.*, p. 948.   [370] *Ibid.*, p. 949.

part of the State would, upon any consideration, relinquish—the education of their children. For this purpose it is only necessary to vest the control of the common schools in a board to be composed of commissioners elected by the people; which board shall apportion the school moneys among all the schools, including those now existing, which shall be organized and conducted in conformity to its general regulations and the laws of the State, in proportion of the number of pupils instructed.[371]

The sections of the governor's message dealing with this subject were submitted to the Committee on Colleges, Academies, and Common Schools, which tendered its report on February 14, 1842. The report was basically in concurrence with the position taken by the governor, and earlier by the superintendent of common schools.

In the first place, there is something exceedingly incongruous with our republican habits of thinking, in the idea of taking the children of a population, approaching half a million souls, taxing them at the same time for the support and maintenance of the schools, and when both the children and taxes are fournished, withdrawing both out of the hands of guardians and tax payers, and handing them over to the management of an irresponsible private chartered company. Such a concentration of power into mammoth machinery of any description, is odious to the feelings, and sometimes dangerous to the rights of freemen. The genius of our institutions is to distribute power where it can be done, and where it cannot, to define and restrict it. . . .

In the next place, the population of the city of New York, is by no means homogeneous; on the contrary, it is the object of education to make it so.—Any system based upon the supposition that that homogeneousness now exists, and all will therefore absolutely conform, or can be obliged to conform, assumes the end to be attained and overlooks the means of its accomplishment.

The error is the same which lies at the basis of established churches; and the failure of the public schools, however assiduous or efficient these schools may be, arises from the very cause, which prevents, in this country, the existence or toleration of an established system of religion. . . .

It is too late to argue that private chartered corporations, with extraordinary powers and privileges, are more suitable or efficient agents for public objects than the community acting under general laws. But the question is not upon the merits or defects of other institutions; it is, whether the Public School Society has or has not failed to accomplish the great object of its establishment—the universal education of the

[371] *Ibid.,* pp. 949–50.

children of the city of New York. That it has signally failed, has been shewn by the statistics of the schools; and there is, moreover, incontrovertible proof in the fact that nearly one half of the citizens of the metropolis protest against the system and demand its modification.[372]

The report of this committee was accompanied by a proposed bill setting up machinery compatible with their basic point of view.[373] The debates over the bill culminated with the passage, on April 9, 1842, of an act "To Extend to the City and County of New York the Provisions of the General Act in Relation to Common Schools." [374] This law established the first Board of Education for the City of New York, to be composed of two commissioners elected in each ward in a special school election every June. The provisions of the general school law of the state were extended to the city, and the several wards making up the city were regarded as towns under the new act. Section 13 of the act placed under the Board's jurisdiction the schools of the Public School Society and

[372] New-York Freeman's Journal and Catholic Register, Vol. 2, No. 35, Feb. 26, 1842, p. 277, col. 2.

[373] Ibid. The report and the bill were warmly supported by the Freeman's Journal. See Vol. 2, No. 34, Feb. 19, 1842, p. 268, col. 1.

[374] Laws of 1842, Chap. CL. It is interesting to note that although the Freeman's Journal endorsed the bill (Vol. 2, No. 39, Mar. 26, 1842, p. 308, col. 1) and acclaimed its passage as a vindication of "the right of the people to exercise an immediate control over the management of the education of their children" (Vol. 2, No. 42, April 16, 1842, p. 332, col. 1), its enthusiasm abated a short time thereafter. Thus, although an editorial on April 30 stated: "As to the State attempting to define a system of religious education for the common schools, we believe it to be totally impracticable, in a community so divided as ours is in religious opinions. Every class of citizens, not excepting the infidels and Jews, is secured in the enjoyment of civil and religious liberty, and it would be clearly an invasion of their rights to establish in the common schools a system of religious education opposed to their conscientious convictions, for it would exclude them from the benefits of the common schools to which they are entitled," yet it criticized the act as superficial and precipitate. "The Legislature," the editoral further stated, "have evaded the responsibility devolved on them, and by their superficial and precipitate legislation, have aggravated the evil which they were required to remove. To abolish or extirpate religion from the schools is impossible; and therefore one of two alternatives remains, either to define a system of religious education, and give it the sanction and authority of law, or to throw the whole matter wide open for the various religious denominations, Christian and Infidel, Protestant, and Romanist, to manage in their own way. The Legislature hav [sic] done neither; they have enacted a law which will be satisfactory only to THOSE WHO WILL BE DISHONEST ENOUGH TO EVADE ITS PROVISIONS, and which, if its provisions are to be fairly carried out, might be properly entitled 'An Act for the nore [sic] effectual exclusion of religion, and for the better establishment and propagation of Atheism." See New-York Freeman's Journal and Catholic Register, Vol. 2, No. 44, April 30, 1842, p. 348, col. 1–2.

of the other private organizations drawing funds under the Act of 1825. These schools were to continue under the "immediate government and management of their respective trustees, managers, and directors." Section 14 distinctly provided that no school "in which any religious sectarian doctrine or tenet shall be taught, inculcated, or practised," shall receive any portion of the school moneys provided for by the terms of the act, and made it the responsibility of the Board to enforce this provision.

Although the system of public ward schools existed for over a decade side by side with the older schools of the Public School Society,[375] the die had been cast by the Act of 1842. Toward the end of the 1840's, the Society was forced to make repeated requests to the Board for money to cover deficits. The Board, while granting them, continued to pare them down.[376] Although the Society obtained state legislation in 1851 authorizing the Board to provide them "with all necessary monies to make all proper repairs, alterations and improvements in the various school premises occupied by them," [377] it still went steadily into debt. The situation became increasingly untenable; and finally in 1853, according to an agreement between the Board and the trustees, a merger of the two systems was effected. The enactment of the legislature[378] provided for the transfer of the Society's property to the city, and the dissolution of the organization itself. However, it also provided for the selection and appointment by the Society, previous to its dissolution, of fifteen of its trustees to act as commissioners at large of the common schools and as members of the Board of Education. They were to serve during the term of office of the then existent Board. On the local level, the provisions called for the Society's appointment, for each ward in which one or more of its schools were established, of three of its members as trustees of common

[375] It is interesting to note that a number of other private schools remained within the scope of public support and under the jurisdiction of the Board as *corporate schools*. See *Report of the Committee on the Annual Apportionment of the School Moneys, Adopted by the Board of Education, March 19th, 1845, and Ordered to be filed with the Chamberlain of the City and County and Printed for the Use of the Members,* pp. 2–3.

[376] The hostility of the Board is well expressed in "The Report of the Special Committee to which was Referred a Communication from the Public School Society, in Answer to a Resolution of Inquiry Passed by the Board of Education, February 11, 1846," Document No. 3, Board of Education, January 20, 1847.

[377] Laws of 1851, Chap. 386.   [378] Laws of 1853, Chap. 301.

schools in that ward, to serve until January 1, 1855, January 1, 1856, and January 1, 1857 respectively.[379]

Thus ended the career of this quasi-public organization which had, for half a century, managed and extended the facilities of public education in the City of New York. The importance of its role in the transition from private to public control of tax-supported facilities in the City of New York cannot be questioned— nor can its effectiveness in actually establishing some kind of school system for the city as a whole. But it is evident that such a private institution, no matter what its composition or benevolent purposes, remained largely an anomaly in view of the tax support on which it thrived and of the developments in other sections of the state and nation. It seems also fitting that the initial movement for the establishment of public control should have come from a minority group which thought itself unjustly deprived, because of this private control, of the benefits which should have accrued from its tax funds. But in spite of their victory in securing the public board, evidences of Catholic dissatisfaction with the public facilities persisted. They continued to find in many of the public school texts passages which they felt derogatory to their faith. But even more fundamentally, their desire for a curriculum providing their children with an education impregnated throughout with Catholic religious teaching had not been fulfilled. And thus, it was probably the results of the controversy of 1840 that gave them the final impetus to apply themselves wholeheartedly to the establishment of their parochial school system.[380]

6. The Principle of Public Control Established

By 1850 the principle of public control of the common school had fairly well taken root throughout the Union. It may well be said that the people by then largely controlled the schools which they had instituted with public funds. As has been indicated, the movement toward establishment of this principle had involved two aspects: (1) the evolution and strengthening of community control in those areas where it developed as a concomitant of public

[379] *Ibid.*
[380] Sister Mary Agnes O'Brien, "History and Development of Catholic Secondary Education in the Archdiocese of New York" (Unpublished Ph.D. thesis, Columbia University, 1949), Chap. III.

support and (2) the assertion of public control over all institutions which enjoyed public support, together with the withdrawal of public funds from schools remaining under private auspices.

By mid-century, every state had experimented in one way or another with representative community control of publicly supported education. Indubitably, the beginnings of such control emerged out of a dual responsibility of the several localities in each state: (1) to receive, raise, and administer the public funds appropriated to education, and (2) to see to it that the schools established were maintained in a manner justifying their support. In effect, these responsibilities merely reflected the community's desire that certain of its representatives be held accountable for what public funds were expended. They were indicated in every one of the previously cited enactments permitting or compelling tax support of common schools.[381]

Over and above this local level, the control of the state over education had also been widely enunciated. Essentially, such control stemmed primarily from two sources: (1) the legal precedents of educational legislation permitting or compelling certain practices throughout the state,[382] and (2) the doctrine that the authority and supervision of the state should follow the support of the state. The symbols of this state authority emerged in a number of forms during the years from 1812 to 1850. The most important of these, perhaps, were the state superintendents of education. By 1850 a majority of the states had legislated into existence some sort of chief state school office.[383] In many cases its responsibilities

[381] See enactments cited on page 127 and Laws of Arkansas, 1842–43, "An Act to establish a system of common schools in the State of Arkansas," passed Feb. 3, 1843.

[382] Reinforced by the Tenth Amendment to the Federal Constitution.

[383] See California (Constitution of 1849, Art. IX, in Francis Newton Thorpe, op. cit., Vol. 1, p. 402); Connecticut (Acts of 1845, Chap. XLVI); Florida (Acts of 1848–49, Chap. 229); Illinois (Laws of 1825, p. 121); Indiana (The Revised Statutes of Indiana, Indianapolis, 1843, Chap. 15); Iowa (Acts of 1846, Chap. XCIX); Kentucky (Acts of 1837, Chap. 898); Louisiana (Acts of 1847, No. 225); Maine (Laws of 1846, Chap. 195); Massachusetts (Laws of 1837, Chap. CLIX); Michigan (Acts of 1835–36, p. 49); Mississippi (Laws of 1846, Chap. 2); Missouri (Laws of 1840–41, p. 142); New Hampshire (Laws of 1846, Chap. 316); New Jersey (Laws of 1846, p. 164); New York (Laws of 1821, Chap. CCXL); Ohio (Laws of 1839, Vol. XXXVIII, p. 130); Pennsylvania (Laws of 1833–34, No. 102); Rhode Island (Laws of June 1845, Appendix); Tennessee (Acts of 1835–36, Chap. XXIII); Vermont (Laws of 1845, No. 37); Wisconsin (Constitution of 1848, Sec. X, in Francis Newton Thorpe, op. cit., Vol. 7, p. 4091).

were merely the ex-officio activities of other state officers; and in virtually all they involved chiefly the collection and dissemination of information and the disbursement of state funds. The establishment of such positions, however, constituted a powerful precedent for the further extension of control at this level, and the increasing frequency of their appearance provides conclusive evidence of an ever stronger affirmation of the principle of public state control.

Within the framework of these developments, the principle of withdrawing public funds from privately controlled institutions also saw general acceptance by 1850. More often than not, this was accomplished through a gradual crystallization in the minds of the people of the meaning of the common school. Thus as more and more states, for instance, began in their constitutions inviolably to appropriate the interest from their school funds "to the support and encouragement of common schools," [384] the question of what exactly was a common school became one of crucial import. The strife which was almost universally connected with this question is well illustrated in the developments which took place in New York City. The eventual prevalence of the conception of a common school fully controlled by the community was there indicated. That this conception was broadly accepted is perhaps best illustrated by the tendency of a great many of the states during succeeding years to reaffirm the position taken in their earlier constitutional provisions; and the quarter of a century following 1850 witnessed such action on the part of a significant number of them.[385]

[384] See, for example, Connecticut (Constitution of 1818, Art. VIII, Sec. 2, in Francis Newton Thorpe, *op. cit.*, p. 545); New York (Constitution of 1821, Art. VI, Sec. 10, in Thorpe, *op. cit.*, p. 2649); Tennessee (Constitution of 1834, Art. XI, Sec. 10, in Thorpe, *op. cit.*, p. 3440); Rhode Island (Constitution of 1842, Art. 12, Sec. 2, in Thorpe, *op. cit.*, p. 3233); New Jersey (Constitution of 1844, Art. IV, Sec. VII, § 6, in Thorpe, *op. cit.*, p. 2604); Texas (Constitution of 1845, Art. X, Sec. 2, in Thorpe, *op. cit.*, p. 3564); California (Constitution of 1849, Art. IX, Sec. 2, in Thorpe, *op. cit.*, p. 402); and Kentucky (Constitution of 1850, Art. XI, Sec. 1, in Thorpe, *op. cit.*, p. 1311). See also Carl Zollman, *Church and School in the American Law* (Concordia Publishing House, St. Louis, 1918), pp. 18–19.

[385] Michigan (Constitution of 1850, Art. 4, Sec. 40, in Francis Newton Thorpe, *op. cit.*, p. 1950); Ohio (Constitution of 1851, Art. VI, Sec. 2, in Thorpe, *op. cit.*, p. 2925); Indiana (Constitution of 1851, Art. I, Sec. 6, in Thorpe, *op. cit.*, p. 1074); Massachusetts (Constitution of 1780, Art. XVIII, May 23, 1855, in Thorpe, *op. cit.*, p. 1918); Oregon (Constitution of 1857, Art. I, Sec. 5, in Thorpe, *op. cit.*, p. 2998);

Essentially, then, the control of the common school by mid-century revolved principally around three basic postulates: (1) that public education was a responsibility and function of the community, with the state as the final level of authority (subject, of course, to the general limitations of the Federal Constitution as in all realms of state authority); (2) that the state exercised its authority largely through the delegation of powers wherever desirable and possible; and (3) that control by the community followed the support by the community. Within these three propositions rested the principle of a common school controlled by the community which supports it.

7. The Fruits of Public Support and Control: the Educational Enrollment Pattern by 1850

Given the establishment of the principles of public support and control of common education, the mid-century already saw unmistakable evidence of a definite movement toward the increasing availability and use of public schools. A brief view of the educational enrollment statistics of that time is most illuminating in this respect. While any citation of the census reports of 1850 must be tempered with a knowledge of their range of probable error, they yet reveal a good over-all picture of the extent of the movement by that time. To gain such a view, then, certain figures have been organized into a table (see p. 180), in which column 1 represents the total aggregate white population of each state;[386]

Kansas (Constitution of 1859, Art. 6, Sec. 8, in Thorpe, *op. cit.*, p. 1253); Nevada (Constitution of 1864, Art. XI, Sec. 9, 10, in Thorpe, *op. cit.*, p. 2420); Nebraska (Constitution of 1867, Article on "Education," Sec. 1, in Thorpe, *op. cit.*, p. 2358); Mississippi (Constitution of 1868, Art. VIII, Sec. 9, in Thorpe, *op. cit.*, p. 2081); South Carolina (Constitution of 1868, Art. X, Sec. 5, in Thorpe, *op. cit.*, p. 3301); Arkansas (Constitution of 1868, Art. IX, Sec. 1, in Thorpe, *op. cit.*, p. 322); Illinois (Constitution of 1870, Art. VIII, § 3, in Thorpe, *op. cit.*, p. 1035); Pennsylvania (Constitution of 1873, Art. X, Sec. 2, in Thorpe, *op. cit.*, p. 3142); Alabama (Constitution of 1875, Art. XII, Sec. 8, in Thorpe, *op. cit.*, p. 177); and Missouri (Constitution of 1875, Art. XI, Sec. 11, in Thorpe, *op. cit.*, p. 2264).

[386] *Statistical View of the United States, Embracing Its Territory, Population—White, Free, Colored, and Slave—Moral and Social Condition, Industry, Property, and Revenue; the Detailed Statistics of Cities, Towns, and Counties; Being a Compendium of the Seventh Census* (J. D. B. DeBow, ed.; Washington, 1854), Table XII, p. 40.

column 2, the enrollment[387] in *all types* of educational institutions[388] in each state;[389] and column 3, the enrollment in public
educational facilities[390] in each state.[391]

Examination of these statistics reveals at least two significant
patterns. First, of the 3,644,928 individuals enrolled in all the
educational institutions of the nation, 3,354,011, or over 90 per
cent, were enrolled in some kind of public facility. This would
imply that by 1850 the publicly supported schools had already
assumed the primary burden of the formal education of the American young. While it is clearly evident that large numbers of children, especially in the South, were denied the availability of such
institutions, it seems equally obvious that the eventual availability
of education to the whole population would depend principally
on the extension of these *public* facilities. The 1860 figure of
4,955,894 for public school enrollment seems clearly indicative of
this fact.[392]

Second, the great disparities in the relations among the three
figures for the several states distinctly reveal the inevitable differences which existed in the character and rate of progress toward
common school systems. One immediately notes the relatively
greater progress of such states as Connecticut, Maine, Massachusetts, Michigan, New Hampshire, New York, and Ohio; and the
relatively slower progress of such states as Alabama, Arkansas, California, Florida, Georgia, Mississippi, South Carolina, Texas, and

[387] These figures represent the average attendance during the year as furnished by
the institutions.

[388] This would include colleges (institutions empowered to grant degrees, including
law, medical, and theological schools), "academies and other schools," and public
schools.

[389] *Statistical View of the United States, Embracing* . . . , Table CXLV (3),
pp. 142–43.

[390] This would include all schools "receiving their support in whole or in part
from taxation or public funds." It is interesting to note, regarding public schools,
that this new classification emerged out of objections to the distinction of the
1840 census reports between "scholars at public charge" and not at public charge,
since, according to DeBow, "in some of the States common schools are supported
by a public tax or by funds provided by the public *for the education of all the
children,* and therefore none of them it was said could be considered as educated
otherwise than at public charge." (See *Statistical View of the United States, Embracing* . . . , p. 140.)

[391] *Statistical View of the United States, Embracing* . . . , Table CXLV (2), p. 142.

[392] See *Statistics of the United States, Eighth Census* (Copy in New York Public
Library, Title Page mutilated), p. 506.

TABLE I

POPULATION, ENROLLMENT IN ALL TYPES OF EDUCATIONAL FACILITIES,
AND ENROLLMENT IN PUBLIC EDUCATIONAL FACILITIES, BY STATES
AND TERRITORIES OF THE UNITED STATES IN 1850

State	Total Aggregate White Population	Enrollment in All Types of Educational Facilities	Enrollment in Public Educational Facilities
Alabama	771,632	37,237	28,380
Arkansas	209,897	11,050	8,493
California	92,597	219	49
District of Columbia	51,687	4,720	2,169
Connecticut	370,792	79,003	71,269
Delaware	91,532	11,125	8,970
Florida	87,445	3,129	1,878
Georgia	906,185	43,299	32,705
Illinois	851,470	130,411	125,725
Indiana	988,416	168,754	161,500
Iowa	192,214	30,767	29,556
Kentucky	982,405	85,914	71,429
Louisiana	517,762	31,003	25,046
Maine	583,169	199,745	192,815
Maryland	183,034	45,025	33,111
Massachusetts	994,514	190,924	176,475
Michigan	397,654	112,382	110,455
Mississippi	606,326	26,236	18,476
Missouri	682,044	61,592	51,754
New Hampshire	317,976	81,237	75,643
New Jersey	489,555	88,244	77,930
New York	3,097,394	727,222	675,221
North Carolina	869,039	112,430	104,095
Ohio	1,980,329	502,826	484,153
Pennsylvania	2,311,786	440,977	413,706
Rhode Island	147,545	25,014	23,130
South Carolina	668,507	26,025	17,838
Tennessee	1,002,717	115,750	104,117
Texas	212,592	11,500	7,946
Vermont	314,120	100,785	93,457
Virginia	1,421,661	77,764	67,353
Wisconsin	305,391	61,615	58,817
Minnesota	6,077	12	—
New Mexico	61,547	40	—
Oregon	13,294	922	80
Utah	11,380	—	—
Total	23,191,876	3,644,928 *	3,354,011

* The total, according to attendance figures from the returns of individual families, is 4,089,507. See *Statistical View of the United States, Embracing* . . . , p. 144.

Virginia. One also notes that there were no states in which no progress had been effected. Such differences point clearly to the fact that the movement toward common school systems, while it assuredly had its principal roots in the period under discussion, was by no means confined to it. Perhaps it was rather more in the nature of an evolution which, though beginning essentially in the first half of the nineteenth century, proceeded at varying rates in the several states of the Union. It achieved relative consummation rather quickly in some states, more slowly in others. In still others, this evolution extended well into the twentieth century.

8. THE PATTERN OF THE COMMON ELEMENTS CURRICULUM

In order to complete the picture of response to the demands for a common school, it is also necessary to give some consideration to the movement of the curriculum in terms of the ideal conceived by the educational reformers. For, given the definite beginnings of movement toward a school common to all children, the possibility of ultimately attaining this ideal would become highly contingent on two factors: (1) whether its curriculum could sufficiently satisfy the needs of the individual and the community to justify continued support, and (2) whether it was such that no pupil was excluded through unjustifiable violation of his individual rights of conscience. It remains, then, to give brief attention to the curricular developments during the birth and infancy of the common school.

I

The curricular tradition of the colonial schools was certainly a rude one at best. Life in the rural, agrarian neighborhood was far from conducive to anything resembling intensive educational effort. The all-demanding efforts to provide the bare necessities of life left the colonial American little energy to use in the pursuit of knowledge. Even those who perceived the need for popular education envisioned but a limited formal effort which would provide only the basic tools of communication. Thus, for instance, William Manning, a Massachusetts farmer "with little in his outward life to distinguish him from the rest of the Yankee yeo-

manry,"[393] wrote in 1798 in *The Key of Libberty: "Learning &
Knowledg is assential to the preservation of Libberty & unless we
have more of it amongue us we Cannot Seporte our Libertyes
Long."*[394] But the principal source of this knowledge, according
to Manning, must be "publick newspapers," operating under "Libberty of the press."[395] The "Larning" necessary to procure this
knowledge must be provided "in the cheepest & best manner pos-
sable,"[396] namely, common schools in which children could learn
to "read write & cifer."[397] Indeed, the plan of Jefferson himself
for the more general diffusion of knowledge in Virginia had as its
cornerstone a universal system of district schools "for teaching
reading, writing, and arithmetic."[398] The principal education of
the young, in colonial society, was to come from their intercourse
with the community in which they matured—the family and the
church. Even for its most interested exponents, the school was to
provide only the basic skills required to gain knowledge from this
intercourse—reading, writing, and perhaps the rudiments of arithmetic.

It will be recalled that the original provisions for compulsory
maintenance of schools in the Massachusetts Bay Colony required
that every township of fifty householders appoint "one wthin [*sic*]
their towne to teach all such children as shall resort to him to write
& reade."[399] Such provision for education in this Calvinist community grew out of the Protestant contention that each man, being
morally responsible for the salvation of his own soul, had to be
able to read and interpret the Bible for himself. No person, ritual,
or agency was to stand between him and the "Word of God." This
contention, however, involved an implicit danger; namely, that
certain individuals might fail to arrive at the one interpretation
by which the Puritans thought man might achieve salvation. Thus
arose the necessity of indoctrinating the Calvinist creed along with
granting of the ability to read. Puritan education, then, demanded

[393] William Manning, *The Key of Libberty, Shewing the Causes why a Free
Government Has Always Failed, and a Remidy against It* (Samuel Eliot Morison,
ed.; The Manning Association, Billerica, Mass., 1922), Foreword.
[394] *Ibid.*, p. 3.   [395] *Ibid.*, p. 36.   [396] *Ibid.*, p. 35.
[397] This curriculum is implied by Manning, *ibid.*, p. 36.
[398] Thomas Jefferson, "Notes on the State of Virginia," in *The Writings of
Thomas Jefferson,* Vol. III, pp. 251–54.
[399] *Records of the Governor and Company of Massachusetts,* Vol. 2, p. 203.

this dual task of the school. The means of its fulfillment was embodied in the *New England Primer,* which was for a hundred years, beyond any other, the principal text of American schools.[400] "With it," Paul Leicester Ford has commented, "millions were taught to read, that they might read the Bible; and with it these millions were catechised unceasingly, that they might find in the Bible only what one of many priesthoods had decided that book contained." [401]

Examination of the *Primer*[402] yields proof throughout of the dual purpose of its existence. It has several pages devoted to the mechanics of reading—the alphabet, simple nonsense syllables, and then words of one, two, three, four, and five syllables.[403] These are followed by the now-famous rhyming couplets accompanied by pictures. Arranged with one for each letter of the alphabet, the couplets and pictures deal with various morally tinged statements.[404] The remainder of the volume is devoted to a variety of verse and prose selections dealing with the basic teachings of Calvinism. These sections are appropriately introduced by the statement, "Now the Child being entred in his Letters and Spelling, let him learn these and such like Sentences by Heart, whereby he will be both instructed in his Duty, and encouraged in his Learning." [405] They include such items as "The Dutiful Child's Promises," "The LORD'S Prayer," "The CREED," "The Ten Commandments," and a catechism. Children were drilled in these moral teachings beginning at an extremely early age; and according to Ford, John Trumbull, the poet, wrote autobiographically that he could say by heart the verses in the *Primer* before he was two years old.[406]

---

[400] It was supplemented by the *Hornbook,* the *Psalter,* the *Testament,* and the *Bible.* See Noah Webster to Barnard, March 10, 1840, in *American Journal of Education,* Vol. XXVI (1876), pp. 195–96.

[401] *The New-England Primer, A Reprint of the Earliest Known Edition, with Many Facsimiles and Reproductions, and an Historical Introduction* (Paul Leicester Ford, ed.; Dodd, Mead and Co., New York, 1899), p. 7. Ford has estimated that in the 150-odd years of their popularity, over 3,000,000 primers were used.

[402] In the following analysis, the representative edition of 1747 included in Ford's book is used.

[403] Even these words were tinged with a religious tone, e.g., bewitching, drunkenness, Godliness, Holiness, etc.

[404] e.g., "In Adam's fall, we sinned all" for the letter "A," etc.

[405] *The New-England Primer.*   [406] Paul Leicester Ford, *op. cit.,* p. 7.

The book enjoyed tremendous circulation during the years of its popularity. It was sold in nearly every New England bookshop, and appeared in nearly every New England home.[407] Other editions, under slightly abridged titles and forms, appeared in and out of New England,[408] and their use spread far and wide throughout the colonies.[409] The *Primer* was increasingly supplemented in the latter half of the eighteenth century by Thomas Dilworth's *A New Guide to the English Tongue,* published in England in 1740. Though this latter text contained material somewhat more secular in tone than the *Primer,* it used much the same type of content—the alphabet, a "large and useful Table of words," a "short but comprehensive *Grammar* of the *English* Tongue," and "An useful collection of *Sentences* n [*sic*] *Prose* and *Verse, Divine, Moral, and Historical.*" [410]

The teaching of reading from these materials was largely by rote and imitation, rendering a good deal of the content relatively meaningless to the pupils. "It scarcely never entered the heads of our teachers," wrote Warren Burton in *The District School As It Was,*[411] "to question us about the ideas hidden in the great, long words and spacious sentences. It is possible that they did not always discover it themselves." [412] The study of reading was considered important enough to appear in both the morning and the afternoon school exercises. Those classes who had mastered a sufficient knowledge of reading[413] also read from the Bible, particularly the New Testament. Burton noted that as far as his own educational experience had been concerned, "reverence for the

---

[407] Clifton Johnson, *Old-Time Schools and School-Books* (Macmillan, New York, 1917), p. 72.

[408] For instance, *The United States Primer, Containing, Besides Other Useful and Instructive Matter, the Assembly of Divines' and the Episcopal Catechism* (Mason, Baker, and Pratt, New York, no date).

[409] Clifton Johnson, *op. cit.,* p. 72.

[410] Thomas Dilworth, *A New Guide to the English Tongue* (Robert Cochran, Philadelphia, 1805), p. 3.

[411] Reverend Warren Burton was born in Wilton, New Hampshire, in 1800, and began attending the local district school at the age of three and a half in the summer of 1804. He attended until the winter of 1817–18, "when he had arrived at the dignity of being one of the big boys on the back seat." (p. vii) This book describing his experiences and impressions during that period was first published in 1833.

[412] Warren Burton, *The District School As It Was* (Clifton Johnson, ed.; T. Y. Crowell Co., New York, 1928), p. 54.

[413] i.e., those who were "adequate to words of more than one syllable."

sacred volume was not deepened by this constant but exceedingly careless use." [414]

About the middle of the century, spurred on somewhat by the introduction of Dilworth's *New Guide,* the study of spelling, formerly a part of reading, began to assume in some sections the stature of an independent subject. Movement in this direction was tremendously stimulated by the publication, in 1782, of a speller by Noah Webster, *The First Part of a Grammatical Institute of the English Language.* Based in some respects on Dilworth's earlier publication, Webster's book sought to institute innovations in the direction of standardized spelling practices. The speller increasingly gained widespread acceptance, and one of its first effects was to make spelling a fad. Whereas spelling had formerly been merely a secondary aspect of reading, it now became one of the primary enthusiasms of pupils and teachers alike. Thus Burton noted: "The child cares no more in his heart about the arrangement of vowels and consonants in the orthography of words, than he does how many chips lie one above another at the school-house woodpile. But he does care whether he is at the head or foot of his class; whether the money dangles from his own neck or another's. This is the secret of the interest in spelling." [415] The methods of teaching spelling, however, conformed rather closely to the patterns established for reading; and there is little doubt that an individual's place in the class spelling hierarchy was in many cases infinitely more important than the meaning of the words he spelled.[416] As with reading and spelling, so with the teaching of writing.[417] Colonial schools had no blackboards or slates, so that the instruction in writing remained largely at the level of rote copying or imitation. That there was much connection of ideas, though, is to be strongly doubted.[418]

Three years after the publication of his reader, Dilworth published *The Schoolmaster's Assistant,* a textbook in elementary arithmetic. Before its publication, no arithmetic text had been available beyond the one or two pages of numbers included in

[414] Warren Burton, *op. cit.,* p. 55.   [415] *Ibid.,* pp. 56–57.   [416] *Ibid.,* Chap. XI.
[417] The lack of practical value in writing for most children, coupled with the scarcity and high cost of paper, tended to make writing much less common than reading.   [418] Warren Burton, *op. cit.,* Chap. XIII.

some editions of the *New England Primer*. As with reading and writing, much of this material was also taught in a somewhat meaningless rote fashion. Burton reported that many of his early hours with arithmetic were spent in copying incomprehensible rules into his notebook.[419] The *Assistant*, like many of the textbooks of the time, was based largely on the catechetical plan of instruction; and it is probable that the rote method of question-and-answer teaching continued after its publication.[420] Dilworth's work held sway until the publication of American texts such as Nicolas Pike's *New and Complete System of Arithmetic*[421] in 1788, Erastus Root's *An Introduction to Arithmetic for the Use of Common Schools*[422] in 1796, and Daniel Adams' *The Scholar's Arithmetic*[423] in 1801.

The inclusion of these items in the elementary school curriculum is effectively reflected in the *Code of Regulations* adopted by the Visitors and Overseers of Schools for Middlesex County, Connecticut, in 1799:

The hours of school ought, as much as possible, to be appropriated in the following, or a similar manner, viz.:

In the morning, the Bible may be delivered to the head of each class, and by them to the scholars capable of reading decently or looking over. This reading with some short remarks, or questions, with the morning prayer, may occupy the *first half hour*. The second, may be employed in hearing the morning lessons, while the younger classes are preparing to spell and read. The third in attention to the writers. The fourth in hearing the under classes ead [*sic*] and spell. The fifth in looking over and assisting the writers and cipherers. The sixth in hearing the under classes spell and read the second time; and receiving and depositing pens, writing and reading books. . . .

In the afternoon, one half hour may be employed in spelling together, repeating grammar, rules of arithmetic, and useful tables, with a clear, and full, but soft voice, while the instructor prepares pens, writing books, &c. The second and third half hours in hearing the under classes and assisting the writers and cypherers. The fourth in

---

[419] Warren Burton, *op. cit.*, pp. 111–12.

[420] Thomas Dilworth, *The Schoolmaster's Assistant; Being a Compendium of Arithmetic Both Practical and Theoretical* (London, 1791).

[421] Nicolas Pike, *New and Complete System of Arithmetic* (John Mycall, Newbury-Port, 1788).

[422] Erastus Root, *An Introduction to Arithmetic for the Use of Common Schools* (Thomas Hubbard, Norwich, 1796).

[423] Daniel Adams, *The Scholar's Arithmetic; or, Federal Accountant* (Second Edition, Larkin, West, West, and Greenleal, Leominster, Mass., 1802).

hearing the upper classes read. The fifth to hearing the under classes read, and spell the second time. The sixth in receiving and depositing the books, &c. as above.

That the school be closed with an evening prayer, previous to which the scholars shall repeat a psalm or hymn—and also the Lord's prayer.

Saturday may be wholly employed in an orderly review of the studies of the week, excepting one hour appropriated to instruction in the first principles of religion and morality; and in repeating, together, the ten commandments. That the Catechism usually taught in schools, be divided, by the master, into four sections, one of which shall be repeated successively on each Saturday.[424]

That the curricular offerings of the New England schools were not peculiar to that section is borne out by records from other sections of the country. Thus, for instance, the South, which had tended to leave education largely in private hands, evidenced signs of similarity in those facilities which did exist. Its schools generally followed a curriculum which strongly resembled the one described above; namely, elementary instruction in reading, writing, and arithmetic as well as drill in the Ten Commandments, the Lord's Prayer, and the Catechism.[425]

Thus, the curriculum of the colonial American schools, where they existed, remained largely confined to the three R's. Though it was, perhaps, an advance in every case over a complete lack of facilities, its value was often slight. The sessions were usually short; the facilities often tragically inadequate.[426] Attendance of the scholars was irregular at best, often sporadic. And the techniques and methods of instruction were, at maximum efficiency, incapable of imparting more than a superficial acquaintance with

[424] *American Annals of Education*, Vol. VII (1837), p. 18. See also Massachusetts Law of 1789, which required towns of fifty or more families to support a school for instruction in reading, writing, orthography, the English language, arithmetic, and decent behavior.

[425] See, for instance, Philip Vickers Fithian, *Journal and Letters*, 1767–1774 (John Rogers Williams, ed.; Princeton Historical Association, Princeton, 1900), pp. 50, 52; "James Wainwright's Will" quoted in Charles L. Coon, *The Beginnings of Public Education in North Carolina, a Documentary History 1790–1840* (North Carolina Historical Association, Raleigh, 1908), pp. 2–3; and Edgar Knight, *Education in the South* (Ginn and Co., New York, 1922), pp. 41–42.

[426] For an excellent illustration of such early facilities, see the description of the school in J. Thomas Scharf, *History of Westchester County, New York, Including Morrisania, Kings Bridge, and West Farms, Which Have Been Annexed to New-York City* (L. E. Preston and Co., Philadelphia, 1886), Vol. 1, Pt. 2, p. 696.

these basic skills.[427] Yet many a pupil, by diligent application during several seasons, was able to gain reasonable proficiency in reading, writing, and ciphering. Some even passed on to the higher branches and into the professions.[428] With slight modifications at more advanced points,[429] this was the curricular tradition within which the American schools were operating at the beginning of the nineteenth century.

II

The response to efforts at making the *common elements* broad enough to encompass the knowledge necessary for citizens of a republic is characterized by a slow but steady movement toward better and more extensive coverage of skills and content areas. But it must be constantly borne in mind that there were tremendous differences among the several sections of the nation. In New England, and in many of the cities, this movement was evidenced by the gradual inclusion of new subjects in the required curriculum. In those areas which had recently instituted new school systems the curriculum more often than not closely resembled the offering of the colonial schools. And in the many areas where the forces opposed to the common school had remained victorious, the curriculum tended to remain even more rigidly within the confines of the older three R's.

The first three decades of the nineteenth century witnessed a tremendous multiplication in the number of available textbooks. In comparing the number of texts offered for sale in the years 1804 and 1832, one writer noted that the "number of Spelling Books, Reading Books, and Arithmetics, has increased nearly fourfold; of Grammars, threefold; of Geographies, sixfold; and of Histories, eightfold; while a number of works have been published in branches of study which were then unknown in our schools." [430]

[427] The monitorial system, by which the schoolmaster taught certain of the older or brighter pupils, and these in turn taught the younger, served only to aggravate the inefficiency of these techniques.

[428] Warren Burton, *op. cit., passim.*

[429] Geography, for instance, and certain other bodies of material were included first in the reading material and later as independent subjects at various places.

[430] *American Annals of Education*, Vol. II (1832), p. 378. The subjects embraced by the 1804 list were: spelling (13), reading (28), grammar (16), geography (6), arithmetic (14), bookkeeping (4), composition (1), surveying (2), history (4), logic and

The total number of texts available had increased from 93 to 407.[431] In seeking further to determine the extent of use of the various books, the same writer turned to the reports of the New York State superintendent of common schools. He discovered that of 125 different books cited by the various town commissioners, those in general use could be reduced to about 20. Of these, there were five kinds of spelling books, six of arithmetics, three of grammars, five of geographies, one dictionary, and ten kinds of reading books.[432]

This breakdown fairly well represents the movement of the curriculum in New England and some of the middle states during this period. Massachusetts, by 1850, had expanded the list of required common school subjects to include orthography, reading, writing, English grammar, geography, and arithmetic.[433] The teaching of good behavior was also enjoined. Moreover, as Horace Mann noted, these "peremptory requisitions are the *minimum*, but not the maximum. Any town may enlarge the course of studies to be pursued in its schools as much as it may choose, even to the preparation of young men for the university, or for any branch of educated labor." [434] Thus, such subjects as history and bookkeeping were included in a number of the town curricula, while vocal music was introduced into the Boston schools through the efforts

---

metaphysics (1), and moral philosophy (1). Three dictionaries were also included. The 1832 list included books on: spelling (45), reading and defining (102), arithmetic (53), grammar (48), geography (39), history (35), geometry (10), astronomy (11), surveying (5), botany (6), logic and metaphysics (3), moral philosophy (4), political science (3), bookkeeping (7), algebra (7), composition (5), chronology (2), natural philosophy (6), and chemistry (5). Ten dictionaries were now included.

[431] Francis Grund observed in his travels that this flourishing book trade, almost wholly monopolized by the eastern states, was carried on more in the "enterprising spirit of trade and commerce than in the timid scrupulousness of literature," *op. cit.*, pp. 287–88.

[432] *American Annals of Education*, Vol. II (1832), p. 378.

[433] The Law of 1647 required reading and writing (*Records of the Governor and Company of Massachusetts*, Vol. 2, p. 203). The Law of 1789 extended these to orthography, reading, writing, the English language, grammar, arithmetic, and decent behavior (Acts of 1789, Chap. XIX). The Laws of 1827 and 1839 added geography to the requirements of 1789 (Laws of 1827, Chap. CXLIII; Acts of 1839, Chap. 56). History of the United States was not required until 1857 (Acts of 1857, Chap. 206).

[434] *Eleventh Annual Report of the Board of Education, Together with the Eleventh Annual Report of the Secretary of the Board.* (Dutton and Wentworth, Boston, 1848), p. 89.

of Lowell Mason.[435] It must be assumed, however, that many of the less populated and less wealthy areas considered themselves doing well if they managed to fulfill the range of subjects prescribed by law.[436]

While this expansion was taking place in these more progressive areas, many others tended to remain within the confines of the older curriculum. Thus, for instance, the schools of Lancaster, Pennsylvania, in 1852, were teaching spelling, reading, writing, tables, and the rudiments of arithmetic and geography as the primary subjects.[437] Until the year 1849, Ohio schools were required to teach only reading, writing, and arithmetic; geography and English grammar were added in that year.[438] The pioneer schools of that state confined themselves largely to rudimentary subjects such as reading, writing, and the simplest operations in numbers; and the great mass of textbooks, published largely in the East, were far from plentiful there. In the first quarter of the century, and continuing into the second, the texts used by western schools were largely those of the Revolutionary period in the East; and books like geographies and grammars were scarce.[439] The southern schools during the ante-bellum period also tended to maintain the narrowest interpretation of the common branches; and most confined themselves to the minimum essentials of an English education—reading, writing, arithmetic, and spelling.[440] Geography, history, and grammar, which were regarded as primary

[435] *The Common School Journal,* Vol. III (1841), pp. 189–90. See also George Combe, *Notes on the United States of North America,* Vol. III, p. 203.

[436] Mention should be made here of some of the work in sewing which appeared at this time and manifested itself in the many samplers which appeared. Aside from this kind of activity, little if any manual training entered the common schools in the first half of the nineteenth century. (See Arthur B. Mays, *The Concept of Vocational Education in the Thinking of the General Educator, 1845 to 1945,* Chap. III.)

[437] *The Pennsylvania School Journal,* Vol. I (1852–1853), p. 21.

[438] The Law of 1825 specified reading, writing, arithmetic, and other necessary branches for all schools (Laws of 1824, Vol. XXIII, p. 37). In another law of 1849, English grammar and geography were sanctioned on demand of three or more householders of a district, and required as qualifications for the teaching certificate (Laws of 1848, Vol. XLVII, p. 43).

[439] Ohio Teachers Association, *A History of Education in the State of Ohio* (Published by authority of the General Assembly, Columbus, 1876), p. 89.

[440] See, for example, "A Report of the President and Directors of the Literary Fund of North Carolina on the Subject of Common Schools, November, 1838," quoted in Charles L. Coon, *The Beginnings of Public Education in North Carolina, A Documentary History 1789–1840* (Raleigh, 1908), Vol. II, pp. 826–50.

subjects in the northeastern states, were still looked upon as more advanced subjects—thus appearing principally in the academies and other higher schools.[441] When geography and history did appear in the elementary curriculum, they were used in much the same way as they had first entered in New England—as reading material, with little emphasis given to meaning.[442]

Thus, the attempts of the reformers broadly to extend the content of the common elements were moderately successful in the more populated places, and in New England where a strong educational tradition was firmly rooted. In many other sections of the nation, the principles of lag implicit in cultural diffusion were operating. Many communities were enjoying their initial experiences with schools, and thus tended to confine their efforts to modest beginnings. Others were fearful of the cost of an over-extended educational effort, and the forces of conservatism and apathy stood firm against expansion. In effect, although the beginnings of the movement toward expansion and improvement of the curriculum were definitely in evidence, the attempt to generalize them to the whole of the educational effort may well lead to a misrepresentation of the actual conditions which prevailed.

III

If the common schools moved slowly toward the broad conception of the common branches held by the reformers, the movement was evolutionary in nature, and little marked by intense conflict or bitterness. In their attempt, however, to include the moral teachings of the common elements of Christianity, the reformers encountered violent opposition from conservative religious interests and the forces allied with them. The period of the establishments

[441] See, for example, Charles L. Coon, *North Carolina Schools and Academies 1790–1840: A Documentary History* (Raleigh, 1915), *passim*.

[442] It is interesting to note the ambitious curricular program proposed in the Virginia Acts of 1845–46. The "ACT for the establishment of a district public school system" required in the district schools reading, writing, and arithmetic, and "(where it is practicable) English grammar, geography, history, (especially of the state of Virginia and of the United States,) and the elements of physical science, and such other and higher branches as the school commissioners may direct." (Acts of 1845–46, Chap. 41.) The special act of February 25, 1846, for counties whose voters had accepted tax support was much similar (Acts of 1845–46, Chap. 42). The failure of this legislation to accomplish its intended ends has already been pointed out (see p. 118 *ante*).

in America was not so distant in the early decades of the nineteenth century as to weaken the traditional ecclesiastical contention that there is no moral life divorced from a particular creed. And the idea that morality could be included in the school curriculum apart from the dogma of any sectarian doctrine was a difficult one to accept. A brief analysis of the controversies which raged in Massachusetts and New York around the acceptance of a common Christianity curriculum will serve to illustrate the dynamics of the movement which ensued.

Regarding moral instruction, the end of the eighteenth century had witnessed in Massachusetts the gradual replacement of the earlier Calvinist religious teachings with a system of ethics and morality growing out of an increasingly milder conception of the Judeo-Christian tradition. The Law of 1789 had illustrated this latter conception when it instructed all teachers of the commonwealth to exert "their best endeavours, to impress on the minds of children and youth committed to their care and instruction, the principles of piety, justice and a sacred regard to truth, love to their country, humanity and universal benevolence, sobriety, industry and frugality, chastity, moderation and temperance, and those other virtues which are the ornament of human society, and the basis upon which the republican Constitution is structured." [443] Although the popularity of the *New England Primer* had begun to wane in favor of newer material, the Bible, the Psalter, and the Testament were still used extensively in the schools. Thus, the provisions of the Law of 1789 must be regarded as requiring the broad principle of Christian teaching to a Christian community rather than as specifically excluding religious instruction in the schools.[444]

It will be remembered that the Law of 1827 went a long way toward strengthening the powers of the town school committees. Around this development arose the question of selecting the books

---

[443] Acts of 1789, Chap. XIX.

[444] Sherman M. Smith, *The Relation of the State to Religious Education in Massachusetts* (Syracuse University Book Store, Syracuse, 1926), pp. 81–82. In terms of the New England influence in the educational provisions of the land ordinances of 1785 and 1787, such provisions must be viewed within a similar framework. Thus, the "Religion, morality, and knowledge" mentioned in Article 3 of the Northwest Ordinance were probably closely related to the moral requirements mentioned in the Law of 1789.

for use in the town schools. Since there had been no specific delegation of this responsibility prior to the passage of this law, there was a feeling among some groups that the great variety of texts had created a harmful nonuniformity. Thus, it was decided to give the school committees the power to regulate the books in the schools under their jurisdiction. Against a background of the movement away from a doctrinal religious-moral base, it was decided to include a precaution to avoid an undue sectarian influence in the choice of books. The following clause was inserted in the law to this effect: "that said committee shall never direct any school books to be purchased or used, in any of the schools under their superintendence, which are calculated to favour any particular religious sect or tenet." [445] This provision, rather than hoping to exclude Christian morality from the schools, merely wrote into law the general sentiment which had come to prevail in the state by that time—that the exclusion of dogmatic theology was to the √ advantage of the school system.[446]

No particular attention was paid to this provision until the establishment of the Board of Education in 1837 and the appointment of a Unitarian as secretary.[447] At that time, however, Mann's opinions on religious teaching in the common schools[448] led the more conservative religious elements to suspect him of attempting to introduce the tenets of *his* distinctive faith into the curriculum. The first attack involving the subject arose in 1838 over the introduction of school libraries in the state. Following the lead of New York,[449] Massachusetts in 1837 passed a law authorizing school districts to raise by taxation funds for the purchase of school equipment and libraries.[450] Because of the permissive nature of the

---

[445] Laws of 1827, Chap. CXLIII, Sec. 7.

[446] The course of the framing of the provision and the rationale behind it are well stated by Samuel M. Burnside, a member of the legislature of 1827 from Worcester and apparently the shepherd of the bill in its course through the legislature. See Burnside to Mann, June 4, 1844, in *The Common School Controversy*, pp. 48–50.

[447] In the choice of the Board itself, the religious and political affiliations of the members had been of great import in their nomination. See *The Common School Controversy*, p. 27.

[448] See Horace Mann, "Means and Objects of Common School Education," in *Lectures* (Ide & Dutton, Boston, 1855), pp. 11–59; and *First Annual Report of the Secretary of the Board of Education*, Senate, Document No. 26, 1838, pp. 61–62.

[449] Laws of 1835, Chap. 80.   [450] Laws of 1837, Chap. CXLVII.

legislation, few of the school districts took advantage of the opportunity. Therefore, in 1838, Mann took steps to stimulate interest in the plan. He obtained the Board's authorization to arrange with a publisher to print two series of books for general use in the schools, "the one adapted for the use of children, the other for a maturer class of readers." [451] The various volumes were to be written by individuals of diverse religious and political convictions; and to avoid infringement of the Law of 1827 (i.e., concerning books of a sectarian character), no book was to be included which did not carry the approval of every member of the Board.[452] In view of a desire to keep certain doctrinal teachings in the curriculum, E. A. Newton, an orthodox Episcopalian member of the Board, submitted his resignation in protest against this policy.[453]

The attack itself grew out of an inquiry of Frederick A. Packard, corresponding secretary and editor of the American Sunday School Union, concerning the use of Abbot's *The Child at Home,* one of a number of books published for children by the Union in a proposed library series.[454] On March 18, 1838, Mann replied that the book contained doctrines peculiar to given sectarian faiths,[455] and therefore could not be introduced in Massachusetts.[456] He further

---

[451] *Second Annual Report of the Board of Education,* Senate, Document No. 13, 1839, pp. 19–21.

[452] *Ibid.,* pp. 20–21. It was felt, in view of the religious heterogeneity of the Board, that such a course would effectively eliminate sectarian views in the materials.

[453] *Everett Papers* (bound in the Massachusetts Historical Society), Vol. 68, July 13, 1838, and September 14, 1838, pp. 55, 100.

[454] Packard to Mann, March 7, 1838. Letter destroyed but alluded to in Mann to Packard, March 18, 1838 [correspondence bound as *Mann Papers* in the Massachusetts Historical Society Library. Also printed as Appendix A of Raymond B. Culver, *Horace Mann and Religion in the Massachusetts Public Schools* (Yale University Press, New Haven, 1929)]. For organization and purposes of the library, see *The Thirteenth Annual Report of the American Sunday-School Union* (American Sunday-School Union, Philadelphia, 1837), p. 8, and *The Fourteenth Annual Report of the American Sunday-School Union* (American Sunday-School Union, Philadelphia, 1838), pp. 17–18. Packard brought the library to the attention of the public in a series of five letters to the *New-York Observer:* Vol. XVI, No. 9, March 3, 1838, p. 36, col. 1; Vol. XVI, No. 10, March 10, 1838, p. 37, col. 4–5; Vol. XVI, No. 11, March 17, 1838, p. 44, col. 3–4; Vol. XVI, No. 12, March 24, 1838, p. 45, col. 1–2; and Vol. XVI, No. 13, March 31, 1838, p. 52, col. 1–2.

[455] Mann to Packard, March 18, 1838: "This book would be in the highest degree, offensive to the Universalists. In this State, we have about 300 towns: & there are more than one hundred *societies* of Universalists; & besides, very many of that denomination are scattered all over the State amongst other denominations."

[456] Packard differed fundamentally with Mann's interpretation of the Law of 1827. He would have the majority of each district, through the school committee,

stated that he would prefer to abandon the plan of libraries completely than to include books of that type in the program.[457]
Packard vigorously attacked Mann and the Board, first at a meeting of orthodox Congregational clergy in New Bedford, and later
in two anonymous letters in the *New-York Observer*. In both
instances, he vehemently questioned the general policies of the
Board, particularly its attitude regarding religious teaching in the
schools.[458] Neither Mann nor the Board replied to the charges.[459]

The embers kindled by the Packard controversy smoldered
more or less for the next six years, and then flared up again in
1844.[460] The immediate impetus of the revived interest was a
United States Supreme Court case involving the will of Stephen
Girard of Pennsylvania[461]—a will which bequeathed several million dollars to the establishment of a school for orphans in that
state. The provisions of the will around which the controversy
flared in Massachusetts were as follows:

. . . I enjoin and require that no ecclesiastic, missionary, or minister
of any sect whatsoever, shall ever hold or exercise any station or duty
whatever in the said college; nor shall any such person ever be admitted
for any purpose, or as a visitor, within the premises appropriated to the
purposes of the said college.

In making this restriction, I do not mean to cast any reflection upon
any sect or person whatsoever; but, as there is such a multitude of sects,
and such a diversity of opinion amongst them, I desire to keep the
tender minds of the orphans, who are to derive advantage from this

---

decide what religion would be taught in each district. Thus, in his letter in the
New-York Observer on March 18, 1838, he stated: ". . . I take it that every school
district in New England, has a right to buy this or any other library, and put it up
in the school-room for the use of school children. Neither the Legislature nor the
Board of Education can control a district in this matter, so long as the law authorizes
the raising of money for this purpose, or so long as the district may see fit in any
other lawful way to obtain possession of it. Each district, is so far, an independent
government." (p. 37, col. 5.)   [457] Mann to Packard, March 18, 1838.

[458] *New-York Observer*, Vol. XVI, No. 42, Oct. 20, 1838, p. 16, col. 2–3; and Vol. XVI,
No. 43, Oct. 27, 1838, p. 172, col. 2–3. Only these two of a series of four letters addressed to the Reverend President Humphrey of Amherst College were published.
The whole series was later published in a pamphlet entitled, "The Question, Will
the Christian Religion Be Recognized As The Basis of The System of Public Instruction In Massachusetts? Discussed In Four Letters to The Rev. Dr. Humphrey,
President of Amherst College" (Whipple and Damrell, Boston, 1839).

[459] *The New Englander*, Vol. 5 (1847), p. 515.

[460] See *The Common School Controversy*.

[461] Vidal *et al. v.* Girard's Executors, *U. S. Reports*, 43, Vol. II, January Term,
1844, p. 126.

bequest, free from the excitement which clashing doctrines and sectarian controversy are so apt to produce; my desire is, that all the instructors and teachers in the college shall take pains to instil into the minds of the scholars the purest principles of morality, so that, on their entrance into active life, they may, from inclination and habit, evince benevolence towards their fellow-creatures, and a love of truth, sobriety, and industry, adopting at the same time such religious tenets as their matured reason may enable them to prefer.[462]

Daniel Webster argued before the court that to teach morality without religion was tantamount to laying "the axe at the root of Christianity itself" while seeking only to lop off the branches of sectarianism.[463] E. A. Newton, the former Episcopalian Board member who had resigned during the school library controversy, asked through the columns of the *Christian Witness and Church Advocate,* an Episcopalian organ, just what was the difference between the proposals of the Girard will and the school policy of the Board and its secretary.[464] In a further elaboration of his position the next month, Newton held that a "book upon politics, morals, or religion, containing no party or sectarian views, will be apt to contain no distinct views of any kind, and will be likely to leave the mind in a state of doubt and *skepticism,* much more to be deplored than any party or sectarian bias." [465] It must be noted at this point that the point of view enunciated by Newton was held by few other than Episcopalians in the state at that time. The closest thing to support they received in the religious press came from the *Christian Reflector,* a Baptist publication which later repudiated the course of the *Witness.*[466] As the controversy drew on, it became more and more evident that Newton was seeking a reaffirmation of the older Calvinist doctrine that there could be no teaching of morality separated from religion.[467]

Mann courteously answered his charges in a letter to the editor of the *Witness,* setting forth the position of the Board as one which favored the teaching of religion but which denied the necessity of its basis in sectarian dogma.[468] The *Witness* replied that according

[462] *Ibid.,* p. 132.   [463] *The Common School Controversy,* p. 3.
[464] *Ibid.,* pp. 3–4.   [465] *Ibid.,* p. 6.   [466] *Ibid.,* pp. 6–7, 55.   [467] *Ibid.,* pp. 22–23.
[468] *Ibid.,* pp. 7–14. Mann's twofold answer to the implication of similarity between the religious aspects of Girard's proposed college and the Massachusetts school system were: (1) Girard's will forbade the clergy from exercising any duties, holding any positions, or even entering, as visitors, the premises of his college. The ad-

to Mann's definition of sectarianism, all religious teaching traditionally associated with Christianity could soon be disbarred from the schools. Mann himself, stated the editorial, was preaching sectarianism for some, in the use of the Bible itself:

Universalism, Millerism, Mormonism, and other "comeoutisms," have sprung up since, and must the liberality of our fathers be interpreted, so as to give place to heresies, which concern the very vitals of Christianity? Presently the papist will give us his interpretation of the word "sectarian," as he does in the "Catholic Herald," to the Philadelphians, "Catholics only ask liberty of Conscience." The Bible may be read in the schools; provided Catholics be not forced to read a *sectarian* version." No; readers—give not to every individual schismatic, comeouter, and infidel, unlimited use of the word "sectarian." They will employ it to rob you of the gospel of Jesus Christ, the good news, that "we who were afar off, alienated from God by wicked works, are made nigh by the blood of Christ.[469]

The arguments of the *Witness* failed to make a potent impression on other religious groups.[470] The people of Massachusetts were still far too homogeneously Protestant Christian, except in specific localities, for the almost prophetic strife predicted in these words to appear as a real or powerful threat; and both the religious and the nondenominational press generally supported Mann's position against that of Newton and the editors of the *Witness*.

The conflict flared again in 1846, in the indictment of the common schools as "Godless" by the Reverend Matthew Hale Smith.[471] Smith charged the Board had removed the spiritual basis from the common schools first, by prohibiting the Bible and all religious instruction, second, by abolishing disciplinary measures, and third, by making "common schools a counterpoise to religious instruc-

---

ministration, control, and visitation of the common schools were entrusted in many cases to committees numbering a large majority of clergymen. (2) The students at the college resided there full time. The pupils of the common schools were subject to the influence of the home and the church in the many hours when they were not in school.

[469] *The Common School Controversy*, pp. 15–16.

[470] *Boston Courier*, March 12, 30, April 15, 1844; *Westfield News Letter*, no date; *Boston Daily Advertiser*, April 8, 1844; *Observer* of Salem, April 13, 1844; *Bay State Democrat*, April 3, May 20, 1844; *Evening Gazette*, April 13, 1844; *National Ægis*, April 3, and May 29, 1844; *New England Puritan*, June 7, 1844; and *Trumpet or Universalist Magazine*, April 1844. (See *The Common School Controversy*, pp. 32–55.)

[471] *The Bible, the Rod, and Religion in Common Schools* (Redding & Co., Boston, 1847).

tion at home in Sabbath schools." [472]   Mann replied that "The whole influence of the Board of Education, from the day of its organization to the present time, has been to promote and encourage, and, whenever they have had any power, as in the case of the Normal Schools, to *direct* the daily use of the Bible in school." [473] This encouragement, coupled with its advocacy of religious instruction in the schools "to the extremest verge to which it can be carried without invading those rights of conscience which are established by the laws of God, and guarantied to us by the Constitution of the State," [474] was Mann's answer to Smith's charge that a secular school was corrupting society to its very core. To Smith's charge that the schools were excluding as sectarian, truths "which *nine-tenths of professed Christians of all names believe,*" [475] Mann replied that "every tyro in ecclesiastical history knows that every persecution from the time of Constantine to St. Bartholomew's and the fires of Smithfield, originated, proceeded, and was justified on the ground that *a few dissenters,* or a *minority,* had no rights." [476] The essence of Mann's position is, perhaps, embodied in one section of the *Sequel* to the correspondence which he published himself—a selection which points clearly his fears surrounding the overwhelming power of religious conflict to destroy the effectiveness of the schools:

I leave you for a moment, Mr. Smith, in order to address a few considerations to those who think that *doctrinal* religion should be taught in our schools; and who would empower each town or school district to determine the *kind* of doctrine to be taught. It is easy to see that the experiment would not stop with having half a dozen conflicting creeds taught by authority of law, in the different schools of the same town or vicinity. Majorities will change in the same place. One sect may have the ascendency, to-day; another, tomorrow. This year, there will be three Persons in the Godhead; next year, but One; and the third year, the Trinity will be restored, to hold its precarious sovereignty, until it shall be again dethroned by the worms of the dust it has made. This year, the everlasting fires of hell will burn, to terrify the impenitent; next year, and without any repentance, its eternal flames will be extinguished,—to be rekindled forever, or to be

---

[472] *Ibid.,* p. 11.   [473] *Ibid.,* p. 24.   [474] *Ibid.,* p. 33.   [475] *Ibid.,* p. 11.
[476] *Sequel to the So Called Correspondence Between the Rev. M. H. Smith and Horace Mann, Surreptitiously Published by Mr. Smith; Containing a Letter from Mr. Mann, Suppressed by Mr. Smith, with the Reply Therein Promised* (William B. Fowle, Boston, 1847), p. 46.

quenched forever, as it may be decided at annual town meetings. This year, under Congregational rule, the Rev. Mr. So and So, and the Rev. Dr. So and So, will be on the committee; but next year, these Reverends and Reverend Doctors will be plain Misters,—never having had apostolical consecration from the Bishop. This year, the ordinance of baptism is inefficacious without immersion; next year one drop of water will be as good as forty fathoms. Children attending the district school will be taught one way; going from the district school to the town high school, they will be taught another way. In controversies involving such momentous interests, the fiercest party spirit will rage, and all the contemplations of heaven be poisoned by the passions of earth. Will not town lines and school district lines be altered, to restore an unsuccessful, or to defeat a successful party? Will not fiery zealots move from place to place, to turn the theological scale, as, it is said, is sometimes now done, to turn a political one? And will not the godless make a merchandise of religion by being bribed to do the same thing? Can aught be conceived more deplorable, more fatal to the interests of the young than this? Such strifes and persecutions on the question of total depravity, as to make all men depraved at any rate; and such contests about the nature and the number of Persons in the Godhead in heaven, as to make little children atheists upon earth.

If the question, "What theology shall be taught in school?" is to be decided by districts or towns, then all the prudential and the superintending school committees must be chosen with express reference to their faith; the creed of every candidate for teaching must be investigated; and when litigations arise,—and such a system will breed them in swarms,—an ecclesiastical tribunal,—some Star Chamber, or High Commission Court, must be created to decide them. If the Governor is to have power to appoint the Judges of this Spiritual Tribunal, he also must be chosen with reference to the appointments he will make, and so too must the Legislators who are to define their power, and to give them the Purse and Sword of the State, to execute their authority. . . . The establishment of the truth faith will not stop with the schoolroom. Its grasping jurisdiction will extend over all schools, over all private faith and public worship; until at last, after all our centuries of struggle and of suffering, it will come back to the inquisition, the fagot and the rack! [477]

If the struggles of sectarian doctrines were allowed to enter the common school, its function as a force promoting a sense of community would be negated. The school itself would actually be turned into an engine of division threatening to wreck the very core of community feeling and relations.

[477] *Ibid.*, pp. 40–42.

The widespread acceptance, at least by public figures, of Mann's principles was verified, to an extent, by a visitor from Europe in 1851. Impressed by the high mental caliber of New Englanders, the Honorable Edward Twisleton, formerly Chief Commissioner of the Poor Laws in Ireland, set about finding out the relationships between these laudable qualities and the system of compulsory schools free of sectarian religion. In pursuit of his task, he addressed the following questions to twelve of the most eminent citizens of Massachusetts:[478]

1. Have you reason to believe that the system of instruction adopted in the common schools of New England interferes with the special religious tenets of any particular denomination of Christians?

2. Is it within your knowledge, that, apart from the common schools, the children educated in them do practically receive instruction in the tenets of the religious denomination to which they respectively belong?

3. If they do receive such instruction, what are the agencies by which it is communicated to them?

4. In your opinion, is the system of instruction pursued in the common schools of New England indirectly favorable to the cultivation of the religious sentiments and to the promotion of morality?

5. Generally, do you approve or do you disapprove of that system; and what are the main grounds on which your approbation or disapprobation of it is founded? [479]

Generally, Twisleton's findings were: (1) that the New England system of free schools was not sectarian in its tendencies; (2) that it was not irreligious; (3) that, if not directly, it was at least indirectly religious "in the sense of being favourable to the cultivation of the religious sentiments and to the promotion of morality"; (4) that by means of Sunday schools, combined with the teaching of

[478] Hon. Daniel Webster, late secretary of state and senator from Massachusetts; Hon. Edward Everett, late American minister in England; Hon. George Bancroft, late American minister to England; Right Rev. Dr. Eastburn, Protestant bishop of Massachusetts; Hon. William Appleton, late representative from Massachusetts; Hon. R. C. Winthrop, late representative from Massachusetts; Hon. F. C. Gray, late senator from Massachusetts and author of a work on prison discipline; Hon. G. S. Hillard, late senator from Massachusetts; William H. Prescott, Esq., the historian; J. Sparks, Esq., president of Cambridge University; George Ticknor, Esq., author; and Henry W. Longfellow, Esq., the poet. Barnas Sears, secretary of the Board of Education, was examined orally by Twisleton. It is interesting to note that the public figures answering the questionnaire were all of the Protestant faith.

[479] Edward Twisleton, *Evidence as to the Religious Working of the Common School in the State of Massachusetts* (James Ridgeway, London, 1854).

parents at home and instruction from the pulpit in church, the children of the free schools were, for the most part, taught the peculiar tenets of the various religious denominations to which they respectively belonged; and (5) that the system of free schools in New England was effective in giving instruction to the children of the poorest classes, and was by dint of this fact deserving of approbation.[480]

Considering the views of these leaders, and the rather striking unanimity they displayed, one may be justified in assuming that continued demands for sectarian instruction would not have met with general support. They attest to a rather widespread acceptance, on the part of Protestant citizens, of the conception of moral instruction founded in the Bible and the common elements of Christianity. Had the population been limited to Protestants, the conception would probably have enjoyed increasingly unchallenged acceptance by the people and their leaders. But a new factor was now entering the picture. The Catholic population, which had been exceedingly small in the 1830's, was beginning to increase rapidly with the great Irish immigrations of the 1840's. From this group came an even more powerful opposition to the unjust and undemocratic elements they saw in the conception. The educational developments in New York City during this period offer a unique opportunity to view the nature and dynamics of this challenge and the results it entailed.[481]

It will be recalled that during the first two decades of the nineteenth century the Free School Society, encouraged by frequent appropriations from the legislature, rapidly became the primary public educational agency in New York City. It will also be recalled that from 1808 on, its influence was directed toward children of all denominations who were "the proper objects of gratuitous instruction." The early reports of the trustees clearly elucidate the policy of the Society in regard to moral and religious instruction. The account of its activities, which the Society published in

---

[480] *Ibid.*, pp. 5–6.

[481] The shift to the New York scene at this point does not imply that there was no Catholic opposition in Massachusetts. It rather indicates the fact that the dynamics were clearer and the issues more well defined in the New York controversy. For a good treatment of the Catholic challenge in Massachusetts, see Sherman M. Smith, *op. cit.*

1814, states that while the trustees had "studiously avoided the inculcation of the peculiar tenets of any religious society," they had also directed "that the Holy Scriptures should be read daily in the schools. . . ." [482] Furthermore, Tuesday afternoons were devoted to instruction in the catechisms of the churches to which the children respectively belonged—this instruction being carried on by "An association of more than fifty Ladies, of distinguished consideration in society, and belonging to the different religious denominations in the city. . . ." [483] On Sunday mornings the children were also assembled to proceed under the care of a monitor to the churches of their respective denominations.[484] Later reports continue to speak of the "common elements" curriculum, but fail to note the continuance of the extracurricular religious training. Thus, the *Nineteenth Annual Report* mentions "That the Schools are open to the children of every denomination, and that while the leading principles of the Christian faith are taught in them, the points of collision between different sects are carefully avoided." [485]

These practices soon became the subject of controversy in the cosmopolitan city, with its increasing Catholic population. As early as 1834, John Dubois, the Roman Catholic Bishop of the Diocese of New York, submitted to the trustees of the Society a six-point program that might better "ensure the confidence of Catholick Parents" in the Society's schools.[486] Significantly included was a request "That no books shall be received in the School, but such as will have been submitted to the Bishop as free from Sectarian principles or calumnies against his Religion, and as many otherwise good books may require only that such passages should be expunged, or left out in binding that on the recommendation of the Bishop, the Board will order it to be done." [487] Though the trustees of the Society felt certain that the Bishop's requests were unconstitutional,[488] they evidenced willingness to cooperate in two ways toward a satisfactory resolution of the text-

---

[482] *An Account of the Free-School Society of New-York*, p. 16.
[483] *Ibid.*, p. 17.   [484] *Ibid.*, p. 18.
[485] *Nineteenth Annual Report of the Trustees of the Free-School Society of New-York*, p. 47.
[486] See *Minutes of the Public School Society* (ms. records at the New York Historical Society), Aug. 1, 1834.   [487] *Ibid.*   [488] *Ibid.*

book problem: first, through the appointment of a committee to confer with him,[489] and second, through a letter stating ". . . if there be in the system of the Schools, or in the Books used in them, any matter which can reasonably be objected to by any Denomination, they would gladly remove the same." [490] No reply was received to this latter communication, however, and the matter was abandoned.[491]

The growing dissatisfaction of the Roman Catholics with the Society's schools reached a climax in the school controversy of 1840. At that time, it will be recalled, the principal Catholic charge against the Society was that its schools, far from being nonsectarian, were vehemently propagating the sectarianism of Protestant Christianity. Several events of interest preceded the actual public hearings on October 29–30, 1840. At a meeting of the Society's trustees on March 24 of the same year, the vice-president reported that the Reverend Felix Varela, a Roman Catholic clergyman, had requested for his inspection a set of the reading books used in the schools.[492] The trustees passed resolutions complying with Varela's request, and assured him of their continued commitment "to remove every objection which the members of the Catholic Church may have to the books used or the studies pursued in the Public Schools." [493] Varela's reply, forwarded on April 8, cited as objectionable certain passages in the "Scripture Lessons" and the geography text.[494] The letter was read at a meeting of the trustees on May 1, and a committee of five was appointed "to examine the books in use in the Public Schools, including those in the Libraries with a view to ascertain and report whether they contain any thing derogatory [sic] to the Roman Catholic Church or any of its religious tenets, with power to communicate with such persons of that Church as may be authorized to meet them in reference to such alterations." [495] The committee early sought and obtained an interview with the Very Reverend John Power, Vicar-General of the Roman Catholic Diocese of New York. At that time the latter requested a set of the committee's school books and led the committee to understand that his communication would

[489] *Ibid.*   [490] *Ibid.*, Nov. 7, 1834.   [491] *Ibid.*, Feb. 6, 1835.
[492] *Ibid.*, March 24, 1840.   [493] *Ibid.*   [494] *Ibid.*, Sept. 25, 1840.
[495] *Ibid.*, May 1, 1840.

be forthcoming pending examination.[496] However, on July 9, Power published a letter in the *Freeman's Journal* outlining his position—a letter which offered terse but excellent insight into the Catholic objections to the public schools:

My second exception is founded on the sectarian character of the public schools. The holy scriptures are read every day, with the restriction, that no specific tenets are to be inculcated—Here, Sir, we find the great demarcating principle between the Catholic church and the Sectaries introduced *silently*. The Catholic church tells her children that they must be taught their religion by AUTHORITY—The Sects say, read the bible, judge for yourselves. The bible is read in the public schools, the children are allowed to judge for themselves. The Protestant principle is therefore acted upon, slily inculcated, and the schools are Sectarian. It may be said that the bible is introduced for the mere purpose of teaching its morality. But recollect Sir, that the morality of the bible is founded on the law of nature, and is a clearer evolution or expression of that law, and as the motive for introducing the bible into the schools is the inculcation of its morality only, a severe logic forces me to say, that the holy book is made ancillary to pure Deism.

There are libraries connected with our public schools, and it is notorious, that books, which to Catholics must be exceptionable as containing the most malevolent and foul attacks on their religion, were placed in the way of Catholic children, no doubt for the very laudable purpose of teaching them to abhor and despise that monster, called Popery. How then, Sir, can we think of sending, under these circumstances, our children to those schools, in which every artifice is resorted to in order to seduce them from their religion? [497]

The position here enunciated was closely similar to the basic reasoning of subsequent Catholic addresses and petitions during the months of August and September.[498] The committee appointed by the Society's trustees on May 1 submitted its report on September 25, 1840. The report was accompanied by a series of suggestions for deletions and revisions of the texts involved.[499] The trustees complied with these suggestions, erasing, pasting, and obliterating objectionable sections, as well as completely removing certain objectionable volumes.[500]

[496] "Report of the Committee appointed on the 1st May 1840 to examine the School books; confer with the Roman Catholic clergy, etc." *Ibid.*, Sept. 25, 1840.
[497] *New-York Freeman's Journal*, Vol. 1, No. 2, July 11, 1840, p. 12, col. 3.
[498] See *Address of the Roman Catholics to Their Fellow Citizens, of the City and State of New York* (Hugh Cassidy, New York, 1840).
[499] *Minutes of the Public School Society*, Sept. 25, 1840.
[500] *Ibid.*, Sept. 25, 1840; Nov. 6, 1840.

In the hearings before the Common Council on October 29 and 30, 1840, regarding the granting of funds to the Catholics, the above-mentioned position was also the crux of Bishop Hughes' arguments.[501] The public schools were sectarian schools, violating the rights of conscience of Catholic citizens, he maintained. And since public schools constituted on a principle of perfect religious neutrality were impossible in his conception,[502] the only means of restoring freedom of conscience to Catholics was the granting of funds. The response of the Society is adequately represented by the speech of Theodore Sedgwick before the Council.[503] Holding that the state requires its children to have some kind of education, Sedgwick examined three possibilities which the state could provide: (1) the purely secular English education, where the child is taught the basic skills and knowledge such as reading, writing, etc.; (2) moral education, teaching "those fundamental principles of morals, about which there is no dispute—at least not in this country, nor in any part of christendom"; and (3) religious instruction, consisting of the peculiar dogmas and doctrines of the various sects and denominations themselves. The state intends to give a secular and moral education, held Sedgwick, but it never intended to give religious instruction.[504] "The common schools have meant from the beginning to teach the children the great moral precepts— 'Thou shalt not steal—thou shalt not lie'—and others; but they have not intended to teach either Episcopalianism, or Methodism, Catholicism, or Unitarianism. . . ." [505] In light of this analysis,

[501] *The Important and Interesting Debate, on the Claim of the Catholics to a Portion of the Common School Fund; with the Arguments of Counsel, Before the Board of Aldermen of the City of New-York, on Thursday and Friday, the 29th and 30th of October, 1840* (Second Edition), pp. 7–16.

[502] *Address of the Roman Catholics to Their Fellow Citizens of the City of New York:* "If the public schools could have been constituted on a principle which would have secured a perfect NEUTRALITY of influence on the subject of religion, then we should have no reason to complain. But this has not been done, and we respectfully submit that it is impossible. The cold indifference with which it is required that all Religions shall be treated in those schools—the scriptures without note or comment—the selection of passages as reading lessons from Protestant and prejudiced authors, on points in which our creed is supposed to be involved—the comments of the teacher, of which the Commissioners cannot be cognizant,—the school libraries, stuffed with sectarian works against us—form against our religion a combination of influences prejudicial, and to whose action it would be criminal in us to expose our children at such an age." p. 12.

[503] *The Important and Interesting Debate, on the Claim of the Catholics . . . , op. cit.,* pp. 16–22. [504] *Ibid.,* p. 18. [505] *Ibid.*

Sedgwick noted the following points about the program of the trustees of the Society:

They have confined themselves in the instruction given in these schools to that which they believe is in conformity with the intentions of the State—a secular education—reading and writing, and the rules of arithmetic, with such instruction on the precepts of the Bible as they did suppose all persons calling themselves Christians could agree in. If this is wrong, the trustees are wrong altogether, and something else must be substituted. If a moral education is not of itself sufficient, if it is not the only proper education for our free schools, something else must be substituted. The religious, the doctrinal, the sectarian education they have hitherto left to the fireside, to the parents, to the Sunday school. They do not pretend to give it; they do not pretend by the use of the Bible to teach more than that moral code which every class of Christians, whether Catholic or Protestant, they conceived would unite to give. In these matters it is worth while to look at the experience of other countries. The same controversy that has arisen here, has arisen also in Ireland; but there—in a country torn by religious schisms . . . both Protestants and Catholics have united in a selection of extracts to be used, some from our version, some from the Douay Bible. I do not say that this could be adopted here, but I do say there is some neutral ground on which both parties can meet. . . . As to the other branch of this double-headed objection, that the books used in the schools are hostile to Catholics, and promote the Protestant interest: if they are so they ought to be expurgated; and if they cannot be satisfactorily expurgated, the books themselves ought to be abandoned and their places supplied by others. The trustees have viewed this matter in the same light—they have done all in their power to remove the Catholic objection so far as it exists. . . . They have expurgated whole passages of text from some books, and in other instances have pasted two leaves together so as to annihilate completely the objectionable passages until a new edition can be procured.—This has been done too, notwithstanding the refusal of the Catholic authorities to give the least aid. . . .[506,507]

It is evident, however, that the Catholics were demanding a reorientation far more fundamental than merely a change in text content. The latter was simply a manifestation of the more

[506] *Ibid.*, p. 22.
[507] The failure of Bishop Hughes to cooperate is noted in his correspondence with Joseph B. Collins of the Society. See Collins to Hughes, Sept. 15, 1840, and Hughes to Collins, Sept. 15, 1840, in "Report of the Committee appointed on the 1st of May 1840 to examine the School books; confer with the Roman Catholic clergy, etc.," *Minutes of the Public School Society*, Sept. 25, 1840.

basic issue—one which held that the public schools, in teaching morality through the common elements of Christianity, were actually teaching the common elements of *Protestant* Christianity. They thereby became sectarian from the Catholic point of view. In spite of an almost deistic quality inherent in Mann's conception of moral instruction, he did establish the Bible as a central figure—never realizing, as the Reverend Edward A. Newton had prophesied, that this too could be regarded as sectarian from certain religious points of view. Whatever might have been their purpose in raising this objection, the Catholics were nevertheless legitimately maintaining their rights to freedom of conscience—a concept implicit in Mann's thinking.[508] And thus, though the challenge they enunciated did not necessarily resolve itself in their peculiar solution alone, it was valid within the framework of such a conception as Mann had enunciated.

When the efforts of the Catholics resulted in the establishment of an elected Board of Education in the city, the problem was not basically alleviated. A conflict developed between the Board and the county superintendent for New York City concerning this matter of Bible reading. Exponents of extreme Protestant points of view vigorously demanded counteraction to Catholic efforts "to get the Bible out of the schools." [509] The superintendent of schools of the city, reflecting this view, actually went beyond his powers and declared two districts in forfeit of their share in the school funds for failure to have the Scriptures read in the morning.[510] A committee of the Board of Education, on the other hand, recommended that the power to choose textbooks be left strictly in the hands of the local committees. It further recommended that selections from the Bible be read both in the morning and in the afternoon—the version of the Scriptures to rest with the respective committees.[511] The superintendent was vigorous in his efforts to secure legislative

---

[508] For this bifocal concept see p. 70 *ante*.

[509] See *An Honest Appeal to Every Voter* (pamphlet published *circa* 1844, in New York Public Library), and George B. Cheever, *Right of the Bible in Our Common Schools*. The implications in such materials indicate that, from this point of view, to Protestantize was definitely one important aspect of the Americanizing role of the schools.

[510] See *Report of the Committee on the Annual Apportionment, on the Communications of the County Superintendent, Relative to the Use of the Bible in the Public Schools of the City of New York* (New York, 1844).   [511] *Ibid.*

interference. On May 7, 1844, he finally secured an amendment to the school law, holding that the Board of Education had no right to exclude the Bible from the schools or to determine which version of the Bible was to be used. Jurisdiction remained in the hands of the people of the districts.[512] Nine years later, a decision of the state superintendent held that prayers could not legitimately constitute school exercises, and that Catholic children in districts where the Bible was read as a school book were privileged to absent themselves both from Bible reading and from the exercises connected with it.[513] The point at which this latter decision violated the commitment of a school fully common to all without distinction is self-evident. The Catholics, on the other hand, having finally secured in the Board of Education a valid vehicle of representative public control, evidenced their continued dissatisfaction with the public system when they turned their efforts to the establishment of their parochial schools.[514]

Thus, in the great majority of places where the population was divided into several sects, but uniformly Protestant, the common elements of Christianity were accepted as a legitimate vehicle of moral instruction. But the beginnings were already evident of the struggle which was to come with the growth of the non-Protestant population. The Catholics, as a non-Protestant sect, had challenged under one aspect of Mann's dual commitment to moral instruction (the provision for freedom of conscience) the consistency of the other aspect (the teaching of morality through the Protestant Bible and common elements). By 1850 the reform group had not yet conceived an adequate solution.

IV

The movement toward providing an adequate education in the values of republicanism was intimately related to and bound up

[512] Laws of 1844, Chap. 320, Sec. 12.

[513] *Decision of the State Superintendent of Common Schools on the Right to Compel Catholic Children to Attend Prayers, and to Read or Commit Portions of the Bible, as School Exercises, Oct. 27, 1853.* In view of the extreme nativist-Protestant position, this decision probably represented a liberal attitude; but it is easy to see how it immediately leads to invidious distinctions among a classroom community.

[514] See Sister Mary Agnes O'Brien, "History of Catholic Secondary Education in the Archdiocese of New York" (Unpublished Ph.D. thesis, Columbia University, 1949).

with inculcation in American patriotic values. As is the case of all such developments, great emphasis was placed on the uniqueness and superiority of America—its physical features, its people, and its institutions. The republican way of life and the republican spirit were so intimately bound up with the destiny of America itself that, in the minds of educators, inculcation of one was tantamount to inculcation of the other. Thus the effort to include training in republican values can be seen in the gradual entry into the curriculum of materials stressing the geographical and historical uniqueness of the American people.

Indicative of the attempt to nurture patriotism was the attitude of textbook authors at the end of the eighteenth and the beginning of the nineteenth centuries. Typical of the sentiments of this group were those of Noah Webster, author of *A Grammatical Institute of the English Language*. The crux of Webster's attitude on patriotism was that if the citizens of the American republic were to feel as a nation, they would have to develop a body of "national prejudices"—those elements of *"political bigotry"* from which *"real allegiance"* springs, and which are "probably necessary . . . to strengthen our government." [515] Thus he sought to develop not only distinctive American textbooks, but textbooks which would also inculcate this sense of distinctiveness. In the preface of his *American Spelling Book* (Part One of the *Grammatical Institute*), he wrote:

To diffuse an uniformity and purity of language in America, to destroy the provincial prejudices that originate in the trifling differences of dialect, and produce reciprocal ridicule—to promote the interests of literature and the harmony of the United States—is the most ardent wish of the Author, and it is his highest ambition to deserve the approbation and encouragement of his countrymen. [516]

And in the preface to the Third Part of the *Grammatical Institute*, which constituted a book of reading selections for youngsters, he noted:

[515] Noah Webster, *The Revolution in France, Considered in Respect to Its Progress and Effects* (New York, 1794), p. 45.
[516] Noah Webster, *The American Spelling Book: Containing an Easy Standard of Pronunciation. Being the First Part of a Grammatical Institute of the English Language. To Which Is Added, an Appendix, Containing a Moral Catechism and a Federal Catechism* (Seventeenth Edition, Thomas and Andrews, Boston, 1798), p. ix.

In the choice of pieces, I have been attentive to the political interest of America. I consider it as a capital fault in all our schools, that the books generally used contain subjects wholly uninteresting to our youth; while the writings that marked the revolution, which are perhaps not inferior to the orations of Cicero and Demosthenes, and which are calculated to impress interesting truths upon young minds, lie neglected and forgotten. Several of those masterly addresses of Congress, written at the commencement of the late revolution, contain such noble sentiments of liberty and patriotism, that I cannot help wishing to transfuse them into the breasts of the rising generation.[517]

This commitment of Webster's was evident in almost every new American reader during the next half century. It was certainly pronounced in the popular early work of Caleb Bingham, *The American Preceptor*,[518] and was similarly prominent in the readers ✓ prepared by William Holmes McGuffey. The latter, published in the late 1830's, sold upwards of 100,000,000 copies during the next fifty years.[519] Even the staid old *New England Primer* reflected the trend in its successive editions published after the Revolutionary War.

The materials of geography and history, and the very fact that geography and history were entering the curriculum as independent studies, offer further support for this movement. The pioneer in the field of American geography textbooks was Jedidiah Morse. His geographies, published in the late eighteenth and early nineteenth centuries, were the most popular books of their kind for many years. Morse, like Webster, saw in American textbooks a vehicle for the inculcation of patriotic republican values; and he viewed the study of geography as a singular instrument for achieving this goal. Thus, he commented in the preface to his *Geography Made Easy:*

NO national government holds out to its subjects so many alluring motives to obtain an accurate knowledge of their own country, and of

[517] Noah Webster, *An American Selection of Lessons in Reading and Speaking. Calculated to Improve the Minds and Refine the Taste of Youth. To Which Are Prefixed Rules in Elocution, and Directions for Expressing the Principal Passions of the Mind. Being the Third Part of a Grammatical Institute of the English Language* (Tenth Edition, Hartford, no date), Preface.

[518] Caleb Bingham, *The American Preceptor; Being a New Selection of Lessons, for Reading and Speaking* (Evert Duyckinck, New York, 1815).

[519] An excellent monograph on the social and moral ideas in the McGuffey readers is provided by Richard D. Mosier, *Making the American Mind* (King's Crown Press, New York, 1947). See Chap. II for patterns of nationalism and patriotism.

its various interests, as that of UNITED AMERICA. By the freedom
of our elections, public honors and public offices are not confined to
any one class of men, but are offered to merit, in whatever rank it may
be found. To discharge the duties of public office with honor and
applause, the history, policy, commerce, productions, particular advantages and interests, of the several States, ought to be thoroughly
understood. It is obviously wise and prudent, then, to initiate our
youth into the knowledge of these things, and thus to form their minds
upon correct principles, and prepare them for further usefulness and
honor. There is no science better adapted to the capacities of youth,
and more apt to captivate their attention, than Geography. An acquaintance with this science, more than with any other, satisfies that
pertinent curiosity, which is the predominating feature of the youthful
mind.[520]

Further enunciating his position, he stated:

Until within a few years, we have seldom pretended to write, and
hardly to think for ourselves. We have humbly received from Great-
Britain our laws, our manners, our books, and our modes of thinking;
and our youth have been educated rather as the subjects of the British
king, than as the citizens of a free and independent nation. But the
scene is now changed. The revolution has been favorable to science
in general; particularly to that of the geography of our own country.[521]

No less potency was attached by enthusiasts to the study of history as an instrument of republican nurture. Gradually history
texts, as they emerged, began to propagate and enhance materials
concerning the events and personalities of the nation's past. A book
such as Davenport's *History of the United States,* for instance,
devoted the major portion of its space to a catechetical coverage of
American history, giving prominence to such documents as the
Declaration of Independence, the Federal Constitution, etc.[522]
Weems's biographies of national heroes circulated widely;[523] and

[520] Jedidiah Morse, *Geography Made Easy; Being an Abridgment of the American Universal Geography. To Which Are Prefixed Elements of Geography* (Thomas & Andrews, Boston, 1809), Preface.   [521] *Ibid.*

[522] Bishop Davenport, *History of the United States, Containing All the Events Necessary to Be Committed to Memory; with the Declaration of Independence, the Constitution of the United States, and a Table of Chronology, for the Use of Schools* (John J. Anderson, ed.; Uriah Hunt & Son, Philadelphia, 1850).

[523] See, for instance, Mason L. Weems, *The Life of Gen. Washington, with Curious Anecdotes, Equally Honourable to Himself, and Exemplary to His Young Country-men* (Ninth Edition, Mathew Carey, Philadelphia, 1809); and M. L. Weems, *The Life of William Penn, the Settler of Pennsylvania, the Founder of Philadelphia, and One of the First Lawgivers in the Colonies, Now United States, in 1682* (Uriah Hunt, Philadelphia, 1836).

the material in "Peter Parley's" (Samuel Goodrich) and William McGuffey's readers devoted a good deal of space to similar material.[524] The tendency to glorify the nation's past in these instances was, for all practical purposes, universal.

Inextricably bound up with the patriotic and moral values in these textbooks were the values of economic individualism.[525] A politically free individual was also an economically free individual. The laissez-faire economic system was so intimately related to the republican system that neither could well exist without the other. One of the best examples of these values in the text material of the early nineteenth century appears in an elementary text by the Reverend John McVickar of Columbia College, entitled *First Lessons in Political Economy*. Every man is the maker of his own fortune, held McVickar; all are dependent on the rigid maintenance of such principles as industry, economy, prudence, resoluteness, contentedness, and thankfulness. Thus: "If he has good health and is industrious, even the poorest boy in our country has something to trade upon; and if he be besides well educated, and have skill in any kind of work, and add to this moral habits and religious principles, so that his employers may trust him and place confidence in him, he may then be said to set out in life with a handsome capital, and certainly has as good a chance of becoming independent and respectable, and perhaps *rich*, as any man in the country. 'Every man is the maker of his own fortune.' " [526]

The remainder of the curriculum was certainly completely permeated with these above-mentioned values. Arithmetic texts universally showed the values of economic individualism in the problem situations they presented;[527] while the political values of

---

[524] Richard D. Mosier, *op. cit., passim.*

[525] See Merle Curti, *The Roots of American Loyalty*, p. 103.

[526] John McVickar, *First Lessons in Political Economy; for the Use of Schools and Families* (Seventh Edition, Saxton and Miles, New York, 1846), p. 113. Lesson XII, entitled "Of Price," is an excellent illustration of instruction in the natural laws of supply and demand. Regarding competition, McVickar wrote: "When men find that with all their labor and pains they are no better off than their lazy and thoughtless neighbors, they will soon learn to be like them, for that is the natural inclination of every one; and thus all industry will cease beyond what is necessary for the immediate wants of nature."

[527] An excellent example is Nicolas Pike, *A New and Complete System of Arithmetick Composed for the Use of the Citizens of the United States* (Fifth Edition, William S. Parker & Son, Troy, 1832). Two problems on p. 365 are as follows:
13. A gay young fellow soon got the better of 2/7 of his fortune; he then gave

patriotism were also often included.[528] Even in singing, patriotic songs figured prominently; and the Scotch traveler, George Combe, reported on several occasions that children, when requested to sing a song of their own selection, sang "I Love My Native Land the Best." [529] Thus it may be generalized that during the first half of the nineteenth century the schools definitely took on the task of inculcating the sentiments of patriotism in the young of the nation. This was to be the means of providing training in and attachment to the principles of republican government. And while political bias had appeared to the reformers as a potential danger equally as destructive as religious bias, the tendency to accentuate the nation's past, its uniqueness, and its institutions, circumvented much of the potential controversy. The role of the schools as Americanizing institutions was definitely established.[530]

V

What, then, was the effect of this curriculum on the behavior patterns of the children who experienced it? To what extent did it actually accomplish the ends envisioned by the educational reform group? Did it really train citizens to live adequately in a republican society and to exercise effectively the prerogatives of citizen-

---

£1500 for a commission, and his profusion continued till he had but £450 left, which he found to be just 6/16 of his money after he had purchased his commission: What was his fortune at first?

14. A merchant begins the world with $5000, and finds that by his distillery he clears $5000 in 6 years: by his navigation $5000 in 7½ years, and that he spends in gaming $5000 in 3 years: How long will his estate last?

[528] Pike's text also illustrates this well. Three problems on page 56 are as follows:

4. Gen. Washington was born in 1732; what was his age in 1799? . . .

6. The Massacre at Boston, by British troops, happened March 5th, 1770, and the Battle at Lexington, April 19th, 1775: How long between? . . .

7. Gen. Burgoyne and his army were captured October 17th, 1777, and Earl Cornwallis and his army, October 19th, 1781: What space of time between?

[529] George Combe, *Notes on the United States of North America*, Vol. I, p. 170.

[530] Brief note must be made here of English as a means of inculcating patriotism. The use of languages other than English as media of instruction—particularly in states like Pennsylvania and Ohio with large German populations—was a source of constant strife in the school histories of these states; and although the wishes of communities to carry on instruction in native languages were often granted in an effort to gain their needed support for school legislation, the practice was deplored by many who viewed the schools as an Americanizing institution. See, for instance, A. D. Mayo, "The Development of the Common School in the Western States from 1830 to 1865," *U. S. Commissioner of Education Report, 1898–99*, Vol. 1, p. 361.

ship? Perhaps a brief examination of its influence is apropos at this point; and the reports and memoirs of the numerous foreign travelers and visitors of the period furnish a rich source from which to draw some basic conclusions.

There is no doubt that in the states where the schools had reached their highest point of development, the level of general knowledge was raised accordingly. Tocqueville noted that every citizen in New England received the simple rudiments of knowledge, the doctrines and evidences of his religion, the history of his country, and the leading features of its Constitution. "In the states of Connecticut and Massachusetts," he remarked, "it is extremely rare to find a man imperfectly acquainted with all these things, and a person wholly ignorant of them is a sort of phenomenon." [531] Although he was fully aware that these generalizations could not be applied to the whole of the nation,[532] he saw fit to generalize on the "middling" state of knowledge in the country, whereby few were destined to brilliance, but few also, to ignorance.[533] Francis Grund noted that the subjects taught in American schools, encompassing arithmetic, geography, geometry, grammar, and reading, were better communicated than in any European school he had seen;[534] and while he saw deficiencies in history and the foreign languages, he was optimistic concerning the whole.[535] The training in republicanism, via patriotism, was so effective, according to Captain Marryat, that Americans were in imminent danger of losing all sight of "humility, good-will, and the other Christian virtues" through the inculcation of national conceit and vanity.[536] Americans were justified, he held, in bringing up their youth to love their institutions, but not to hate others. The elements of patriotism, he noted, were "drilled into the ears of the American boy, until he leaves school, when he takes a political part himself, connecting himself with some young men's society, where he spouts about tyrants, crowned heads, shades of his forefathers, blood flowing like water, independence, and glory." [537] And pos-

---

[531] Alexis de Tocqueville, *Democracy in America*, Vol. I, p. 315.
[532] *Ibid.*, p. 316.   [533] *Ibid.*, p. 52.
[534] Francis Grund, *The Americans, in Their Moral, Social, and Political Relations,* p. 128.   [535] *Ibid.*
[536] Frederick Marryat, *A Diary in America*, Vol. III, p. 294.
[537] *Ibid.*, p. 298.

sibly no one sang the glories of the republican atmosphere of the schoolroom as well as Grund when he wrote:

Who, upon entering an American school-room, and witnessing the continual exercises in reading and speaking, or listening to the subject of their discourses, and watching the behavior of the pupils towards each other and their teacher, could, for a moment, doubt his being amongst a congregation of young republicans? And who, on entering a German academy, would not be struck with the principle of authority and silence, which reflects the history of Germany for the last half dozen centuries? What difficulty has not an American teacher to maintain order amongst a dozen unruly little urchins; while a German rules over two hundred pupils in a class with all the ease and tranquillity of an Eastern monarch? . . .

The majority of the pupils of an American school will imprint their character on the institution; the personal disposition of the teacher in Germany can always be read in the behavior of his pupils. There is as little disposition on the part of American children to obey the uncontrolled will of their masters, as on the part of their fathers to submit to the mandates of kings; and it would only be necessary to conduct some doubting European politician to an American schoolroom, to convince him at once that there is no immediate prospect of transferring royalty to the shores of the New World.[538]

But if these reflections represent optimism regarding the influence of the American common schools, indications of pessimism were by no means lacking. Perhaps the most vehement of these came from the writings of George Combe, the Scotch phrenologist. Fully aware of the necessity for education in a republic,[539] Combe saw a curriculum confined to reading, writing, and arithmetic, supplemented by moral and religious training, as the effort of a dominant ruling class to perpetuate a lowly "laboring-class" patterned after the European autocracy.[540] Such an education, he held, was little different from or better than the education which the king of Austria provided his subjects.[541] His conclusions regarding the effectiveness of the moral instruction which was to make American instruction uniquely republican are worthy of note:

[538] Francis Grund, *op. cit.*, pp. 133–34. These observations on lack of respect for authority in American children are also cited by Marryat, *op. cit.*, Vol. II, Part 2, p. 90; Charles Dickens (See John Forster, *The Life of Charles Dickens*, Vol. I, p. 364); and Sir Charles Lyell, *A Second Visit to the United States of North America*, Vol. II, p. 169.

[539] George Combe, *Notes on the United States of North America*, Vol. I, pp. 161–62.

[540] *Ibid.*, pp. 162–64.   [541] *Ibid.*, pp. 162–63.

Making allowance for individual exceptions, it may be stated, that an American young man, in emerging from school, has scarcely formed a conception that he is subject to any natural laws, which he must obey in every step of his progress in life, or suffer. He has not been taught the laws of health, the laws by which the production and distribution of wealth are regulated, or the laws which determine the progress of society; nor is he trained to subject his own inclinations and will to those of any similar laws as indispensable to his well-being and success. On the contrary, he comes forth a free-born, self-willed, sanguine, confident citizen, of which he considers to be the greatest, the best, and the wisest nation on earth, and he commences his career in life guided chiefly by the inspirations of his own good pleasure.[542]

Thus Combe was forced to conclude that the schools had failed in their task of teaching "all that . . . young voters should know . . . all that the best . . . citizens would wish them to know, when they act as electors and arbitrators of the public welfare." [543]

Insight may be gained perhaps from the fact that in most places in the nation, the school still represented only an insignificant aspect of the experience of the young. While schools teaching an expanding range of subjects with ever greater systematization were now maintained for the better part of the year in New England [544] and in the cities, education in the great remaining rural areas was by no means as effective or efficient. In many states where tax-supported systems had recently been instituted, only rude beginnings were in evidence. Teachers were untrained, and the curriculum revolved around the three R's. In other states, educational systems had made little progress, remaining largely in the blueprint stage or in the imaginations of reformers. And thus, in many places, reminiscent of William Manning, the schools furnished "larning" while the experience of life yet provided "knowledge." Tocqueville noted this, and apparently acquiesced to its fundamental validity when he wrote:

It cannot be doubted that in the United States the instruction of the people powerfully contributes to the support of the democratic republic; and such must always be the case, I believe, where the instruction which enlightens the understanding is not separated from the

---

[542] *Ibid.*, Vol. I, pp. 235–36.   [543] *Ibid.*, Vol. III, p. 412. See also pp. 251–52.

[544] The reports of the various superintendents and Board secretaries indicate that a steady increase in the average number of weeks of schooling was maintained during this period.

moral education which amends the heart. But I would not exaggerate this advantage, and I am still further from thinking, as so many people do think in Europe, that men can be instantaneously made citizens by teaching them to read and write. True information is mainly derived from experience; and if the Americans had not been gradually accustomed to govern themselves, their book-learning would not help them much at the present day. . . .

The citizen of the United States does not acquire his practical science and his positive notions from books; the instruction he has acquired may have prepared him for receiving those ideas, but it did not furnish them. The American learns to know the laws by participating in the act of legislation; and he takes a lesson in the forms of government from governing. The great work of society is ever going on before his eyes, as it were, under his hands.[545]

One American writer succinctly concurrred, noting that: "As a nation, we are educated more by contact with each other, by business, by newspapers, magazines, and circulating libraries, by public meetings and conventions, by lyceums, by speeches in congress, in the state legislatures, and at political gatherings, and in various other ways, than by direct instructions imparted in the school room." [546]

In light of this, then, one may well ponder, for instance, just what proportion of the republican spirit which Grund found in the schoolroom was generated by the school itself, and what proportion was simply a reflection of the peculiar quality of the relationships maintained by the young in the family[547] and in the wider

[545] Alexis de Tocqueville, *op. cit.*, Vol. I, pp. 317–18.

[546] E. C. Wines, *Hints on a System of Popular Education*, p. 158.

[547] Marryat gives an interesting example of this relationship which bears quotation in full:

'Imagine a child of three years old in England behaving thus:—

"Johnny, my dear, come here," says his mamma.

"I won't," cries Johnny.

"You must, my love, you are all wet, and you'll catch cold."

"I won't," replies Johnny.

"Come, my sweet, and I've something for you."

"I won't."

"Oh! Mr. ——, do, pray make Johnny come in."

"Come in, Johnny," says the father.

"I won't."

"I tell you, come in directly, sir—do you hear?"

"I won't," replies the urchin, taking to his heels.

"A sturdy republican, sir," says his father to me, smiling at the boy's resolute disobedience.

community. The fruitfulness of carrying on such cogitation at too great length, however, seems questionable. Suffice it to say that the common school of 1850, in its influence on society, was just one of many contemporary educative institutions—profound, perhaps, insofar as it uniquely provided the basic skills of communication to the population—infinitely less profound, perhaps, as more than one contributing agency in shaping the values, attitudes, and standards of the young. It remained for the facilities, insights, techniques, and methods emerging out of another century of educational endeavor for the school's power in this latter sphere to be anywhere near adequately harnessed and realized.

Be it recollected that I give this as one instance of a thousand which I witnessed during my sojourn in the country.' *Op. cit.*, Vol. III, pp. 284–85.

This, and the other statements concerning lack of respect for authority in American children, must of course be set against the more authoritarian family and community patterns of Europe out of which these travelers came.

PART 4

THE AMERICAN COMMON
SCHOOL: 1850

EMERGING out of the early life of the American nation the common school by 1850 had in its own right become a genuine part of that life, standing as a principal positive commitment of the American people. The essence of this commitment had come basically to center in four fundamental meanings:

1. A common school was a school ideally common to all, available without cost to the young of the whole community.
2. A common school was a school providing students of diverse backgrounds with a minimum common educational experience, involving the intellectual and moral training necessary to the responsible and intelligent exercise of citizenship. It was carefully to avoid in the process those areas which in terms of conscience would prove so emotionally and intellectually divisive as to destroy the school's paramount commitment to universality.
3. A common school was a school totally supported by the common effort of the whole community as embodied in public funds.
4. A common school was a school completely controlled by the whole community (usually through its representatives) rather than by sectarian political, economic, or religious groups.

These four aspects had originally stood in the relation of means to ends, the first two representing the objectives and the latter two the instruments. However, in the intricate mesh of interrelationships which inevitably came to characterize their application in practice, it became increasingly difficult always to delineate sharply their functions in this respect. Thus, for instance, the use of public funds, which had originally stood as an instrument, in turn made it incumbent upon the community to preserve the public nature of the enterprise. The adoption of a pattern of public control provided similar reinforcement. On the other hand, this public availability was itself the most pressing claim both on the public purse and on the public agencies of control and administration. Such interrelationships served only to strengthen the basic idea implicit in common education: that a school common to all, teaching a body of materials considered necessary to all, was vital to the maintenance of a healthy republic. In the primacy of this conviction rested the crux of the common school.

It seems evident that the conception of an educational experience common to all citizens goes to the very heart of some of the most crucial problems of social and political democracy. Premising their arguments on the proposition that democracy is a complicated and exacting way of life, the proponents of the common school were urging that the young be adequately trained for participation in its processes. They were seeking universally to acquaint the citizenry with those basic elements of the intellectual and moral heritage of the race which were considered the necessary tools of intelligent and effective self-government.

Equally fundamental, however, was their attempt to cope with the problem of the one and the many, of reconciling individual liberty with the responsibility of group membership. For granted the pluralism implicit in any valid historical or philosophical conception of democracy, there yet remain the claims of the common, of the community. As Carl Becker has so incisively observed: "Freedom unrestrained by responsibility becomes mere license; responsibility unchecked by freedom becomes mere arbitrary power. The question, then, is not whether freedom and responsibility shall be united, but how they can be united and reconciled to the best advantage." [1]

[1] Carl L. Becker, *Freedom and Responsibility in the American Way of Life* (Alfred A. Knopf, New York, 1947), p. 3.

In essence, the proponents of the common school were seeking the nurture of a common core of sentiment, of value, and of practice *within which* pluralism would not become anarchy. They were seeking, in a sense, a means of constant regeneration whereby the inevitable inequities arising out of freedom would not from generation to generation become destructive of its very sources. And realizing the threat of disunity potentially inherent in heterogeneity, they were seeking to build and inculcate a sense of community which would function, not at the expense of individualism, but rather as a firm framework within which individuality might be most effectively preserved. What they set out to do, and in large measure accomplished, was to convince the American people that a common educational experience was the only means potentially capable of coping with these Herculean tasks. And while by 1850 this potential yet remained largely unfulfilled, their faith in its ultimate success had already become a cardinal American ideal.

BIBLIOGRAPHY

[*Note.* Because of the difficulties arising out of the tendency of early printers to set single titles in many different type styles, standard present-day capitalization has been used in the following listings. This bibliography has been shortened for publication. A complete list of materials used has been placed in the library of Teachers College, Columbia University.]

I. PRIMARY SOURCES

A. BOOKS, PAMPHLETS, AND ARTICLES

ABBOTT, JACOB. "The Duties of Parents, in Regard to the Schools Where Their Children Are Instructed," *The Introductory Discourse and the Lectures Delivered before the American Institute of Instruction, in Boston, August, 1834. Including the Journal of Proceedings, and a List of the Officers* (Carter, Hendee and Co., Boston, 1835), pp. 84–98.

ADAMS, DANIEL. *The Scholar's Arithmetic; or, Federal Accountant* (Second Edition, Larkin, West, West, and Greenleal, Leominster, Mass., 1802).

ALCOTT, WILLIAM A. "On the Construction of School-Houses," *Introductory Discourse and Lectures Delivered Before the American Institute of Instruction* (No place, no date), pp. 241–59.

ANDREWS, CHARLES C. *The History of the New-York African Free-Schools, from Their Establishment in 1787, to the Present Time: Embracing a Period of More than Forty Years: Also a Brief Account of the Successful Labors, of the New-York Manumission Society: With an Appendix* (New York, 1830).

BANCROFT, GEORGE. "The Office of the People in Art, Government, and Religion," *Literary and Historical Miscellanies* (Harper & Brothers, New York, 1855).

BANCROFT, GEORGE. *History of the United States from the Discovery of the American Continent* (D. Appleton and Co., 1892–95). 6 Vols.

BARNARD, HENRY. *Report of Public Schools of Rhode Island* (1848).

BARNARD, HENRY. *National Education in Europe; Being an Account of the Organization, Administration, Instruction, and Statistics of Public Schools of Different Grades in the Principal States* (Charles B. Norton, New York, 1854).

BINGHAM, CALEB. *The American Preceptor; Being a New Selection of Lessons, for Reading and Speaking* (Every Duyckinck, New York, 1815).

"A Review of the Second Annual Report of the Board of Education, Together with the Second Annual Report of the Secretary of the Board," *The Boston Quarterly Review*, Vol. 2 (1839), pp. 393–434.

BROOKS, CHARLES. "On the Duties of Legislatures in Relation to Public Schools in the United States," *The Lectures Delivered before the American Institute of Instruction, at Montpelier, Vt., August, 1849; Including the Journal of Proceedings, and a List of the Officers* (Ticknor, Reed, & Fields, Boston, 1850), pp. 175–91.

BROOKS, CHARLES. "School Reform or Teachers' Seminaries," *The Introductory Discourse, and the Lectures Delivered before the American Institute of Instruction, at Worcester, (Mass.) August, 1837. Including the Journal of Proceedings, and a List of the Officers* (James Munroe & Co., Boston, 1838), pp. 161–79.

BRUCE, JAMES C. "Popular Knowledge the Necessity of Popular Government," *Southern Literary Messenger*, Vol. 19 (1853), pp. 292–302.

BURNSIDE, SAMUEL M. "On the Classification of Schools," *The Introductory Discourse and the Lectures Delivered before the American Institute of Instruction, in Boston, August, 1833. Including a List of Officers and Members* (Carter, Hendee & Co., Boston, 1834), pp. 73–94.

BURTON, WARREN. *The District School as It Was* (Clifton Johnson, ed.; T. Y. Crowell Co., New York, 1928).

BUSHNELL, HORACE. "Christianity and Common Schools," *Common School Journal*, Vol. 2 (1840), pp. 102–03.

CAREY, MATHEW. *Appeal to the Wealthy of the Land, Ladies as Well as Gentlemen, on the Character, Conduct, Situation, and Prospects of Those Whose Sole Dependence for Subsistence Is on the Labour of Their Hands* (Second Edition, Philadelphia, 1833).

CARTER, JAMES G. *Essays upon Popular Education, Containing a Particular Examination of the Schools of Massachusetts, and an Outline of an Institution for the Education of Teachers* (Bowles and Dearborn, Boston, 1826).

CARTER, JAMES G. *Letters to the Hon. William Prescott, LL.D. on the Free Schools of New England, with Remarks upon the Principles of Instruction* (Cummings, Hilliard and Co., Boston, 1824).

CHEEVER, GEORGE B. *Right of the Bible in Our Public Schools* (Robert Carter & Brothers, New York, 1854).

CHEVALIER, MICHEL. *Society, Manners, and Politics in the United States* (Weeks, Jordon & Co., Boston, 1839).

CLINTON, DEWITT. *An Address to the Benefactors and Friends of the Free School Society of New York, Delivered on the Opening of That Institution, in Their New and Spacious Building on the Eleventh of the Twelfth Month (December) 1809* (New York, 1810).

COMBE, GEORGE. *Notes on the United States of North America during a Phrenological Visit in 1838–39–40* (Maclachlan, Stewart, & Company, Edinburgh, 1841). 3 Vols.

CONDORCET. *Esquisse d'un Tableau Historique des Progrès de l'Esprit Humain* (Librairie de la Bibliothèque Nationale, Paris, 1886).

DABNEY, G. E. "Education in Virginia," *Southern Literary Messenger*, Vol. 7 (1841), pp. 631–37.

DAVENPORT, BISHOP. *History of the United States, Containing All the Events Necessary to Be Committed to Memory; with the Declaration of Independence, the Constitution of the United States, and a Table of Chronology, for the Use of Schools* (John J. Anderson, ed.; Uriah Hunt & Son, Philadelphia, 1850).

DILWORTH, THOMAS. *A New Guide to the English Tongue* (Robert Cochran, Philadelphia, 1805).

DILWORTH, THOMAS. *The Schoolmaster's Assistant; Being a Compendium of Arithmetic both Practical and Theoretical* (London, 1791).

DOANE, GEORGE W. "Address to the People of New Jersey," *American Journal of Education*, Vol. 15 (1865), pp. 5–11.

DURGIN, CLEMENT. "On Natural History as a Branch of Common Education," *Intro-*

ductory Discourse and Lectures Delivered Before the American Institute of Instruction (No place, no date), pp. 209–36.

DWIGHT, T., JR. "On the Management of a Common School," *The Introductory Discourse and the Lectures Delivered before the American Institute of Instruction, in Boston, August, 1835. Including the Journal of Proceedings and a List of the Officers* (Charles J. Hendee, Boston, 1836), pp. 205–32.

EDSON, THEODORE. "On the Comparative Merits of Private and Public Schools," *The Introductory Discourse, and the Lectures Delivered before the American Institute of Instruction, at Worcester (Mass.) August, 1837. Including the Journal of Proceedings, and a List of the Officers* (James Munroe & Company, Boston, 1838).

ELLIOT, JONATHAN, ed. *The Debates in the Several State Conventions, on the Adoption of the Federal Constitution, as Recommended by the General Convention at Philadelphia in 1787* (J. B. Lippincott Company, Philadelphia, 1888). 5 Vols.

ELLIS, GEORGE EDWARD. *History of the Battle of Bunker's (Breed's) Hill, on June 17, 1775, from Authentic Sources in Print and Manuscript* (Lockwood, Brooks, and Company, Boston, 1875).

"Elm." "Christianity and Patriotism," *Southern Literary Messenger,* Vol. 8 (1842), pp. 600–06.

ELY, ALFRED B. *American Liberty, Its Sources,—Its Dangers, and the Means of Its Preservation* (New York, 1850).

Emerson's Complete Works (Houghton Mifflin and Co., Boston, 1894). 14 Vols.

EVERETT, EDWARD. *Papers* (Bound in the Massachusetts Historical Society).

EVERETT, EDWARD. "Remarks at the Taunton Common School Convention," *Common School Journal,* Vol. I (1839), pp. 219–23.

FARLEY, STEPHEN. "On the Improvement Which May Be Made in the Condition of Common Schools," *The Introductory Discourse and the Lectures Delivered before the American Institute of Instruction, in Boston, August, 1834. Including the Journal of Proceedings, and a List of the Officers* (Carter, Hendee and Co., Boston, 1835).

FITHIAN, PHILIP VICKERS. *Journals and Letters, 1767–1774* (J. R. Williams, ed.; Princeton Historical Society, Princeton, 1900).

FOOTE, JOHN P. *The Schools of Cincinnati, and Its Vicinity* (C. F. Bradley, Cincinnati, 1855).

FOWLER, WILLIAM C. "Influence of Academies and High Schools on Common Schools," *Introductory Discourse and Lectures Delivered before the American Institute of Instruction* (No place, no date), pp. 185–206.

FRELINGHUYSEN, THEODORE. "Essay on the Propriety of Introducing the Study of the Constitution and Political Institutions of the United States, as Subjects of Instruction in Common Schools," *American Annals of Education and Instruction,* Vol. 2 (1832), pp. 505–09.

GOODRICH, SAMUEL G. "On Man the Subject of Education," *The Lectures Delivered before the American Institute of Instruction at Lowell (Mass.) August, 1838; Including the Journal of Proceedings, and a List of the Officers* (William D. Ticknor, Boston, 1839), pp. 165–87.

GOULD, A. A. "On the Introduction of Natural History as a Study to Common Schools," *The Introductory Discourse and the Lectures Delivered before the American Institute of Instruction, in Boston, August, 1834. Including the Journal of Proceedings and a List of the Officers* (Carter, Hendee and Co., Boston, 1835), pp. 225–45.

GREEN, BERIAH. "On Uniting a System of Education, Manual with Mental Labor," *The Introductory Discourse and the Lectures Delivered before the American Institute of Instruction, in Boston, August, 1834. Including the Journal of Proceedings, and a List of the Officers* (Carter, Hendee and Co., Boston, 1835), pp. 189–206.

GRAY, A. "On the Importance of the Natural Sciences in Our System of Popular Education," *The Lectures Delivered before the American Institute of Instruction, at Boston, August, 1841; Including the Journal of Proceedings, and a List of the Officers* (William D. Ticknor, Boston, 1842).

GRUND, FRANCIS J. *The Americans, in Their Moral, Social, and Political Relations* (Marsh, Capen & Lyon, Boston, 1837).

HALL, BAYNARD RUSH. *The New Purchase or, Seven and a Half Years in the Far West* (James Albert Woodburn, ed.; Princeton University Press, Princeton, 1916).

HAMILTON, THOMAS. *Men and Manners in America* (W. Blackwood, Edinburgh, 1833). 2 Vols.

Gen. Jackson's Farewell Address to the People of the United States, together with His Proclamation to South Carolina (J. M. G. Lescure, Harrisburg, 1850).

The Writings of Thomas Jefferson (Paul Leicester Ford, ed.; G. P. Putnam's Sons, New York, 1892–99). 10 Vols.

JOCELYN, EDWIN. *A Prize Essay on the Duties of Parents in Relation to Their Schools* (Ives & Pease, 1845).

KING, RUFUS. *Ohio, First Fruits of the Ordinance of 1787* (H. E. Scudder, ed.; American Commonwealth, Boston, 1888).

KINMONT, ALEXANDER. "Report on Anatomy and Physiology as a Branch of Study in Schools," *Transactions of the Fifth Annual Meeting of the Western Literary Institute, and College of Professional Teachers, Held in Cincinnati, October, 1835* (Cincinnati, 1836).

KIRKLAND, C. M. "The Log Schoolhouse," *Western Literary Messenger,* Vol. 14 (1850), pp. 95–99.

LABAREE, BENJAMIN. "The Education Demanded by the Peculiar Character of Our Civil Institutions," *The Lectures Delivered before the American Institute of Instruction, at Montpelier, Vt., August, 1849; Including the Journal of Proceedings and a List of the Officers* (Ticknor, Reed, & Fields, Boston, 1850), pp. 27–58.

LANG, JOHN DUNMORE. *Religion and Education in America: With Notices of the State and Prospects of American Unitarianism, Popery, and African Colonization* (Thomas Ward & Co., London, 1840).

LATROBE, CHARLES JOSEPH. *The Rambler in North America* (Harper and Brothers, New York, 1835). 2 Vols.

LAWRENCE, EDWARD A. "On the Elementary Principles of Constitutional Law, as a Branch of Education in Common Schools," *The Lectures Delivered before the American Institute of Instruction, at Boston, August, 1841; Including the Journal of Proceedings, and a List of the Officers* (William D. Ticknor, Boston, 1842), pp. 179–94.

LEONARD, L. W. "On the Present Condition and Wants of Common Schools," *The Lectures Delivered before the American Institute of Instruction, at Keene, N. H., August, 1851. Including the Journal of Proceedings, and a List of the Officers* (Ticknor, Reed, and Fields, Boston, 1851).

LEWIS, SAMUEL. *First Annual Report of the Superintendent of Common Schools,*

Made to the Thirty-Sixth General Assembly of Ohio, January, 1838 (No place, no date).

LEWIS, SAMUEL. *Second Annual Report of the Superintendent of Common Schools, Made to the Thirty-Seventh General Assembly of the State of Ohio, December 24, 1838* (S. Medary, Columbus, 1839).

LEWIS, SAMUEL. *Third Annual Report of the Superintendent of Common Schools, Made to the Thirty-Eighth General Assembly of the State of Ohio, December 13, 1839* (No place, no date).

LEWIS, SAMUEL. "Remarks on Common Schools," Appendix of Calvin Stowe, *The Prussian System of Public Instruction* (Truman and Smith, Cincinnati, 1836).

LIEBER, FRANCIS. *The Stranger in America: Comprising Sketches of the Manners, Society, and National Peculiarities of the United States in a Series of Letters to a Friend in Europe* (Richard Bentley, London, 1835). 2 Vols.

LINCOLN, LUTHER B. "On the Means of Cultivating a Classic Taste in Our Common Schools," *The Introductory Discourse, and the Lectures Delivered before the American Institute of Instruction, at Springfield, (Mass.) August, 1839. Including the Journal of Proceedings and a List of the Officers* (Marsh, Capen, Lyon, and Webb, Boston, 1840).

LYELL, CHARLES. *Lyell's Travels in North America in the Years 1841–42* (John P. Cushing, ed.; Charles E. Merrill Co., New York, 1909).

LYELL, CHARLES. *A Second Visit to the United States of North America* (Harper and Brothers, New York, 1849). 2 Vols.

MACLEAN, JOHN. *A Lecture on a School System for New-Jersey* (Princeton Press, Princeton, 1829).

McVICKAR, JOHN. *First Lessons in Political Economy; for the Use of Schools and Families* (Seventh Edition, Saxton and Miles, New York, 1846).

The Writings of James Madison (Gaillard Hunt, ed.; G. P. Putnam's Sons, New York, 1900–10). 9 Vols.

MANN, HORACE. *Annual Report on Education* (Rand & Avery Co., Boston, no date).

MANN, HORACE. *Answer to the "Rejoinder" of Twenty-Nine Boston Schoolmasters, Part of the "Thirty-One" Who Published "Remarks" on the Seventh Annual Report of the Secretary of the Massachusetts Board of Education* (William B. Fowle and Nahum Capen, Boston, 1845).

MANN, HORACE. *Lectures on Education* (Ide & Dutton, Boston, 1855).

MANN, HORACE. *Life and Works of Horace Mann* (Lee and Shepard, Boston, 1891). 5 Vols.

Life of Horace Mann by His Wife (Lee and Shepard, Boston, 1891). Vol. 1 of *Life and Works of Horace Mann.*

MANN, HORACE. *Papers* (Bound in Massachusetts Historical Society).

MANN, HORACE. *Reply to the "Remarks" of Thirty-One Boston Schoolmasters on the Seventh Annual Report of the Secretary of the Massachusetts Board of Education* (William B. Fowle and Nahum Capen, Boston, 1844).

MANN, HORACE. *Sequel to the So Called Correspondence between the Rev. M. H. Smith and Horace Mann, Surreptitiously Published by Mr. Smith; Containing a Letter from Mr. Mann, Suppressed by Mr. Smith with the Reply Therein Promised* (William B. Fowle, Boston, 1847).

MANNING, WILLIAM. *The Key of Libberty, Shewing the Causes Why a Free Government Has Always Failed, and a Remidy Against It* (Samuel Eliot Morison, ed.; The Manning Association, Billerica, Mass., 1922).

MARRYAT, FREDERICK. *A Diary in America* (Longman, Orme, Brown, Green and Longmans, London, 1839). 3 Vols.

"Education of the People," *The Massachusetts Quarterly Review*, Vol. 1 (1848), pp. 198–224.

MERCER, CHARLES FENTON. *A Discourse on Popular Education* (Princeton, Sept. 26, 1826).

MORSE, JEDIDIAH. *Geography Made Easy; Being an Abridgement of the American Universal Geography. To Which Are Prefixed Elements of Geography* (Thomas & Andrews, Boston, 1809).

MORSE, SAMUEL F. B. *Imminent Dangers to the Free Institutions of the United States Through Foreign Immigration* (New York, 1835).

"Common Schools," *The New-England Magazine*, Vol. 3 (1832), pp. 194–207.

The New-England Primer, A Reprint of the Earliest Known Edition, with Many Facsimiles and Reproductions, and an Historical Introduction (Paul Leicester Ford, ed.; Dodd, Mead and Company, New York, 1899).

NORTHEND, WILLIAM D. "Importance of Moral and Religious Education in a Republic," *The Lectures Delivered before the American Institute of Instruction, at Keene, N. H., August, 1851. Including the Journal of Proceedings, and a List of the Officers* (Ticknor, Reed, and Fields, Boston, 1851), pp. 103–22.

NOTT, SAMUEL JR. "On a Proper Education for an Agricultural People," *The Introductory Discourse and the Lectures Delivered before the American Institute of Instruction, in Boston, August, 1835. Including the Journal of Proceedings and a List of the Officers* (Charles J. Hendee, Boston, 1836), pp. 35–59.

PACKARD, FREDERICK A. *The Question, Will the Christian Religion Be Recognized as the Basis of the System of Public Instruction in Massachusetts? Discussed in Four Letters to the Rev. Dr. Humphrey, President of Amherst College* (Whipple and Damrell, Boston, 1839).

PACKARD, FREDERICK A. *Thoughts on the Condition and Prospects of Popular Education in the United States* (No place, no date).

PALMER, THOMAS H. "The Essentials of Education," *The Lectures Delivered before the American Institute of Instruction, at Montpelier, Vt., August, 1849; Including the Journal of Proceedings, and a List of the Officers* (Ticknor, Reed, & Fields, Boston, 1850), pp. 79–118.

PALMER, THOMAS H. "On the Evils of the Present System of Primary Instruction," *The Introductory Discourse, and the Lectures Delivered before the American Institute of Instruction, at Worcester, (Mass.) August, 1837. Including the Journal of Proceedings, and a List of the Officers* (James Munroe & Company, Boston, 1838), pp. 211–39.

PARK, R. "On Religious Education," *The Introductory Discourse and the Lectures Delivered before the American Institute of Instruction, in Boston, August, 1835. Including the Journal of Proceedings and a List of the Officers* (Charles J. Hendee, Boston, 1836), pp. 101–10.

PARKER, THEODORE. "On the Education of the Laboring Class," *The Lectures Delivered before the American Institute of Instruction, at Boston, August, 1841; Including the Journal of Proceedings, and a List of the Officers* (William D. Ticknor, Boston, 1842), pp. 65–90.

PERRY, GARDNER BRAMAN. "On Primary Education," *The Introductory Discourse and the Lectures Delivered Before the American Institute of Instruction, in Boston,*

1833. Including a List of Officers and Members (Carter, Hendee, and Co., Boston, 1834), pp. 97–128.

PIKE, NICOLAS. *New and Complete System of Arithmetic* (John Mycall, Newbury-Port, 1788).

PIKE, NICOLAS. *A New and Complete System of Arithmetic Composed for the Use of the Citizens of the United States* (Fifth Edition, William S. Parker & Son, Troy, 1832).

Public School Society. *Minutes 1833–51* (Bound at the New York Historical Society).

RANDALL, HENRY STEPHENS. *Decision of the State Superintendent of Common Schools, on the Right to Compel Catholic Children to Attend Prayers, and to Read or Commit Portions of the Bible, as School Exercises, Oct. 27, 1853* (New York, 1853).

RANTOUL, ROBERT, JR. "The Education of a Free People," *The Introductory Discourse, and the Lectures Delivered before the American Institute of Instruction, at Springfield, (Mass.) August, 1839. Including the Journal of Proceedings and a List of the Officers* (Marsh, Capen, Lyon, and Webb, Boston, 1840), pp. 3–33.

ROBINSON, E. W. "Moral Culture Essential to Intellectual Education," *The Lectures Delivered before the American Institute of Instruction, at Boston, August, 1841; Including the Journal of Proceedings, and a List of the Officers* (William D. Ticknor, Boston, 1842), pp. 119–36.

ROOT, ERASTUS. *An Introduction to Arithmetic for the Use of Common Schools* (Thomas Hubbard, Norwich, 1796).

SANBORN, E. D. "Education—The Condition of National Greatness," *The Lectures Delivered before the American Institute of Instruction, at Montpelier, Vt., August, 1849; Including the Journal of Proceedings and a List of the Officers* (Ticknor, Reed, & Fields, Boston, 1850), pp. 149–73.

SMITH, BENJAMIN MOSBY. *The Prussian Primary School System as Seen by a Virginia Traveler a Century Ago with Suggestions as to Its Application to the State of Virginia; a Report Submitted to the Governor of Virginia on January 15, 1839, by the Rev. Benjamin Mosby Smith of Danville, Virginia, Reprinted from a Photostat of House Document 26, Virginia* (McClure, Staunton, Va., 1936).

STORY, JOSEPH. *Commentaries on the Constitution of the United States: With a Preliminary Review of the Constitutional History of the Colonies and States, before the Adoption of the Constitution* (Third Edition, Little, Brown and Company, Boston, 1858). 2 Vols.

STORY, JOSEPH. "On the Science of Government as a Branch of Popular Education," *The Lectures Delivered before the American Institute of Instruction, at Montpelier, Vt., August, 1849; Including the Journal of Proceedings, and a List of the Officers* (Ticknor, Reed, & Fields, Boston, 1850), pp. 234–75.

STOWE, CALVIN. *The Prussian System of Public Instruction* (Truman and Smith, Cincinnati, 1836).

STOWE, C. E. *Report on Elementary Public Instruction in Europe, Made to the Thirty-Sixth General Assembly of the State of Ohio, December 19, 1837* (Dutton and Wentworth, Boston, 1838).

TAYLOR, J. ORVILLE. *The District School; or, National Education* (Carey, Lea, and Blanchard, Philadelphia, 1835).

TOCQUEVILLE, ALEXIS DE. *Democracy in America* (Phillips Bradley, ed.; Alfred A. Knopf, New York, 1946). 2 Vols.

TOUMLIN, HARRY. *The Western Country in 1793* (Marion Tinling and Godfrey Davies, ed.; Huntington Library, San Marino, 1948).

TWISLETON, EDWARD. *Evidence as to the Religious Working of the Common Schools of the State of Massachusetts* (James Ridgway, London, 1854).

The United States Primer, Containing, Besides Other Useful and Instructive Matter, the Assembly of Divines' and the Episcopal Catechism (Watson, Baker, and Pratt, New York, no date).

WASHBURN, E. "On the Political Influence of School-Masters," *The Introductory Discourse and the Lectures Delivered before the American Institute of Instruction, in Boston, August, 1835. Including the Journal of Proceedings and a List of the Officers* (Charles J. Hendee, Boston, 1836), pp. 63–87.

The Writings of George Washington from the Original Manuscript Sources (John C. Fitzpatrick, ed.; United States Government Printing Office, Washington, 1940). 39 Vols.

WATERSTON, R. C. "On Moral and Spiritual Culture in Early Education," *The Introductory Discourse and the Lectures Delivered before the American Institute of Instruction, in Boston, August, 1835. Including the Journal of Proceedings and a List of the Officers* (Charles J. Hendee, Boston, 1836), pp. 235–50.

WEBSTER, NOAH. *An American Selection of Lessons in Reading and Speaking. Calculated to Improve the Minds and Refine the Taste of Youth. To Which Are Prefixed Rules in Elocution, and Directions for Expressing the Principal Passions of the Mind. Being the Third Part of a Grammatical Institute of the English Language* (Tenth Edition, Hartford, no date).

WEBSTER, NOAH. *The American Spelling Book: Containing an Easy Standard of Pronunciation. Being the First Part of a Grammatical Institute of the English Language. To Which Is Added, an Appendix, Containing a Moral Catechism and a Federal Catechism* (Seventeenth Edition, Thomas and Andrews, Boston, 1798).

WEBSTER, NOAH. *The Revolution in France, Considered in Respect to Its Progress and Effects* (New York, 1794).

WEEMS, MASON L. *The Life of Gen. Washington, with Curious Anecdotes, Equally Honourable to Himself, and Exemplary to His Young Countrymen* (Ninth Edition, Mathew Carey, Philadelphia, 1809).

WEEMS, MASON L. *The Life of William Penn, the Settler of Pennsylvania, the Founder of Philadelphia, and One of the First Lawgivers in the Colonies, Now United States, in 1682* (Uriah Hunt, Philadelphia, 1836).

WHITE, CHARLES. "On the Literary Responsibility of Teachers," *The Lectures Delivered before the American Institute of Instruction, at Lowell, (Mass.) August, 1838; Including the Journal of Proceedings, and a List of the Officers* (William D. Ticknor, Boston, 1839), pp. 1–30.

WINES, E. C. *Hints on a System of Popular Education* (Hogan & Thompson, Philadelphia, 1838).

WRIGHT, FRANCES and OWEN, ROBERT. *Tracts on Republican Government and National Education* (J. Watson, London, 1847).

B. MISCELLANEOUS PAMPHLETS

An Account of the Free-School Society of New York (Collins and Co., New York, 1814).

Address of His Excellency Marcus Morton, to the Two Branches of the Legislature, on the Organization of the Government for the Political Year Commencing January 1, 1840 (Bay State Democrat, Boston, 1840).

Address of the Roman Catholics to Their Fellow Citizens, of the City and State of New York (Hugh Cassidy, New York, 1840).

Annual Reports of the American Sunday-School Union, 1836–37.

Annual Reports of the Trustees of the Free-School Society of New-York, 1824–25.

Annual Reports of the Trustees of the Public School Society of New-York, 1826–53.

The Bible, the Rod, and Religion, in Common Schools (Boston, 1847).

The Common School Controversy: Consisting of Three Letters of the Secretary of the Board of Education, of the State of Massachusetts, in Reply to Charges Preferred Against the Board, by the Editor of the Christian Witness and by Edward A. Newton Esq. of Pittsfield, Once a Member of the Board; to Which Are Added Extracts from the Daily Press, in Regard to the Controversy (Boston, 1844).

An Honest Appeal to Every Voter (Pamphlet published *circa* 1844, in New York Public Library).

The Important and Interesting Debate, on the Claim of the Catholics to a Portion of the Common School Fund; with Arguments of Counsel, before the Board of Aldermen of the City of New York, on Thursday and Friday, the 29th and 30th of October, 1840 (Second Edition, published by the proprietor of the *New-York Freeman's Journal*, New York, 1840).

Memorials, Presented to the Legislature in the Session of 1823, Praying the Repeal of the Section of a Law Granting Peculiar Privileges to the Trustees of the Bethel Baptist Church, in the Appropriation of the Common School Fund. Together with Introductory Observations and Facts (Board of Trustees of the Free-School Society of New-York, New York, 1823).

Rejoinder to the "Reply" of the Hon. Horace Mann, Secretary of the Massachusetts Board of Education, to the "Remarks" of the Association of Boston Masters, upon His Seventh Annual Report (Charles C. Little and James Brown, Boston, 1845).

Remarks of John L. Mason, Esq., and Jos. S. Bosworth, Esq. before the Board of Education, March 17 and 24, 1847, upon the Right and Power Claimed by the Public School Society to Establish New Common Schools Entitled to a Participation in the School Monies, and to Use Those Monies in Establishing Such Schools (Casper C. Childs, New York, 1847).

Remarks on Mr. Carter's Outline of an Institution for the Education of Teachers (Bowles and Dearborn, Boston, 1827).

Remarks on the Seventh Annual Report of the Hon. Horace Mann, Secretary of the Massachusetts Board of Education (Charles C. Little and James Brown, Boston, 1844).

Report of a Committee of the Trustees of the Free-School Society, on the Distribution of the Common School Fund (New York, 1825).

Report of the Committee on the Annual Apportionment, on the Communications of the County Superintendent, Relative to the Use of the Bible in the Public Schools of the City of New York (New York, 1844).

Reasons of the Trustees of the Public School Society, for Their Remonstrances Against the Petition of the Roman Catholic Benevolent Society, to Be Admitted to a Common Participation in the School Fund (New York, 1831).

C. PUBLIC DOCUMENTS

ALABAMA

Statutes Passed by the General Assembly of the State of Alabama, 1825.

ARKANSAS

Statutes Passed by the General Assembly of the State of Arkansas, 1842/43.

CONNECTICUT

The Public Records of the Colony of Connecticut (Charles J. Hoadley, ed.; Hartford, 1868).
Acts and Laws of the State of Connecticut in America (Hudson and Goodwin, Hartford, 1796).
Statutes Passed by the General Assembly of the State of Connecticut, 1845.

DELAWARE

Laws of the State of Delaware, from the Fourteenth Day of October, One Thousand Seven Hundred, to the Eighteenth Day of August, One Thousand Seven Hundred and Ninety-Seven (Samuel and John Adams, New-Castle, 1797). 2 Vols.
Statutes of the State of Delaware, 1817, 1829.

ENGLAND

Pulton, Fardinando, *Collection of Sundrie Statutes, Frequent in Use: With Notes in the Margent, and References to the Booke Cases and Bookes of Entries and Registers, Where They Be Treated of. Together with an Abridgement of the Residue Which Be Expired, Repealed, Altered, and Worne out of Use, or Doe Concerne Privat Persons, Places, or Things, and Not the Whole Commonwealth. Whereunto Be Added Certaine Materiall Statutes, Never Printed Before in English. Also a Necessarie Table, or Kalender Is Annexed Hereunto, Expressing in Titles the Most Materiall Branches of Those Statutes in Use, and Practise* (Printed for the Societie of Stationers, London, 1618).

FLORIDA

Statutes of the General Assembly of the State of Florida, 1848/49.

GEORGIA

Statutes of the General Assembly of the State of Georgia, 1838, 1843.

ILLINOIS

Statutes of the General Assembly of the State of Illinois, 1824/25.

INDIANA

Statutes of the State of Indiana, 1842, 1848.

IOWA

Statutes of the General Assembly of the State of Iowa, 1846.

KENTUCKY

Statutes of the General Assembly of the Commonwealth of Kentucky, 1837.

LOUISIANA

Statutes of the Legislature of the State of Louisiana, 1847.

MAINE

Statutes Passed by the Legislature of the State of Maine, 1846.
Laws of the State of Maine; to Which Are Prefixed the Constitution of the U. States and of the Said State, with an Appendix (William Hyde, Portland, 1822).

MARYLAND

Statutes Passed by the General Assembly of the State of Maryland, 1825.

MASSACHUSETTS

Records of the Governor and Company of the Massachusetts Bay in New England (Nathaniel B. Shurtleff, ed.; William White, Boston, 1853). 5 Vols.
The Colonial Laws of Massachusetts (William H. Whitmore, ed.; Boston, 1889).
The Acts and Resolves, Public and Private, of the Province of Massachusetts Bay: to Which Are Prefixed the Charters of the Province, with Historical and Explanatory Notes, and an Appendix (Wright & Potter, Boston, 1869–1922). 21 Vols.
Statutes of the Commonwealth of Massachusetts, 1789–1850, 1857.
Resolves Passed by the Legislature of Massachusetts, 1839–1850, 1857.

MASSACHUSETTS DOCUMENTS

Document No. 27: "Memorial of the American Institute of Instruction, Praying for the Appointment of a Superintendent of the Common Schools," in bound volume of *Documents of the Massachusetts House of Representatives* (New York Public Library).
Document No. 1: "Address of His Excellency Edward Everett, to the Two Branches of the Legislature, on the Organization of the Government, for the Political Year Commencing January 4, 1837" (Dutton and Wentworth, Boston, 1837), in bound volume of *Documents of the Massachusetts Senate* (New York Public Library).
Document No. 3: "Address of His Excellency Edward Everett, to the Two Branches of the Legislature, on the Organization of the Government, for the Political Year Commencing January 3, 1838" (Dutton and Wentworth, Boston, 1838).
Report of the Secretary of the Board of Education, on the Subject of Schoolhouses, Supplementary to His First Annual Report (Dutton and Wentworth, Boston, 1838).
Annual Reports of the Board of Education, Together with the Annual Reports of the Secretary of the Board, 1838–1848.

MICHIGAN

Statutes of the Legislature of the State of Michigan, 1835–1837.

MISSISSIPPI

Statutes of the State of Mississippi, 1846.

MISSOURI

Statutes of the State of Missouri, 1838, 1841.

NEW HAMPSHIRE

The Laws of the State of New-Hampshire, the Constitution of the State of New-Hampshire, and the Constitution of the United States with Its Proposed Amendments (John Melcher, Portsmouth, 1797).
Statutes of the State of New-Hampshire, 1846.

NEW JERSEY

Statutes of the General Assembly of the State of New-Jersey, 1816/17, 1837, 1846.

NEW YORK

Laws of the State of New York Passed at the Sessions of the Legislature Held in the Years 1785, 1786, 1787 and 1788, Inclusive, Being the Eighth, Ninth, Tenth and Seven Sessions (Weed, Parsons and Company, Albany, 1886).

Laws of the State of New York Passed at the Sessions of the Legislature Held in the Years 1785, 1786, 1787 and 1788, Inclusive, Being the Eighth, Ninth, Tenth and Eleventh Sessions (Weed, Parsons and Company, Printers, 1886).

Statutes of the State of New-York, 1789–1853.

Journal of the Senate of the State of New-York, 1842.

Journal of the Assembly of the State of New-York, 1842.

Report of the Debates and Proceedings of the Convention for the Revision of the Constitution of the State of New York (Reported by William G. Bishop and William H. Attree, Office of the Evening Atlas, Albany, 1846).

Messages from the Governors (Charles Z. Lincoln, ed.; State of New York, Albany, 1909). 11 Vols.

NEW YORK STATE DOCUMENTS

Document No. 86, April 26, 1841: "Report of the Secretary of State, Respecting the Distribution of the Common School Moneys in that City, Referred to Him by the Senate," in *Documents of the Senate of the State of New-York, Sixty-Fourth Session, 1841,* Vol. III (Thurlow Weed, Albany, 1841).

Document No. 97, May 22, 1841: "Memorial and Remonstrance of the Trustees of the Public School Society of the City of New-York," in *Documents of the Senate of the State of New-York, Sixty-Fourth Session, 1841,* Vol. III (Thurlow Weed, Albany, 1841).

NEW YORK CITY

Minutes of the Common Council of the City of New York 1734–1831 (City of New York, New York, 1917). 19 Vols.

Proceedings of the Board of Assistants, 1831–1834.

Proceedings of the Board of Assistant Aldermen, 1834–1836.

Documents of the Board of Assistants, 1831–1845.

Journal of the Board of Assistants, 1836–1845.

Proceedings of the Board of Aldermen, 1836–1845.

Documents of the Board of Aldermen, 1835–1845.

Proceedings of the Boards of Aldermen and Assistant Aldermen, 1835–1845.

NEW YORK CITY DOCUMENTS

Document No. XXI, September 19, 1831: "Report of the Law Committee on the Constitutionality of the Ordinance Appropriating to the School Fund," in *Documents of the Board of Assistants, from No. 1 to No. 78, and from A to O, Inclusive,* Vol. 1 (New York, 1837), pp. 67–79.

Document No. LXXVIII, May 7, 1832: "Report of the Committee on Arts and Sciences, and Schools, on the Petition from the Trustees of the Methodist Church, in Relation to School Fund," in *Documents of the Board of Assistants, from No. 1 to No. 78, and from A to O, Inclusive,* Vol. 1 (New York, 1837), pp. 311–14.

Document No. 80, April 27, 1840: "Report of the Committee on Arts and Sciences and Schools, on the Petition of the Officers and Members of the Roman Catholic and Other Churches, in the City of New-York, for an Apportionment of School Moneys, to the Schools Attached to Said Churches. Presented by Mr. Dodge. Adopted, and Two Thousand Copies Ordered to Be Printed, with the Accompanying Petitions and Remonstrances, under the Direction of the Committee," in *Journal and Documents of the Board of Assistants, of the City of New-York,* Vol. 15 (1840), pp. 335–89.

Document No. 40, Jan. 11, 1841: "The Special Committee, to Whom Was Referred the Petition of the Catholics for a Portion of the School Fund, Together with the Remonstrances Against the Same, Presented the Following Report Thereon, Which Was, on Motion Accepted, on a Division Called by Alderman Grahm, viz:—In the Affirmative, the President, Aldermen Bales, Woodhull, Benson, Jones, Rich, Chamberlain, Campbell, Hatfield, Jarvis, Smith, Nichols, Grahm, Cooper and Nash—15. In the Negative, Alderman Pentz—1. and 1000 Copies Thereof Ordered Printed, with the Vote Taken on the Report," in *Documents of the Board of Aldermen, of the City of New-York,* Vol. VII (Bryant and Boggs, New York, no date), pp. 555–85.

NEW YORK CITY BOARD OF EDUCATION

Document No. 3, January 20, 1847: *Report of the Select Committee, to Which Was Referred a Communication from the Public School Society, in Answer to a Resolution of Inquiry, Passed by the Board of Education, February 11th, 1846, Which Was Ordered to Lie on the Table and Be Printed.*

October 20, 1847: *Report of the Conference Committee, in Reference to a Communication from the Board of Trustees of the Public School Society.*

November 15, 1848: *Report of the Finance Committee, to Which Was Referred an Application of the Public School Society of New York, for an Appropriation of $10,152.63, to Supply a Deficiency to Meet the Necessary Legal Expenses of the Schools of Said Society, Which Was Read, and Ordered to Lie on the Table and Be Printed.*

October 17, 1849: *Report of the Finance Committee, on the Application of the Public School Society of New York, for an Appropriation of $26,103.48, to Supply a Deficiency in Its Means to Meet the Necessary Legal Expenses of the Schools of Said Society; Which Was Ordered to Lie on the Table and Be Printed.*

NORTH CAROLINA

Statutes of the State of North Carolina, 1840/41.

OHIO

Statutes of the State of Ohio, 1803–1806; 1811–1850.
Journals of the House of Representatives, 1823–1824.

PENNSYLVANIA

Statutes of the Commonwealth of Pennsylvania, 1801–1811; 1813–1850.
Journal of the House of Representatives of the Commonwealth of Pennsylvania, 1823.

RHODE ISLAND

Statutes, 1839, 1845.

SOUTH CAROLINA

Statutes of the General Assembly of the State of South-Carolina, 1811.

TENNESSEE

Statutes of the General Assembly of the State of Tennessee, 1832, 1835/36.

UNITED STATES

Journals of the Continental Congress 1774–1789.

CENSUS OFFICE

Statistical View of the United States, Embracing Its Territory, Population—White, Free, Colored, and Slave—Moral and Social Conditions, Industry, Property and Revenue; the Detailed Statistics of Cities, Towns, and Counties; Being a Compendium of the Seventh Census (J. D. B. DeBow, ed.; Washington, 1854).
Statistics of the United States, Eighth Census (Copy in New York Public Library, title page mutilated).

BUREAU OF THE CENSUS

A Century of Population Growth (Government Printing Office, Washington, 1909).
Fifteenth Census of the United States: 1930 Population, Vol. I (Government Printing Office, Washington, 1931).

SUPREME COURT

Vidal *et al.* v. Girard's Executors, January Term, 1844.

VERMONT

Statutes of the Legislature of the State of Vermont, 1845, 1850.

VIRGINIA

Hening, William Waller, *The Statutes at Large; Being a Collection of All the Laws of Virginia from the First Session of the Legislature, in the Year 1619* (Samuel Pleasants, Richmond, 1809). 13 Vols.
Shepherd, Samuel, *The Statutes at Large of Virginia, from October Session 1792, to December Session 1806, Inclusive* (Samuel Shepherd, Richmond, 1835). 3 Vols.
Statutes of the General Assembly of the Commonwealth of Virginia, 1807–1810; 1815–1850.
Journals of the House of Delegates of the Commonwealth of Virginia, 1815–1816.
Journals of the Senate of the Commonwealth of Virginia, 1815–1817.
Proceedings and Debates of the Virginia State Convention, of 1829–30 (Ritchie and Cook, Richmond, 1830).

VIRGINIA DOCUMENTS

Document No. 7, Dec. 13, 1841: "Education Convention of Northwestern Virginia," in *Journal of the House of Delegates of Virginia. Session 1841–42* (Samuel Shepherd, Richmond, 1841).
Document No. 35: Henry Ruffner, "Proposed Plan for the Organization and Support of Common Schools in Virginia: Prepared and Presented to the Legislature, at the Request of a School Convention Held in Lexington, on the Seventh Day of October Eighteen Hundred and Forty-One, and Composed of Delegates from the Counties of Both, Augusta and Rockbridge," in *Journal of the House of Delegates of Virginia. Session 1841–42* (Samuel Shepherd, Richmond, 1841).
Document No. 53: "Project for a District School System, Accompanying the Report of the President and Directors of the Literary Fund to the General Assembly, Called for by an Act of Eighth of March, One Thousand Eight Hundred and

Forty-One," in *Journal of the House of Delegates of Virginia. Session 1841–42* (Samuel Shepherd, Richmond, 1841).

Document No. 1: "Annual Message of the Governor of the Commonwealth and Accompanying Documents," in *Journal of the House of Delegates of Virginia. Session 1845–46* (Samuel Shepherd, Richmond, 1845).

D. PERIODICALS

American Annals of Education (Boston), 1838–39.

American Annals of Education and Instruction (Boston), 1831–37.

American Journal of Education (Boston), 1826–30.

American Journal of Education (Hartford), 1855–80.

American Journal of Education and College Review (New York), 1856–57.

American Quarterly Review (Philadelphia), 1827–35.

Boston Quarterly Review (Boston), 1838–41.

Chautauquan (Meadville, Pa.), 1895–96.

Commercial Review of the South and West (New Orleans), 1846–50.

Common School Advocate (Cincinnati), 1837–38.

Common School Advocate and Journal of Education (Jacksonville, Ill.), 1837.

Common School Assistant (Albany), 1836–40.

Common School Journal (Boston), 1839–52.

Connecticut Common School Journal (Hartford), 1838–42.

Dial (Boston), 1840–44.

Free Enquirer (New Harmony), 1828–33.

Hazard's Register of Pennsylvania (Philadelphia), 1831–36.

Literary and Evangelical Magazine (Richmond), 1819–25.

Massachusetts Quarterly Review (Boston), 1848–50.

National Gazette and Literary Register (Philadelphia), 1829–31.

Newburgh Telegraph (Newburgh, N. Y.), 1846.

New-England Magazine (Boston), 1831–35.

New York Evening Post (New York), 1833–35.

New-York Freeman's Journal and Catholic Register (New York), 1840–43.

New-York Observer (New York), 1837–39.

New-York Weekly Tribune (New York), 1845–48.

North American Review (Boston), 1830–50.

Pennsylvania School Journal (Lancaster), 1852–70.

Register of Pennsylvania (Philadelphia), 1828–31.

Richmond Enquirer (Richmond), 1818–46.

Richmond Whig and Public Advertiser (Richmond), 1835–45.

Southern Literary Messenger (Richmond), 1837–50.

Western Literary Messenger, A Family Magazine of Literature, Science, Art, Morality, and General Intelligence (Buffalo), 1849–50.

Western Quarterly Review (Cincinnati), 1849.

Working Man's Advocate (New York), 1830–33.

II. SECONDARY SOURCES

AMERICAN BUREAU OF INDUSTRIAL RESEARCH. *A Documentary History of American Industrial Society:* Vol. I–II (Ulrich B. Phillips, ed.; The Arthur H. Clark Company, Cleveland, 1910).

AMERICAN BUREAU OF INDUSTRIAL RESEARCH. *A Documentary History of American*

Industrial Society: Vol. V. (John R. Commons and Helen L. Sumner, eds.; The Arthur H. Clark Company, Cleveland, 1910).

BEARD, CHARLES A. and BEARD, MARY R. *The Rise of American Civilization* (The Macmillan Co., New York, 1936).

BECKER, CARL. *Freedom and Responsibility in the American Way of Life* (Alfred A. Knopf, New York, 1947).

BELL, SADIE. *The Church, the State, and Education in Virginia* (The Science Press, Philadelphia, 1930).

BIDWELL, PERCY WELLS. "Rural Economy in New England at the Beginning of the Nineteenth Century," in *Transactions of the Connecticut Academy of Arts and Sciences* (New Haven, April, 1916), Vol. 20, pp. 241–399.

BISHOP, CORTLANDT F. *History of Elections in the American Colonies* (Columbia University Studies in History, Economics, and Law, New York, 1893).

BLACKMAR, FRANK WILSON. *History of Federal and State Aid to Higher Education,* U. S. Bureau of Education, Circular of Information, No. 1, 1890 (Government Printing Office, Washington, 1890).

BLACKMAR, FRANK W. "History of Suffrage in Legislation in the United States," in *The Chautauquan,* Vol. 22, pp. 28–34.

BLAU, JOSEPH L., ed. *Social Theories of Jacksonian Democracy* (Hafner Publishing Co., New York, 1947).

BOURNE, WILLIAM OLAND. *History of the Public School Society of the City of New York* (William Wood & Co., New York, 1870).

BRUCE, WILLIAM CABELL. *John Randolph of Roanoke 1773–1833* (G. P. Putnam's Sons, New York, 1922). 2 Vols.

BURNS, JAMES J. *Educational History of Ohio* (Historical Publishing Co., Columbus, 1905).

BURR, NELSON R. *Education in New Jersey 1630–1871* (Princeton University Press, Princeton, 1942).

BUTTS, R. FREEMAN. *A Cultural History of Education* (McGraw-Hill Book Co., New York, 1947).

CARLTON, FRANK T. *Economic Influences upon Educational Progress in the United States 1820–1850* (Bulletin of the University of Wisconsin, Madison, 1908).

CHADBOURNE, AVA HARRIET. *The Beginnings of Education in Maine* (Teachers College, Columbia University, New York, 1928).

COMMAGER, HENRY STEELE. *Documents of American History* (Third Edition, Crofts, New York, 1944).

COON, CHARLES L. *The Beginnings of Public Education in North Carolina, A Documentary History 1790–1840* (North Carolina Historical Association, Raleigh, 1908). 2 Vols.

COON, CHARLES L. *North Carolina Schools and Academies, 1790–1840: A Documentary History* (Raleigh, 1915).

CULVER, RAYMOND B. *Horace Mann and Religion in the Massachusetts Public Schools* (Yale University Press, New Haven, 1929).

CUROE, PHILIP R. V. *Educational Attitudes and Policies of Organized Labor in the United States* (Teachers College, Columbia University, New York, 1926).

CURTI, MERLE. *The Growth of American Thought* (Harper and Brothers, New York, 1943).

CURTI, MERLE. *The Roots of American Loyalty* (Columbia University Press, New York, 1946).

CURTI, MERLE. *The Social Ideas of American Educators* (Charles Scribner's Sons, New York, 1935).

DEWEY, JOHN. "James Marsh and American Philosophy," in *Problems of Men* (Philosophical Library, New York, 1946).

DORFMAN, JOSEPH. *The Economic Mind in American Civilization—1606–1865* (The Viking Press, New York, 1946). 2 Vols.

FINEGAN, THOMAS E. *Free Schools* (University of the State of New York, Albany, 1921).

FISH, CARL RUSSELL. *The Rise of the Common Man* (The Macmillan Co., New York, 1927).

FITCH, CHARLES E. *History of Common School in New York* (Albany, 1904).

FITZPATRICK, EDWARD A. *The Educational Views and Influence of De Witt Clinton* (Teachers College, Columbia University, New York, 1911).

FORSTER, JOHN. *The Life of Charles Dickens* (J. P. Lippincott, Philadelphia, 1872–74). 3 Vols.

FREID, JACOB H. "The Log Cabin Symbol in American Presidential Politics" (Unpublished Ph.D. Thesis, Columbia University, 1948).

GABRIEL, RALPH H. *The Course of American Democratic Thought* (The Ronald Press Co., New York, 1940).

GARLAND, HUGH A. *The Life of John Randolph of Roanoke* (D. Appleton, New York, 1850). 2 Vols.

GOODRICH, CARTER and DAVIDSON, SOL. "The Wage-Earner in the Westward Movement," in *Political Science Quarterly*, Vol. 50, pp. 161–85, and Vol. 51, pp. 61–116.

GREENE, EVARTS B. *Religion and the State* (New York University Press, New York, 1941).

HACKER, LOUIS M. *The Shaping of the American Tradition* (Columbia University Press, New York, 1947).

HACKER, LOUIS M. *The Triumph of American Capitalism* (Simon and Schuster, New York, 1949).

HALES, DAWSON. "The Rise of Federal Control in American Education" (Unpublished Ph.D. Thesis, Teachers College, Columbia University, 1949).

HALL, ARTHUR JACKSON. *Religious Education in the Public Schools of the State and City of New York* (Chicago, 1914).

HARRIS, HERBERT. *American Labor* (Yale University Press, New Haven, 1938).

HAYES, CECIL BRANNER. *The American Lyceum; Its History and Contribution to Education*, U. S. Office of Education, Bulletin No. 12, 1932 (Government Printing Office, Washington, 1932).

HENDERSON, JOHN C. *Thomas Jefferson's Views on Public Education* (G. P. Putnam's Sons, New York, 1890).

HILL, JAMES WILSON. "Secondary Education in North Carolina" (Unpublished Ed.D. Project, Teachers College, Columbia University, 1948).

HINSDALE, B. A. *Horace Mann and the Common School Revival in the United States* (Charles Scribner's Sons, New York, 1898).

HOBSON, ELSIE GARLAND. *Educational Legislation and Administration in the State of New York from 1777 to 1850* (University of Chicago, Chicago, 1918).

HOUGH, FRANKLIN B. *Historical and Statistical Record of the University of the State of New York During the Century from 1784 to 1884* (Albany, 1885).

JAMESON, J. FRANKLIN. *The American Revolution Considered as a Social Movement* (Princeton University Press, Princeton, 1940).

JOHNSON, CLIFTON. *Old-Time Schools and School-Books* (The Macmillan Co., New York, 1917).

KNIGHT, EDGAR W. *Public Education in the South* (Ginn and Co., Boston, 1922).

KNIGHT, EDGAR W., ed. *Reports on European Education* (McGraw-Hill Book Co., New York, 1930).

KNIGHT, GEORGE W. "History and Management of Land Grants for Education in the Northwest Territory," in *Papers of the American Historical Association* (G. P. Putnam's Sons, New York, 1885), Vol. 1, No. 3.

LEOPOLD, RICHARD W. *Robert Dale Owen, A Biography* (Harvard University Press, Cambridge, 1940).

LEWIS, WILLIAM G. W. *Biography of Samuel Lewis* (Cincinnati, 1857).

LINTON, RALPH, ed. *The Science of Man in the World Crisis* (Columbia University Press, New York, 1945).

MADDOX, WILLIAM A. *The Free School Idea in Virginia Before the Civil War* (Teachers College, Columbia University, New York, 1918).

MALINOWSKI, BRONISLAW. "Culture," in *Selections from the Encyclopaedia of the Social Sciences* (Edwin R. A. Seligman, ed.; The Macmillan Co., New York, 1947).

MARTIN, GEORGE N. *The Evolution of the Massachusetts Public School System* (D. Appleton and Co., New York, 1908).

MATHEWS, LOIS KIMBALL. *The Expansion of New England* (Houghton Mifflin Co., Boston, 1909).

MATZEN, MATHIASON. *State Constitutional Provisions for Education* (Teachers College, Columbia University, New York, 1931).

MAYO, A. D. "The American Common School in New England from 1790 to 1840," *Report of the Commissioner of Education for the Year 1894–95* (Government Printing Office, Washington, 1896), Vol. 2, pp. 1551–1615.

MAYO, A. D. "The American Common School in New York, New Jersey, and Pennsylvania During the First Half Century of the Republic," *Report of the Commissioner of Education for the Year 1895–96* (Government Printing Office, Washington, 1897), Vol. 1, pp. 219–66.

MAYO, A. D. "The American Common School in the Southern States During the First Half Century of the Republic," *Report of the Commissioner of Education for the Year 1895–96* (Government Printing Office, Washington, 1897), Vol. 1, pp. 267–338.

MAYO, A. D. "The Common School in the Southern States Beyond the Mississippi River, from 1830 to 1860," *Report of the Commissioner of Education for the Year 1900–01* (Government Printing Office, Washington, 1902), Vol. 1, pp. 357–401.

MAYO, A. D. "The Development of the Common School in the Western States from 1830 to 1865," *Report of the Commissioner of Education for the Year 1898–99* (Government Printing Office, Washington, 1900), Vol. 1, pp. 357–450.

MAYO, A. D. "Education in the Northwest During the First Half Century of the Republic, 1790–1840," *Report of the Commissioner of Education for the Year 1894–95* (Government Printing Office, Washington, 1896), Vol. 2, pp. 1513–50.

MAYO, A. D. "Henry Barnard," *Report of the Commissioner of Education for the Year 1896–97* (Government Printing Office, Washington, 1898), Vol. 1, pp. 769–810.

MAYO, A. D. "Horace Mann and the Great Revival of the American Common School, 1830–1850," *Report of the Commissioner of Education for the Year 1896–97* (Government Printing Office, Washington, 1898), Vol. 1, pp. 715–67.

MAYO, A. D. "The Organization and Development of the American Common

School in the Atlantic and Central States of the South, 1830 to 1860," *Report of the Commissioner of Education for the Year 1899–1900* (Government Printing Office, Washington, 1901), Vol. 1, pp. 427–561.

MAYO, A. D. "The Organization and Reconstruction of State Systems of Common-School Education in the North Atlantic States from 1830 to 1865," *Report of the Commissioner of Education for the Year 1897–98* (Government Printing Office, Washington, 1899), Vol. 1, pp. 355–486.

MAYO, A. D. "Public Schools During the Colonial and Revolutionary Period in the United States," *Report of the Commissioner of Education for the Year 1893–94* (Government Printing Office, Washington, 1896), Vol. 1, pp. 639–738.

MAYS, ARTHUR B. *The Concept of Vocational Education in the Thinking of the General Educator, 1845 to 1945* (University of Illinois, Urbana, 1946).

MILLER, EDWARD ALANSON. *The History of Educational Legislation in Ohio from 1803 to 1850* (University of Chicago, Chicago, 1920).

MORRISON, A. J. *The Beginnings of Public Education in Virginia, 1776–1860* (State Board of Education, Richmond, 1917).

MORSE, EDWARD LIND, ed. *Samuel F. B. Morse, His Letters and Journals* (Houghton Mifflin Company, Boston, 1914). 2 Vols.

MOSIER, RICHARD D. *Making the American Mind* (King's Crown Press, New York, 1947).

NICHOLLS, GEORGE. *A History of the English Poor Law, in Connexion with the Legislation and Other Circumstances Affecting the Condition of the People* (John Murray, London, 1854). 2 Vols.

O'BRIEN, MARY AGNES. "History and Development of Catholic Secondary Education in the Archdiocese of New York" (Unpublished Ph.D. Thesis, Columbia University, New York, 1949).

OHIO TEACHERS ASSOCIATION. *A History of Education in the State of Ohio* (Published by authority of the General Assembly, Columbus, 1876).

PARKES, HENRY BAMFORD. *The American Experience* (Alfred A. Knopf, New York, 1947).

PARRINGTON, VERNON LOUIS. *Main Currents in American Thought* (Harcourt, Brace, and Co., New York, 1930).

PERRY, RALPH BARTON. *Puritanism and Democracy* (Vanguard Press, New York, 1944).

PHILLIPS, ULRICH BONNELL. *Life and Labor in the Old South* (Little, Brown and Co., Boston, 1929).

PICKERING, OCTAVIUS and UPHAM, CHARLES W. *The Life of Timothy Pickering* (Little, Brown and Co., Boston, 1867). 4 Vols.

PORTER, KIRK H. *A History of Suffrage in the United States* (University of Chicago Press, Chicago, 1918).

RANDALL, JOHN HERMAN JR. *The Making of the Modern Mind* (Houghton Mifflin Company, Boston, 1926).

RANDALL, S. S. *History of the Common School System of the State of New York* (Ivison, Blackman, Taylor and Co., New York, 1871).

REISNER, EDWARD H. *The Evolution of the Common School* (The Macmillan Co., New York, 1930).

RUSK, RALPH LESLIE. *The Literature of the Middle Western Frontier* (Columbia University Press, New York, 1925). 2 Vols.

SCHARF, J. THOMAS. *History of Westchester County, New York, Including Morrisania,*

Kings Bridge, and West Farms, Which Have Been Annexed to New-York City (L. E. Preston and Co., Philadelphia, 1886).

SCHLESINGER, ARTHUR M., JR. *The Age of Jackson* (Little, Brown and Co., Boston, 1946).

SCHNEIDER, HERBERT W. *A History of American Philosophy* (Columbia University Press, New York, 1946).

SHANNON, FRED ALBERT. *Economic History of the People of the United States* (The Macmillan Co., New York, 1934).

SMITH, SHERMAN M. *The Relation of the State to Religious Education in Massachusetts* (Syracuse University Book Store, Syracuse, 1926).

STEWART, ROLLAND MACLAREN. *Co-operative Methods in the Development of School Support in the United States* (Iowa City, 1914).

SUZZALLO, HENRY. *The Rise of Local School Supervision in Massachusetts* (Teachers College, Columbia University, New York, 1906).

SWIFT, FLETCHER HARPER. *A History of Public Permanent Common School Funds in the United States, 1795–1905* (Henry Holt and Co., New York, 1911).

TAYLOR, HOWARD CROMWELL. *The Educational Significance of the Early Federal Land Ordinances* (Teachers College, Columbia University, New York, 1922).

THORPE, FRANCIS NEWTON. *The Federal and State Constitutions, Colonial Charters, and Other Organic Laws of the States, Territories, and Colonies Now or Heretofore Forming the United States of America* (Government Printing Office, Washington, 1909).

TREAT, PAYSON JACKSON. *The National Land System* (E. B. Treat & Co., New York, 1910).

TURNER, FREDERICK JACKSON. *The Frontier in American History* (Henry Holt and Co., New York, 1921).

TYLER, ALICE FELT. *Freedom's Ferment* (The University of Minnesota Press, Minneapolis, 1944).

UPDEGRAFF, HARLAN. *Origin of the Moving School in Massachusetts* (Teachers College, Columbia University, New York, 1908).

WATERMAN, WILLIAM RANDALL. *Frances Wright* (Columbia University, New York, 1924).

WICKERSHAM, JAMES P. *History of Education in Pennsylvania* (Inquirer Publishing Co., Lancaster, 1886).

WRIGHT, LOUIS BOOKER. *The First Gentlemen of Virginia: Intellectual Qualities of the Early Colonial Ruling Class* (The Huntington Library, San Marino, 1940).

ZOLLMAN, CARL. *Church and School in the American Law* (Concordia Publishing House, St. Louis, 1918).

INDEX